S0-ADU-314

DISCARD

CRITICAL INSIGHTS

The Outsiders

CRITICAL INSIGHTS

The Outsiders

Editor
M. Katherine Grimes
Ferrum College, Virginia

SALEM PRESS
A Division of EBSCO Information Services, Inc.
Ipswich, Massachusetts

GREY HOUSE PUBLISHING

Copyright © 2018 by Grey House Publishing, Inc.

All rights reserved. No part of this work may be used or reproduced in any manner whatsoever or transmitted in any form or by any means, electronic or mechanical, including photocopy, recording, or any information storage and retrieval system, without written permission from the copyright owner. For information, contact Grey House Publishing/Salem Press, 4919 Route 22, PO Box 56, Amenia, NY 12501.

∞ The paper used in these volumes conforms to the American National Standard for Permanence of Paper for Printed Library Materials, Z39.48 1992 (R2009).

Publisher's Cataloging-In-Publication Data
(Prepared by The Donohue Group, Inc.)

Names: Grimes, M. Katherine, editor.
Title: The outsiders / editor, M. Katherine Grimes, Ferrum College, Virginia.
Other Titles: Critical insights.
Description: [First edition]. | Ipswich, Massachusetts : Salem Press, a division
     of EBSCO Information Services, Inc. ; Amenia, NY : Grey
     House Publishing, [2018] | Includes bibliographical references
     and index.
Identifiers: ISBN 9781682176863 (hardcover)
Subjects: LCSH: Hinton, S. E. Outsiders. | Hinton, S. E.--Criticism and
     interpretation. | Teenagers in literature. | Maturation (Psychology) in
     literature.
Classification: LCC PS3558.I548 O985 2018 | DDC 813/.54--dc23

First Printing

PRINTED IN THE UNITED STATES OF AMERICA

Contents _____

Resources _____

About This Volume

M. Katherine Grimes

The writers of *Critical Insights: The Outsiders* began our project in 2017, the year S. E. Hinton's first published novel turned fifty. Like Hinton herself, many of us waxed a bit nostalgic about a book from our past, one we read in our youth, probably at about the age when Hinton wrote her famous book. Now looking at *The Outsiders* as adults, we find it richer than we did when we first read it, filled with themes and concepts we missed when we found it just "a really good book."

Laurie Adams wrote much of the background material on the book's author, as well as researching the bibliographic material, works by and about S. E. Hinton. Because Ms. Adams' educational background is in the field of criminal justice, her Historical Background chapter, "Lawyer Up, Ponyboy: Reconciling Delinquency Outcomes in S. E. Hinton's *The Outsiders* with Trends in Modern Juvenile Justice," explores the legal issues, especially crime and punishment, that the characters in *The Outsiders* might have faced in the mid-1960s and what they might face under similar circumstances today.

Lana A. Whited and M. Katherine Grimes in the Critical Reception chapter look at what critics said about the novel when it was first published, again on the book's fortieth anniversary, and on *The Outsiders*' recent semicentennial. Both Dr. Whited and Dr. Grimes have also written additional essays for this volume.

Dr. Whited's major field of study is twentieth-century British and American literature, and recently much of her writing has been about novels for children and adolescents, works including the Harry Potter and Hunger Games series. For this volume, she has written an essay about parallels among *The Outsiders'* narrator, Ponyboy Curtis; the narrator and titular character of Mark Twain's *Adventures of Huckleberry Finn*; and Stephen Daedelus, the protagonist of James Joyce's *A Portrait of the Artist as a Young Man*; her essay is called "A Portrait of the Artist as a Young Greaser: *The Outsiders* as *Künstlerroman*."

In the essay "S. E. Hinton's *The Outsiders* and Theories of Moral Development," Dr. Grimes combines her study in English with her undergraduate work in psychology, using the research of psychological theorists Lawrence Kohlberg and Carol Gilligan to examine the moral maturation of the novel's major characters.

Jake Brown's Critical Lens chapter entitled "'You greasers have a different set of values': Othering, Violence and the Promise of Reconciliation in S. E. Hinton's *The Outsiders*" looks at the concept of binaries in the theories of Jacques Derrida, whose ideas Mr. Brown explains as clearly as possible—not an easy task. Mr. Brown is also the author of "'It's like being in a Halloween costume we can't get out of': Identity and Authenticity in S.E Hinton's *The Outsiders*," an essay exploring the way Ponyboy defines himself as both a member of a group and a stranger within it.

Julia Hayes, whose primary field of specialization is African American literature, explores the ways that the characters in a short story by James Baldwin and S. E. Hinton's first published novel cope with hardships. Both works examine relationships between or among brothers, with both the joy and the anguish that can permeate those kinships. The title of Ms. Hayes' Comparative Analysis chapter refers, perhaps ironically, to a comment by Cherry Valance about the difficulties of being a Soc: "'Things Are Rough All Over' Indeed: Suffering and Salvation in James Baldwin's 'Sonny's Blues' and S. E. Hinton's *The Outsiders*."

Robert C. Evans has examined and compiled excerpts from numerous interviews with S. E. Hinton, providing the reader with her descriptions of writing and publishing *The Outsiders*, her reasons for writing the novel, and her views on the book and the movie version decades after the publication and filming. Dr. Evans' essay, entitled "S. E. Hinton on *The Outsiders*: A Compendium of Interviews," also quotes some of Hinton's advice to up-and-coming writers.

Sarah E. Whitney's essay "'I'm going to look just like him': S.E. Hinton's Young Adult Novels and the Fraternal Lens" looks not just at *The Outsiders* but at Hinton's other published novels: *That Was Then, This Is Now*; *Rumble Fish*; *Tex*; and *Taming the Star Runner*. Dr. Whitney focuses especially on male characters' interactions with brothers; surrogate brothers; and even, in her latest young adult novel, with a girl who acts as a surrogate sibling.

Mary Baron discusses three poems by Robert Frost in relation to Hinton's novel. In addition to "Nothing Gold Can Stay," which, of course, features prominently in *The Outsiders*, Dr. Baron writes about "The Oven Bird" and "The Road Not Taken," especially as they apply to choices that Ponyboy Curtis makes and lessons he must learn. Her essay, entitled "Robert Frost's Seasons of the Self in *The Outsiders*," uses the poet's own explanation that he writes about nature not just as something to be observed and enjoyed but as a force that helps us understand ourselves.

Michelle Ann Abate's journal article "'Soda attracted girls like honey draws flies': *The Outsiders*, the Boy Band Formula, and Adolescent Sexuality," reprinted in this volume from *Children's Literature Association Quarterly*, explains how the descriptions of the characters in *The Outsiders* match the appearances of members of popular 1960s bands. Examples in Dr. Abate's essay sometimes read like teen magazines of the time.

Paige Gray is the author of two essays in this book. The first, "Greasers and Gallants: Writing Realism, Romanticism, and Identity in *The Outsiders*," examines the role of Margaret Mitchell's novel *Gone With the Wind* in S. E. Hinton's book, especially in the ways the boys view themselves and in what they aspire to be. Dr. Gray's essay "'You've seen too much to be innocent': *The Outsiders*, the Myth of American Youth, and Young Adult Literature" explores the way that most adults, especially adult writers of literature for adolescents, view young people as innocent, while S. E. Hinton, a teenager herself at the time she penned *The Outsiders*, exposes the truth behind the façade of innocence.

Mária I. Cipriani in the essay entitled "Gold and Magic—Ponyboy Curtis and Harry Potter: Binaries, Hierarchies, and Privilege" explores the ways that *The Outsiders* and J. K. Rowling's *Harry Potter and the Prisoner of Azkaban* reinforce male and female stereotypes, as well as the presumptions that maleness is superior and that heterosexuality is the norm. Dr. Cipriani sees both novels as reflecting society's opinions about these issues and presenting the ideas as though they are instructive.

The breadth of topics that the essayists represented in this book explore is impressive, as are the depth of research and richness of critical thought. All of these speak to the importance of S. E. Hinton's *The Outsiders* in helping to shape the psyches of American youth and young people from around the world, as well as the necessity for more mature readers to interpret the deeper themes of the novel.

On *The Outsiders*

M. Katherine Grimes

The story of Susan Eloise Hinton as prodigy is well known: she wrote *The Outsiders* when she was a teenager and received a contract for the book the same week she graduated from high school. It is the sort of happily-ever-after, fairy-tale ending that most young people only dream about.

The story behind young Susie Hinton's success has other fairy-tale elements, as well. The author came from a working-class background in Tulsa, Oklahoma, a city not known for glamour. Her parents were not rich and famous, nor were they very understanding of their bookworm daughter and her authorial ambitions. She went to a high school where she was academically successful but not a member of the elite clique.

Out of this background came S. E. Hinton, who wrote *The Outsiders*, one of the best known, best remembered, and best loved books ever read by high school students. Like Cinderella, she has qualities that are recognized as superior and that grant her a promising future. Like Belle from *Beauty and the Beast*, she loves to read, and that passion leads to her finding success. And like Harper Lee of *To Kill a Mockingbird* fame, she has written a book that teachers assign and young readers love.

The Outsiders, which was published in 1967, turned fifty years old in 2017. It was written during a memorable decade:

- the Vietnam War was going full force, with no end in sight;
- the Civil Rights movement was achieving huge successes, including the Voting Rights Act;
- the space race between the United States and the Soviet Union was going strong;
- Rock and Roll was in its heyday, with both the British invasion (The Beatles, the Rolling Stones, The Who) and Motown (The

Supremes, the Temptations, the Jackson Five) burning up the radio and *The Monkees* bursting from the television screen;

- the free speech movement began at Berkeley (Duddy);

- laws against birth control were outlawed;

- the women's movement, which had been relatively dormant since the Suffragettes won women the right to vote, ramped up again; and

- as *The Columbia Guide to America in the 1960s* tells us, *Time* magazine in 1966 chose for its "Man of the Year" not a man, but "Twenty-Five and Under" (Farber and Bailey 441), recognizing the importance of the youth movement.

Watching 1960s television shows would make one think that we had never left the 1950s. *Leave It to Beaver, My Three Sons, Gidget,* and *The Andy Griffith Show* might lead a viewer to believe that almost all Americans were white, middle class, and funny. But watching the news was a different story, for, as Bob Dylan sang in 1964, "The times, they [were] a-changin'." Images of civil rights marches with policemen using dogs and fire hoses to attack protesters were followed by images of soldiers and Marines being killed in Vietnam. The assassination of President John F. Kennedy in 1963 was still on the minds of Americans, too, when S. E. Hinton began writing *The Outsiders*.

Hinton's world must have seemed as confusing to her as 1960s television. People were being attacked in the streets of America and fighting in a country half a world away, yet the entertainment media showed happy homemakers feeding their happy, middle-class families while teenagers worried about such problems as having their brothers steal their girlfriends. One of Hinton's friends was beaten up by other teenagers, yet the books she was reading about young people were about dating and dances.

How could anyone reconcile these two visions of the world, either the larger one or the one she saw every day? Susan Eloise Hinton decided to try—at least try to understand and explain her own high school world in Tulsa, Oklahoma—and thus *The Outsiders* was born.

Oklahoma is a state with an unusual identity, too. It is not exactly Western or Southern or Midwestern, but a sort of combination of the three. It was put together from lands acquired in the Louisiana Purchase in 1803 and as a result of the Mexican-American War (1846–48), and it became the destination of numerous Native Americans who were removed by the United States government from their lands in the Southeastern part of the country as part of the Trail of Tears in the mid-1800s. Yet it did not become a state until 1907, sixty years before the publication of *The Outsiders*.

Known primarily for its oil industry and art deco architecture, Tulsa, Oklahoma, does not seem like the setting of a fairy tale, and at first, *The Outsiders* does not seem to have fairy tale ingredients. It features violence involving children and contains dead parents, drunk parents, neglectful parents, and abusive parents. The main characters are working-class members of a gang-like group, often high school dropouts, and sometimes petty criminals or even felons.

S. E. Hinton's novel tells the story of these characters through the eyes of narrator Ponyboy Curtis, a fourteen-year-old orphan who lives with his older brothers, twenty-year-old Darrel "Darry" and sixteen-year-old Sodapop, because their parents were victims of a fatal car crash eight months before the story begins. Darry works construction; Sodapop has dropped out of high school to work in a service station to help pay the bills; and Ponyboy is in college-preparatory classes in high school. The Curtis brothers are members of a group of boys who call themselves and are called by others "greasers" because of the amount of hair grease they use on their long hair. Their group also includes the hardened Dallas "Dally" Winston, who has been in New York gangs; Johnny Cade, whose parents alternately neglect and beat him; Keith "Two-Bit" Mathews, a petty criminal; and Steve Randle, Sodapop's best friend.

The greasers are continually in conflict with the Socs, or Socials, teenagers whose families have the money and prestige to make their offspring believe that they are better than other students at their school. A band of Socs sometimes attacks a solitary greaser if they catch him alone; in fact, both Ponyboy and Johnny have recently been jumped. Sometimes the altercations are larger and more formal, as on occasion the groups arrange a rumble to fight one another, usually without weapons.

Early in the novel, Johnny and Ponyboy are in a drive-in theatre, which attracts both moviegoers in cars and people who want to sit outside and watch the film. The boys sit behind two girls they identify as Socs, and their friend Dally joins them, then begins taunting the girls, one of whom stands up to him. Finally Johnny, usually quiet and shy, tells Dally to stop. After Dally sulks away, the girls, who introduce themselves as Sherri "Cherry" Valance and Marcia, invite Johnny and Ponyboy to join them.

Two-Bit Mathews joins them also, and the five teenagers are walking together when Bob Sheldon, Cherry's boyfriend, and other Soc boys drive by and threaten to attack the greasers if Cherry and Marcia don't leave their new friends. The girls go with the Soc boys, but the Socs' resentment is not completely squashed.

Later that night, when Ponyboy gets home late because he has fallen asleep in the lot near his house, Darry becomes angry with him, and Ponyboy runs out of the house, meeting up with Johnny and going to the park. There, they are attacked by the still-angry Socs, who hold Ponyboy's head under water in the fountain. To save his friend, Johnny stabs Bob, killing him.

Ponyboy and Johnny find Dally, who gives them money and a gun and directs them to an abandoned church building in the country to hide out. There the boys eat bologna sandwiches, smoke cigarettes, and read Margaret Mitchell's novel about the Civil War, *Gone With the Wind*. When Dally drives to visit them, he takes them to the nearest town to get food, and when the three return to the church building, it is on fire. Johnny and Ponyboy learn that children are inside and go in to save them. Both are burned, as is Dally, who rescues his two friends.

Ponyboy and Dally soon leave the hospital, but Johnny is much more seriously injured and remains hospitalized. Meanwhile, the greasers rumble with the Socs in a fight that Cherry has helped negotiate to make sure the only weapons used are fists and feet. Randy Adderson, a Soc and a good friend of Bob's, meets with Ponyboy before the rumble and explains to Ponyboy why Randy cannot fight. The greasers win the battle, but Johnny dies almost immediately afterward, leaving Ponyboy a copy of *Gone With the Wind* and reminding him to "Stay gold," a reference to a Robert Frost poem that Ponyboy had recited to Johnny while the two were hiding out.

Dally, who loved Johnny like a little brother, runs distraught through the streets, and when police confront him, he waves an unloaded pistol in front of officers, who fatally shoot him. The deaths of two of his friends and one of his enemies and the discussions with Randy and Cherry lead Ponyboy to question the rivalries and divisions between the greasers and the Socs. He thinks beyond his own friends and enemies to other boys who suffer from a society that doesn't seem to care about them, and he decides to tell their story, in the form of a project for an English class. That story, of course, is *The Outsiders*.

Hinton's novel is generally noted for its realism and is in many ways far too depressing to feel like a fairy tale. Yet the book does contain folk- and fairy-tale elements. Like Jack of Jack Tales fame, the narrator of *The Outsiders*, Ponyboy Curtis, is the third son; in folk tales, the third son is special, often the cleverest and luckiest. Like Cinderella, he is orphaned, and he often feels that the oldest sibling, Darry, doesn't really like him. Like Beowulf, who in killing the man-eating monster Grendel becomes both a folk and an epic hero, Ponyboy fights, and he risks his own life to save others when he pulls children from the burning church building. Also like Beowulf, he inspires great friendship; after all, Johnny Cade kills a boy to save Ponyboy's life, as Wiglaf fights alongside Beowulf to save the Geats from the dragon.

Is it difficult to see the ending of *The Outsiders* as having any elements of a fairy tale or folktale. Johnny Cade has died from injuries he suffered in the church building fire from which he pulled children to safety. Grieving for his lost friend, Dally Winston has committed suicide by cop. The earlier death of Bob Sheldon at Johnny's hand has taken the boys' childhood, and it can never return.

However, our hero survives, and he will thrive. The youngest of the greaser bunch and the youngest Curtis brother, a poor orphan, and a sensitive reader in a world that emphasizes physical ability, he is the underdog. Yet when he is called on to risk his life to save the children from the burning church building, he does just that. He realizes how much his brothers love him, but he also realizes that he doesn't have to be like his brothers and their friends. He makes connections with those who could have been his enemies, and he grows through these interactions. Thus, the underdog wins, as the folk hero must, but he also matures and grows from his experiences, making the novel much richer than a typical folk or fairy tale.

From the typical folk tale, we learn that we can succeed if we are clever, like Jack. From fairy tales, we learn that our wildest dreams can come true if we are beautiful and lucky like Cinderella, especially if we have a fairy godmother. From S. E. Hinton's personal story, we learn that success comes when we are persistent and true to ourselves and what we know.

From S. E. Hinton's own words in interviews, we also know that young people are often fed fairy tales long after they are too old for them. Hinton says that her reality did not mesh at all with the trite books that she found for people her age, so she wrote the reality that she saw, but not without some optimism that such reality could be changed for the better. In fact, many scholars believe *The Outsiders* to be the first true young adult, or YA, novel.

Hinton's comments and scholars' reactions led me to think about books I read when I was in high school. I come from a family of readers. More than once my parents had to pry books out of our hands to get us to eat, and two of my three siblings, like me, were English majors. By the time I got to high school, I had been through Trixie Belden, Nancy Drew, and even the Bobbsey Twins, old books I found in my church library. From the school and county libraries, I had checked out numerous biographies and Laura Ingalls Wilder's *Little House* books and Louisa May Alcott's works, not just *Little Women* but *Jo's Boys* and *Little Men* and *Jack and Jill*. Dickens and I were old friends—*Great Expectations*, *David Copperfield*, *Oliver Twist*. When I got to high school, my English teacher Helen Comer Pulliam assigned *To Kill a Mockingbird*, and for some reason, that's when I knew that I would go to college (that part was never in doubt at my house) and major in English. Before that time, reading was just for fun. Now I knew that it was a serious undertaking, a life-changing action, for books could explain everything about our world.

When I think about S. E. Hinton's saying that the books she was reading didn't represent her world, I started to wonder why it didn't bother me that I was reading about boys in England a hundred years ago and girls in New England and the American Midwest from the century before I was born. Even Harper Lee's novel is set in 1940. And I realized that I didn't want the real world; I wanted escape. That's why J. D. Salinger's *The Catcher in the Rye* had a real "ick" factor for me and why *Go Ask Alice* by Beatrice Sparks, presented as the diary of a real girl who did drugs and feared pregnancy, scared me much more than did Alfred Hitchcock films.

So why were all the books I read as an adolescent not enough for S. E. Hinton? Salinger's novel predates *The Outsiders* by sixteen years; Lee's, by seven. Of the works listed in the paragraphs above, only *Go Ask Alice* came out after Hinton's book (I'm a little younger than S. E. Hinton). My theory is that Hinton did not want the escapism of the past or of another country. I think she did not identify with the wealthy (and, I thought, whiny) Holden Caulfield. The problems in *To Kill a Mockingbird* are really created by adults and must be solved by adults; the child is an observer. S. E. Hinton wanted books about the world in which she lived, for she needed not just emotional escape but real escape, a way to figure out how not to continue to live the way her parents and those around her lived. Writing was her way to get through the maze that was her life, her teenage life, by creating adolescent characters with agency, even if they sometimes misused it.

And so she created Ponyboy Curtis, a character who might be her male alter ego. Like Hinton, he is intelligent, academically successful, and economically challenged. His social group is on the bottom of the high school ladder, and he feels the pile atop him, just as S.E. Hinton felt her own lower socioeconomic status. Like Ponyboy, Hinton writes to try to explain her world and the people in it—the teenagers, not the adults (who seem inexplicable to both Ponyboy and Hinton).

The connection between Ponyboy and S. E. Hinton seems obvious; many readers and critics have seen the similarities between the real author and her fictional one. But I believe that Hinton has three alter egos, three fictional selves: Ponyboy, Randy Adderson, and Cherry Valance.

Randy Adderson removes himself from the situation when he realizes that violence is no solution to the disparities in the world, but he believes that, in fact, there **is** no solution. Randy sees individuals as individuals, both Bob Sheldon and Ponyboy Curtis, loving Bob despite his bullying and violence and reaching out to Ponyboy even though Ponyboy is from the group that killed Bob. However, Randy believes that the two groups, the greasers and the Socs, will always exist and that he can do nothing to improve the situation. All he knows to do is to remove himself from the violence, to refuse to fight. In short, he can diagnose the problem, but he doesn't see a means of solving it, so he cannot see himself as part of the solution.

Cherry, on the other hand, does not give up hope that a solution can be found. Even though other characters might consider her a traitor or a disloyal spy, she is neither. Cherry is the uniter, the negotiator, the open-minded person from one world who does not discount people from the other. In fact, she has decided that there needn't be two worlds. She reaches across the divide, trying to pull the two sides together. She knows that unity cannot happen at once, so she tries to keep people safe in the meantime by negotiating less destructive fighting rules. However, Cherry realizes that change cannot happen overnight. Like the characters in the movie *The Breakfast Club* who know that Monday morning they will all go back to their own groups, Cherry knows that when she sees Ponyboy in the hall at school, she will pretend not to notice him. She won't go visit Johnny in the hospital. But she does see Ponyboy as a person, not a greaser. She just realizes that her friends will not.

S. E. Hinton has created a book to make sure that we see Ponyboy and his family and friends as people, not greasers. She helps us understand that Randy and Cherry are also caught in a world that divides itself, forcing people into groups that continue to try to maintain what they see as their superiority or to pull down those they grudgingly see as enviable. In short, Hinton has written a book to help us understand her own world.

The characters in *The Outsiders*, in true teenage form, see their world as isolated. They don't discuss the war in Vietnam, even though any one of the boys could have been drafted in just a few years. They don't talk about the Civil Rights movement, although the fight by the establishment—that is, powerful white people supported by powerless white people—to maintain the status quo so as to keep those not in the establishment—that is, African American people—from having a piece of the pie of democracy parallels the actions of the Socs in trying to keep the greasers in their place. What the greasers discuss is how to maintain their own turf, to keep what they have, to keep from being beaten up by the Socs. We don't hear the Socs talking to one another, only to Ponyboy. When they do reach out, tentatively, we see some hope, but not enough to save Bob or Dally.

Even though S. E. Hinton, through Ponyboy, doesn't write about the larger world of the 1960s, her book could be a metaphor for that time. Teenagers often felt alienated from adults—the "generation gap" at its height. Some even became "hippies," young people who checked out of the establishment, celebrated peace and love, and protested against war. Supporters of the Vietnam War and those who fought in it certainly felt alienated from those who refused to fight and those who protested for peace. The women's movement pointed out how underrepresented in the world of power women were, one of the points that Hinton herself makes when she explains why her protagonist is male. The differences in the ways that society treated men and women at the time were not nearly as prominent in the news media, though, as were the discrepancies in the treatment of white people and African Americans. *The Outsiders* is a cautiously optimistic novel. The divide between Socs and greasers still exists, and Randy and Cherry haven't straddled the aisle, but at least they've reached across it.

The turmoil of the 1960s continued long after Hinton published her novel. The Vietnam War became even more intense, with the Tet Offensive in February of 1968, the year in which both Martin Luther King Jr. and Robert F. Kennedy were assassinated. However, eventually the Vietnam War ended; voting rights laws were passed; Jim Crow laws were overturned; integration of public schools was finally realized; and women entered many professions formerly seen as all male. Young people went to college or got jobs, married, and had children, just as Susan Eloise Hinton did. The 1970s seemed almost peaceful after the 1960s.

When Barack Obama was elected president in 2008, it seemed that our divisions were growing still smaller. Winning more votes than any president before him, a man whose mother was American and whose father was Kenyan seemed to represent a United States that could move beyond racial and ethnic divisions to prove that, as Theodore Parker said, "The arc of the moral universe is long, but it bends toward justice."

Susan Eloise Hinton's reasons for writing about boys instead of girls and her publisher's rationale for putting her initials rather than her full name on her book seemed verified thirty years later when Joanne Rowling published her first Harry Potter book, *Harry Potter and the Philosopher's Stone* (*Sorcerer's Stone*, in the United States). Rowling, too, published under her initials to make sure that boys would read her book, and Harry Potter is obviously male. Soon, however, Rowling revealed her gender, and boys by the millions still read her novels, just as they had read S. E. Hinton's *The Outsiders* even after they learned that the writer was a woman. In addition, Suzanne Collins' *The Hunger Games* trilogy, published in 2008, 2009, and 2010, features a strong female protagonist who is also the narrator, and millions of both male and female adolescents read those books and watch the movies based on them.

So fifty years after the publication of *The Outsiders*, has the nation of Hinton's birth realized the promise of tolerance that a reader glimpses in Ponyboy's conversations with Randy Adderson and Cherry Valance? In many ways, we seem back where we started. Gaps between rich and poor have increased, with CEOs of companies making over 200 times what the people who are paid the least in those companies make and Congress passing a tax bill that greatly benefits the wealthy. Neo-Nazis and members of the Ku Klux Klan are rallying on one side, while Black Lives Matters members and women are marching on the other. A woman ran for president and won the popular vote, but she was defeated in the electoral college by a man who encouraged supporters to yell "Lock her up" at her, who loomed behind her in one of the presidential debates, and who boasted on tape about groping women. Thus, the divide between men and women is obviously still not healed. The divide between white people and African Americans is evident in the resurgence of white supremacists. The divide between people born in this country and immigrants from Spanish-speaking countries is evident in the shouts at rallies for the man who became president in 2017 to "build that wall" between the United States and Mexico. Immigrants, to some Americans, are a problem to be solved.

The Outsiders is a book that illustrates the poem "Outwitted" by Edwin Markham:

> He drew a circle that shut me out—
> Heretic, rebel, a thing to flout.
> But love and I had the wit to win:
> We drew a circle that took him in!

While *The Outsiders* doesn't show us a utopia, the novel does show us that people can rise above pettiness and groupthink and can learn to break the cycle of violence and feuding.

The Hunger Games trilogy, by contrast, is dystopian. It shows the way that division and power can become exaggerated to the point that the only resolution is more extreme division and more extreme violence. It is a warning designed to try to steer us back toward social and cultural reconciliation.

Ponyboy and Randy and Cherry can perceive one another's humanity beyond their differences and find reconciliation because of an adolescent optimism and innocence not yet worn down by the worries and woes of adult life. If this innocence is the viewpoint that Johnny encourages Ponyboy to cling to in his admonition "Stay gold," then perhaps Johnny Cade is a prophet for our times as well. Yet we must add to that optimism and innocence the wisdom that Ponyboy gains. In the aftermath of the most divisive election in modern US history, many of us are afraid. But we should overcome our fear, and like Hinton's characters, we should stop fighting, step back, and reach out.

Works Cited

Duddy, Karen. Personal Interview, Ferrum College, 9 Jan. 2018.

Farber, David, and Beth Bailey. *The Columbia Guide to America in the 1960s.* Columbia UP, 2001.

Hinton, S. E. *The Outsiders*. Viking, 1967. Platinum ed., Speak / Penguin, 2012.

Krischer, Haley. "Why *The Outsiders* Lives On: A Teenage Novel Turns 50." *The New York Times*, 12 Mar. 2017, www.nytimes. com/2017/03/12/books/the-outsiders-s-e-hinton-book.html/.

S. E. Hinton: Matriarch of Young Adult Literature, Observer in the Moment

Laurie Adams

> I feel like an outsider, but it's not a bad feeling . . . . It just means being your own person.
>
> (S.E. Hinton)[1]

There always has to be a first: a first human-made fire, a first walk on the moon, a first book to view teenagers as they view themselves instead of as adults wish to script them. The journey towards firsts of all kinds begins with a person attempting to solve a problem, often without knowing he or she is embarking on a journey by doing so, and certainly without any notion of where that journey will have led some fifty years hence.

In 1965 in Tulsa, Oklahoma, fifteen-year-old Susan Eloise Hinton saw a problem: there was a stultifying sameness in the books marketed to people her age, books that she found wholesome but rather vapid. Hinton would later describe her frustration with finding the books meant for teenaged readership filled with trope-laden plots revolving around whether their main characters would go to prom or help their team win a championship game (Franklin & Wilson 12). Their characters did not get jumped on their way home from school, as did one of her friends (Daly 4), and in no way did they portray youngsters being tormented as members of an out group, scorned for being less athletic, academic, or well-dressed than their in-group peers. While the stories may have had one or more characters playing the heavy, they somehow failed to address the factions and polarization Hinton saw among her classmates. Furthermore, they did nothing to explain why such groups would form or what sway they held over their members that prevented one group from associating with any of the others (Daly 4). "Susie" Hinton set out to write a book for her own amusement and to try to capture in words the teen universe as she was observing it. Fifty years on, the product of her efforts, *The Outsiders*, is still allowing teenagers to find an echo of their own experiences with not fitting in.

Positioned as an Outsider/Observer, Writing *The Outsiders*

S. E. Hinton was born in 1948[2] to a working-class family; her father, Grady, was a door-to-door salesman, and her mother, Lillian, was a factory worker. S. E. Hinton describes the area where she and her younger sister, Beverly, grew up in Tulsa, Oklahoma, as a "greaser" neighborhood (Smith).

According to the film *Great Women Writers*, even as a young child, Hinton had a complex personality. Uninterested in what were considered at the time to be traditionally girl-y things, she eschewed dolls as a youngster and avoided the rigidly narrow expressive outlets of hair and makeup afforded to her 60s-era female peers as a teen. She instead preferred to spend time participating in the more active, outdoorsy pursuits of her male cousins and boys from her neighborhood.

Despite having friends, Hinton says she was "kind of an introvert" and never a "joiner." She noted in the 1999 documentary *Great Women Writers*, "I somehow was born without this gene that everybody else seems to have that they've got to be in a group; but I don't have to be in a group." This tendency ultimately may have proved to be as asset for Hinton as she moved through her early life. A "tomboy," "introvert," and "avid reader," she found herself the odd one out, caught between the "greaser" and the "Soc" groups at her high school—friends with both due to her home neighborhood and college-prep classes, but not truly belonging to either. Biographer Jay Daly quoted Hinton as saying, "I didn't have any label in high school. I think I was considered a little eccentric. I'm still considered a little eccentric. If I had a label at all, it was probably something like 'The School Nut'" (Daly 1-2)

Despite being a loner, upon entering Tulsa's Will Rogers High School as a freshman, Hinton noticed that not only had her peers sequestered themselves into well-defined groups, but that those groups had little to nothing to do with one another, and this stratification "made [her] angry" ("S. E. Hinton on Location").

It wasn't only the exclusionary tendencies of the groups, but the mindset that took over when those walls went up. Hinton stated, "I knew both sides and I could see there were human beings in both places." But she says that once polarized into their cliques, the attitude appeared to be "the other guys aren't even human" (*Great Women Writers*). It was this sort of thought process that often escalated into violence between the cliques. In one such event, a friend of Hinton's was jumped on his way home from school and beaten by "the rich kids" (Lang). As she had been doing for eight years prior (Hinton says she began writing in third grade), she began to incorporate all of those elements into a short story: forty pages, typed, single-spaced. She began to write the kind of book for teens she'd wanted for herself, the story that was playing out before her eyes but that nobody seemed to be telling.

The Outsiders was Hinton's third manuscript (*Great Women Writers*). The two others, "horse stories" that she never sought to publish, are what Hinton considers the "practice" that prepared her with the skills and discipline needed to capture the moment she was witnessing. Her keen observation meant that any detail that helped define her own experiences would be captured and translated into the story.

Beginning with the assault of her friend and the in-group/out-group tension in her high school, Hinton has pointed out a number of events and locations that went into the creation of *The Outsiders* universe. Tulsa's Admiral Twin Drive-In became the backdrop for a major plot-building scene in the book. It was here that Hinton witnessed a fight between a girl and her boyfriend that she took as inspiration for a means of introducing the character of Sherry "Cherry" Valance into the story ("S.E. Hinton on Location").

For Johnny Cade's less-than-doting mother, Hinton, sadly, may not have had to struggle for a model. According to writer Dinitia Smith, Hinton's mother resented the time her daughter spent in her literary worlds. Hinton told Smith, "When I was writing, she'd come into my room, grab my hair and throw me in front of the TV . . . . She'd say 'you're part of this family, now act like it!'" Smith says that on one occasion, Hinton's mother threatened Hinton's writing by throwing her work into a trash burner, though she did not actually destroy the pages.

With this life experience, it makes sense that Hinton could so easily imagine youngsters like Johnny Cade and Dallas Winston turning to their friends for caring, shelter, and community after not finding it at home. Smith's revelation about this aspect of Hinton's early home life is at odds with Jay Daly's biography of Hinton, which makes no mention of any abuse within the family; Daly only quotes Hinton's mother's recollections of Hinton's being closer to her father, and his illness and death spurring the young writer to work harder and harder (Daly 2). It bears mentioning, however, that Daly's work was published in 1989, while Hinton's mother and sister were still living, while Smith's account in the *New York Times* was published years after their deaths, possibly allowing such a disclosure to be made without upsetting Hinton's relatives.

Once her book was completed, Hinton enjoyed what may have been the simplest of all possible paths to publication, missing the dreaded slush pile and never once querying an agent for the book. Instead, her manuscript was read by the mother of one of her friends, who passed it along to an agent. The agent began to submit the manuscript to publishers, and it was accepted by the second publisher (*Great Women Authors*). She later joked that receiving contracts for *The Outsiders* "absolutely ruined graduation day, because I was sitting there going 'eh—this is nothing. I've sold my book!'" ("*Outsiders* Author").

The book was initially marketed to adult readers, but then as Hinton puts it, it "began to spread by word of mouth from 'astute kids,' helped along by the group most motivated to pique teen interest in literature: teachers ("S. E. Hinton at Bumbershoot").

Enter the Teachers

Teachers' key role in the continued success of *The Outsiders* cannot be overstated, and Hinton frequently praises them for their support of the book. By using it as a lure to engage recalcitrant non-readers into the world of books and as a platform to open up dialogue about the issues their students confront, teachers are in Hinton's words "the best damn advertising anybody could ever want" ("S.E. Hinton at Bumbershoot").

As early as 1968, reviews for *The Outsiders* began to appear in journals, touting the book's readability and relatability for students. That accessibility has maintained the book's appeal over time. As of 2014, *The Outsiders* had sold 14 million copies, with the yearly number of copies sold averaging roughly 500,000 (Tipping).

Continuing Career

Hinton has noted that the writer she was at the time she wrote *The Outsiders* and the writer she matured and evolved to become over the course of her career might not have arrived at the same manuscript. Hinton has noted she was "very lucky" to have written *The Outsiders* in her teens, adding that "even by the time I was 20, I couldn't write *The Outsiders* again" (*Great Women Writers*). By age twenty, Hinton had enrolled in university and been exposed to works of literature that made her feel by comparison, when she re-read her own work, that it "was the worst piece of trash [she'd] ever read" ("S.E. Hinton," Oklahoma Historical Society). She initially saw her assistance with the screen adaptation of *The Outsiders* as a chance to "fix everything that was wrong with it" ("S.E. Hinton," Oklahoma Historical Society) before being overruled by Francis Ford Coppola's insistence on remaining faithful to the text to avoid alienating the book's fans.

Hinton was a freshman at the University of Tulsa when *The Outsiders* was released. Initially majoring in journalism, she switched to education but ultimately decided that teaching was not the right career for her. Instead, she married David Inhofe, whom she had met in one of her classes. The wedding took place in September 1970, following her graduation that spring (Daly).

In the wake of *The Outsiders*, Hinton remained true to her voice, audience, and subject matter with *That Was Then, This Is Now* in 1971, *Rumble Fish* (which she initially published in 1968 as a short story in her university's alumni magazine) in 1975, and *Tex* in 1979. Each of these novels features young people struggling—sometimes against their circumstances, sometimes against others, and sometimes both. Hinton even allowed Ponyboy Curtis and Randy the Soc to re-emerge briefly in *That Was Then, This Is Now.* When asked about her preference in writing male narrators, Hinton would often tell interviewers that it was simply "easier" for her and referred back to her tomboyish traits: "I felt like I literally could not think like a girl. If I couldn't think like a girl, I couldn't write like a girl" (*Great Women Writers*). Once again, Hinton's quirks worked to her benefit. She has said, "I find writing from a male point of view I reach a larger audience, because girls will read boys' books, but boys won't read girls' books" (*Great Women Writers*).

In 1988, Hinton published *Taming the Star Runner*, her last truly teen-oriented book. She followed this with two books for younger readers: *Big David, Little David* and *The Puppy Sister*, both published in 1995. *Hawkes Harbor* followed in 2004. It was a departure for Hinton, involving elements of the supernatural instead of coming-of-age turmoil, and reviews were mixed. In 2007, Hinton published *Some of Tim's Stories*, which she called her best writing to date because she reached the goal of conciseness that she had set for herself. All but one of the tales within the collection are kept to around 900 words ("S.E. Hinton," Oklahoma Historical Society).

Throughout her career, except for a three-year bout with writer's block, S.E. Hinton has worked steadily, whether writing novels, helping to develop screenplays for her novels, or assisting in the production of the resulting films. She continues to write, meeting with a writer's group weekly, now allowing herself to create things she considers merely frivolous and fun ("S. E. Hinton," Oklahoma Historical Society).

If she should be remembered best for having written *The Outsiders*, this is still an enviable legacy. Beyond the millions of copies sold and the book's remarkable longevity, having been continuously in print for fifty years, *The Outsiders* accomplished Hinton's original goals for it and more. It changed the way teenagers were presented in media, gave rise to the young adult genre as we know it, and demanded that young people and their issues be given thoughtful consideration and sympathetic treatment despite their flaws. Beyond recognition, awards, or royalties, the untold number of new readers it helped to create is Hinton's greatest and most deeply felt success with the book. She told the audience while accepting the 2008 *Chicago Tribune* Young Adult Book Prize, "Reading has been one of the major influences in my life, not just professionally, but mentally, emotionally, my morals, my values, reading has played such a humongous part of my life that to think I've opened that door for somebody else is just really the best thing I could ever get" ("S. E. Hinton, Pt. 1").

Notes

1. Quoted from *This Land Presents: SE Hinton*, a YouTube video.
2. See the Chronology of the Life of S.E. Hinton endnote for details regarding the ambiguity surrounding the author's birthdate.

Works Cited

Barnard, Matt. "*The Outsiders* Author S.E. Hinton Headlines Event at Circle Cinema." *Tulsa World TV*, n.d., www.tulsaworldtv.com/ The-Outsiders-author-SE-Hinton-headlines-event-at-Circle-Cinema-32173450/. Accessed 9 Sept. 2017.

"Beverly Ada Hinton." *Geni*, 31 Aug.2017, www.geni.com/people/ Beverly-Hinton/6000000001193200085/.

Daly, Jay. *Presenting S. E. Hinton*. Updated ed, Twayne, 1989.

"Deaths: Aug. 9, 1997." *Tulsa World*, 9 Aug. 1997, www.tulsaworld.com/ archives/deaths/article_8a885498-3d63-51e5-b284-05bfac7d90ec. html/.

Franklin, Joseph, and Antoine Wilson. *S.E. Hinton*. Rosen, 2016.

"Grady Pulaski Hinton." *Geni*. 31 Aug. 2017. https://www.geni.com/ people/Grady-Hinton/6000000066037858912/.

Great Women Writers: Rita Dove, S. E. Hinton, and Maya Angelou. Hacienda Productions, 1999.

Lang, George. "S.E. Hinton Recalls *The Outsiders* 45 years Later—E-book Due in Spring 2013." *NewsOK.com*, 10 May 2012, newsok. com/article/3770291/.

"Lillian Hinton." *Geni*, 31 Aug. 2017, www.geni.com/people/Lillian-Hinton/6000000001193200065/.

"S.E. Hinton." *IMDB.com*, n.d., www.imdb.com/name/nm0386023/?ref_=fn_al_nm_1/. Accessed 18 Aug. 2017.

"S.E. Hinton on Location in Tulsa." *Youtube*, uploaded by micalaux, 14 Nov. 2010, www.youtube.com/watch?v=wJnfleLeOZg/.

"S.E. Hinton." *Oklahoma Historical Society*, n.d., www.okhistory. org/writers/bio.php?/name=hinton&fname=s.%20E/. Accessed 6 Sept. 2017.

"S. E. Hinton at Bumbershoot, Sept. 6th, 2009." *Youtube*, uploaded by PennyLayner, 9 Sept. 2009, www.youtube.com/ watch?v=yLUR0RYoQvU/.

"S.E.Hinton, Pt. 1." *Youtube*, uploaded by Michael Doherty, 7 Jun. 2008, www.youtube.com/watch?v=KBs4BSXukM8/.

"S.E. Hinton.com." *S.E. Hinton.com*, n.d., www.sehinton.com/. Accessed 18 Aug. 2017.

Smith, Dinitia. "An Outsider out of the Shadows." *New York Times*, vol. 154, no. 53330, 07 Sept. 2005, p. E1. *EBSCOhost*, 0nesearch. ebscohost.com.library.acaweb.org/login.aspx?direct=true&db=f5h& AN=18139141&site=eds-live/.

Taylor, Elizabeth. "An Interview with S.E. Hinton." *Chicago Tribune*, 31 May 2008, articles.chicagotribune.com/2008-05-31/ entertainment/0805300368_1_hinton-outsiders-gender/.

Tipping, Joy. "S.E. Hinton on how *The Outsiders* Worked Its Way into the Mainstream." *Dallas News*, 4 Apr. 2014. www.dallasnews.com/ arts/books/2014/04/18/s.e.-hinton-on-how-the-outsiders-worked-its- way-into-the-mainstream/.

'This Land Presents: S. E. Hinton.' *YouTube*, uploaded by thislandpress, 10 Aug. 2012. www.youtube.com/watch?v=Ei707lyoow8.

CRITICAL
CONTEXTS

Lawyer Up, Ponyboy: Reconciling Delinquency Outcomes in S. E. Hinton's *The Outsiders* with Trends in Modern Juvenile Justice_____

Laurie Adams

> I often lie awake during the wee hours of the morning, staring at cracks in a white, concrete ceiling, pondering my life. Every crevice inspires a thought, every thought a memory; thus, an introspective journey begins, guiding me through scenes resembling an S.E. Hinton novel.
>
> (Robert Pruett, Texas death row inmate executed October 12, 2017 for a secondary offense after initially being given a ninety-nine year sentence as a fifteen-year-old.)[1]

S. E. Hinton has mentioned on numerous occasions that she could not write *The Outsiders* again and couldn't have done so even in her early twenties after she had matured beyond her high school experiences and observations (*Great Women Writers*). Her rationale is that she could not have recaptured the intensity of teen emotions and all-or-nothing angst with the same immediacy and conviction as she had at sixteen, but there are other compelling reasons why the book might not have been able to be written at a later point. Given changes to the legal realities surrounding juvenile offenses, *The Outsiders* almost certainly could not be written in its original form in the twenty-first century.

From a criminal justice point of view, *The Outsiders'* plot includes outcomes that would be out of sync outside the time period in which the novel was written and very much at odds with the realities of juvenile justice as it exists in the United States today, not to mention the expectations of readers who have witnessed the outcomes of various forms of delinquency and violence in media or their own communities, or both. *The Outsiders* could not be written today without substantial changes to outcomes for various forms of juvenile delinquency depicted in its plot, given changes in the criminal and juvenile justice systems over the course of the book's fifty years of continuous publication, and given readers' increased social awareness of and exposure to criminality through media or personal experience.

Four major changes have come about since *The Outsiders*' 1967 release: the increase in minors being tried as adults, the increase in American litigiousness in pursuit of civil suits, the proliferation of privatized correctional facilities, and the institution of three-strikes laws. All of these point to far different outcomes for Ponyboy Curtis and his friends were *The Outsiders* to take place in a modern setting.

Getting Reacquainted with *The Outsiders*

The Outsiders takes place in Tulsa, Oklahoma, and was written to reflect the late 1960s surroundings of its author. S. E. Hinton had grown up in a "greaser" neighborhood (Smith), where most of the families were working class or not quite working class, and teens from her community often found themselves at odds with or outright targets of the wealthier kids from across town, whom Hinton refers to as "Socs." *The Outsiders* timeline runs quickly—the action in the novel covers the span of only a few weeks, though the book refers to the deaths of the Curtis boys' parents eight months before the events of the story take place.

In *The Outsiders*' Tulsa, the greasers and Socs mostly stick to their own neighborhoods unless meeting up for a rumble, although as in the episode that sets the tone for the remainder of the book, the Socs sometimes cross their territorial lines to jump a random greaser for fun and to make sure greasers know their place. The greasers do the same, to settle scores (S. E. Hinton 48).

The greasers are headed by twenty-year-old Darrel (Darry) Curtis. The older brother of narrator Ponyboy, Darry is the straight arrow of the group. Darry avoids trouble at all costs, primarily out of fear of losing his underage brothers to the foster care system, and works two jobs to make sure they can pay their bills and stay together. He nevertheless is bound by a sense of loyalty to his group, participates in their rumbles, and is aware of his friends' illegal activities without reporting them. The last element might make him an accessory after the fact, or possibly guilty of obstruction of justice.

Sodapop Curtis is the sixteen-year-old middle brother, who very much follows Darry's lead. A high school dropout due to low motivation, distractibility, and poor grades, Sodapop also works to support the family and selflessly anticipates continuing to do so in order to put Ponyboy through college when the time comes. Sodapop charms his way through the book with good looks and an engaging personality, being the brother who is more sympathetic to Ponyboy. Like Darry, he'll answer the call of his gang and not report their law-breaking behaviors and he generally steers clear of legal trouble.

Ponyboy Curtis is fourteen, grappling with the deaths of his parents, and he can't stay out of trouble even when he's engaged enough in the present moment to realize that it is about to befall him. An attack on Ponyboy by the "Socs" at the beginning of the book that establishes the high stakes and suddenness of the violence that can be visited upon teens from his neighborhood whose only fault is existing on a lower socioeconomic rung than their tormentors. For Ponyboy, though he never deliberately incites it, violence in *The Outsiders* occurs with the rapidity and lack of warning of a teenager's mood swings. A deep thinker and good student, Ponyboy rumbles alongside the older greasers; isn't above using a weapon to scare off a would-be attacker; sneaks into movies without paying to keep up with his crowd; and, when hard pressed, resorts to breaking and entering when he and Johnny go into hiding.

Dallas Winston is the gang member with the longest rap sheet and the only one of Ponyboy's crowd to have had experience with actual New York City street gangs. Apart from unspecified criminal priors, Dallas indulges in theft and vandalism, and he is absolutely an accessory after the fact for aiding and abetting Johnny and Ponyboy when they skip town after the death of Bob the Soc. He later engages in simple assault by threatening nurses with a switchblade, battery in the rumble afterward, and armed robbery after Johnny Cade's death. In and out of jail (with a first arrest at age ten), seventeen-year-old Dallas is the greaser furthest along on his way to becoming a career criminal.

Johnny Cade is sixteen, meek and unassuming. He rumbles with the group but doesn't seek out fights as some of his peers tend to do. He runs away from home frequently to avoid his parents' abuse and neglect. Johnny kills in defense of Ponyboy when the two boys are set upon by a group of Socs. He brandishes a knife to fend them off, saving Ponyboy from being drowned in a fountain, but fatally stabbing Bob (the leader of the Socs) in the process. Johnny and Ponyboy go on the lam and break into an abandoned church building for shelter.

Keith "Two-Bit" Mathews and Steve Randle round out the group. Apart from Ponyboy's assessment that Steve "fights for hate" and his propensity for stealing car parts, very little about Steve stands out. He is mostly defined by his annoyance at Ponyboy for tagging along and Ponyboy's dislike for him. "Two-Bit" is a cheerful no-gooder with a penchant for shoplifting, cracking jokes, and flashing switchblades.

The Socs, including presumptive leader Robert "Bob" Sheldon, Randy, David, and Paul Holden, are mainly guilty of fighting and underage drinking—though their fights sometimes come close to beating their victims to death. Johnny Cade is the victim of such an attack by the Socs when he's caught out alone in an empty lot where he'd gone to practice football kicks.

With this background in place, readers are given to understand that several members of Ponyboy's group, as well as the Socs, are not only moderately to seriously delinquent, but that they're repeat offenders with no plans to alter their lifestyle—what the criminal justice system would view as incorrigibles. At the end of the book, both groups are battered, scarred, and minus at least one of their number (Johnny through a horrible accident, Dallas through self-destruction, and Bob through Johnny's defensive act). However, all the boys are almost miraculously absolved of legal culpability for their latest and most serious skirmishes. This is the point at which the text might fall apart for editors with an eye toward realistic criminal justice outcomes in fiction, as well as modern readers who weigh the lack of legal ramifications of the group's acts against what they may personally be aware of through media or experience.

It might be tempting for readers to imagine that the changes to the criminal and juvenile justice systems that have come about since 1967 have built up slowly and incrementally to the current day, but that is not what happened. Major changes came in fits and starts, sometimes pushed equally by political expediency and perceived public need. Key pieces of legislation, including the Omnibus Crime Bill and Safe Streets Act of 1968, The Juvenile Justice and Delinquency Prevention Act of 1974 and 2002, and the Violent Crime Control and Law Enforcement Act of 1994 have shaped the juvenile justice system as we know it today (Regoli and Hewitt 9). The Omnibus Crime Bill and Safe Streets Act set aside money for research grants aimed at developing new and more effective means of juvenile corrections ("Omnibus"). The Juvenile Justice and Delinquency Prevention Act of 1974 and 2002 required that juveniles be removed from adult facilities, forbade detention in a juvenile facility for "status offenses" including running away, drinking alcohol or smoking cigarettes, and other minor infractions, and set aside funds to improve existing juvenile justice programs ("Juvenile Justice Reform"). The Violent Crime Control and Law Enforcement Act of 1994, among other things, set rules for trying juveniles as adults for violent crimes and participation in violent street gangs ("HR3355"). Those laws, as well as others that were adopted at the state level, meant that over time, *The Outsiders'* depiction of juvenile contacts with the justice system slipped further and further from the realism for which the book was lauded.

The Outsiders vs. Trial as an Adult

On their way to the rumble with the Socs, Ponyboy's gang sing and joke about being juvenile delinquents. Considering the laundry list of their various infractions, that's a fairly self-aware assessment—but crimes committed by an underage person don't necessarily end in juvenile detention.

During the 1980s, lawmakers began to adopt a "get tough" approach to juvenile crimes in response to increases in the crime rate, a perception of youngsters as smugly confident of their immunity from serious legal consequences, and a perception of the punishment of juveniles as too mild to be effectual (Bernard and Kurlychek 155). Had this 'get tough' approach been represented in *The Outsiders*, this alone would have led to one or more of the characters' facing more serious, possibly adult consequences.

By 1994, the Violent Crime Control and Law Enforcement Act had set guidelines for trying youth as adults. While this legislation was aimed at curbing urban youth involvement in serious street gangs, it could certainly have been applicable to members of Ponyboy's neighborhood gang, given the repetitive nature of their criminal behaviors. In 1996, First Lady Hillary Clinton addressed the perceived need to push further to address gang activity at Keene State College, saying, "They're not just gangs of kids anymore; they're often the kind of kids that are called 'super-predators.' No conscience, no empathy. We can talk about why they ended up that way, but first we have to bring them to heel" ("1996"). This language sounds very much like Ponyboy's description of Dallas Winston, Tim Shepherd, and the Brumly greasers, "Young hoods who would grow up to be old hoods" (S. E. Hinton 117). Arguing for legislation that would encourage more states to try juveniles as adults for violent crimes, Florida Republican Representative Porter Goss exhorted his peers to act, saying, "Our youngest career criminals are getting away with the most heinous crimes over and over again, and it's not just gang warfare . . . . Wake up!" That bill, known as The Juvenile Crime Control Bill of 1997, ultimately died in the Senate, but not before passing in the House of Representatives with the support of 209 Republicans and 77 Democrats (Gray).

Throughout the 1990s, several states made changes to their laws regarding the status of sixteen or seventeen-year-old offenders that excluded them from juvenile court and tried them instead as adults. In its publication *Juvenile Justice Reform Initiatives in the States 1994–1996*, the Office of Juvenile Justice and Delinquency Prevention noted that juveniles were sent to adult criminal court for nonviolent as well as violent offenses:

> Of the small number of juvenile cases waived to criminal court, more nonviolent offenders were waived than violent offenders. Nonviolent

offenders comprised 66 percent of all juveniles waived to adult court in 1992, according to [the General Accounting Office]. ("Juvenile Justice Reform")

Crime control and being tough on crime in general were planks in most politicians' political platforms at that time because safety sells and allows otherwise partisan voters to meet in the middle. There often appeared to be an effort on the part of liberal and moderate politicians to prove they would be as tough on crime as their conservative opponents if elected, and campaign rhetoric was heavily slanted toward crime control throughout the 80s and 90s, to the degree that elections could be won or lost because of it. *Mother Jones* reporter Patrick Caldwell noted in an article detailing former Vice President Joe Biden's history with the movement toward mass incarceration in the United States, "As crime rates spiked across the country, Democrats adopted a harsh tough-on-crime posture. Yet few pushed the issue quite as hard as Biden." Caldwell notes that Biden's "career-defining victory" was the passage of the 1994 Violent Crime Control and Law Enforcement Act, which he had helped to clear the Senate with the support of 188 of his fellow Democrats (Caldwell).

The get-tough mentality and the push to stem the tide of youth crime, and thereby crime overall, meant that by 1997, as author Elizabeth Hinton writes, "all fifty states had laws on the books allowing children as young as ten to be tried as adults" (E. Hinton 241). Today, estimates put the yearly number of juveniles prosecuted as adults across the United States at around 250,000, with as many as 10,000 juveniles being housed in adult correctional facilities ("Key Facts"). The Juvenile Justice and Delinquency Prevention Act of 1974 and 2002 forbade juveniles from being housed in adult prisons, but that protection does not extend to juveniles tried as adults. At most, *The Outsiders* refers to the possibility of brief stints in jail, but certainly never years or decades in adult prison other than potentially for Johnny and Ponyboy after Bob's killing. Cavalierly singing about holding up gas stations makes far less sense in a contemporary context when arrest for armed robbery could result in the character's spending half his life in prison.

In 2005, the Supreme Court's *Roper v. Simmons* decision ruled that those under the age of eighteen at the time they committed capital offenses were not eligible for the death penalty (Regoli and Hewitt 470). In 2010, *Graham v. Florida* held that minors prosecuted as adults for crimes that had not resulted in a death could not be given life sentences without parole (Agnew and Brezina 19). In 2016, the *Montgomery v. Louisiana* decision effectively ended mandatory life without parole sentences for juveniles. Even with these rulings, spending the majority of their lives behind bars is a very real possibility for youngsters tried as adults, hardly the slap on the wrist juvenile justice was perceived to be in the time period leading up to the "get tough" era. *The Outsiders* simply doesn't go far enough in the legal outcomes it presents for juvenile offenses despite its characters' worries about jail or boys' homes. A realistic book that involves juvenile contacts with the criminal justice system would have to reflect the gravity of spending decades—if not life—behind bars.

The Outsiders vs. Three Strikes

The relationship among politicians, the media, and the public is dynamic and fluid, with pressure exerted to change the behaviors of one of those entities also potentially affecting either or both of the other two. Throughout the 1990s, changes to juvenile and criminal justice were taking place at the federal and state levels, and beyond those previously mentioned, another type of legislation began to catch on with lawmakers seeking to assure the public that every possible measure was being taken to curtail crime. It was dubbed the "Three Strikes and You're Out" law.

First adopted by Washington State in 1993, the concept quickly took hold elsewhere. Though there was some variation amongst its iterations, three-strikes laws generally meant that a third arrest and conviction after one arrest and conviction of a felony would result in a maximal prison term for the current conviction, plus an "enhancement" of five years for each prior felony conviction. Michael Vitiello of the University of the Pacific McGeorge School of Law notes that three-strikes laws began their rise, paradoxically,

---

at a point when the number of incarcerated persons had trebled from the previous decade and crime rates had begun to ebb (395). Vitiello says despite the reduction, "most Americans felt more vulnerable to violent crime than they did a decade earlier. At a time when crime rates were declining modestly, politicians in several states seized on the fear of crime as a powerful political issue" (395).

Three-strikes laws, and the dynamics among politicians, the media, and public that led to their passage, are important here for three reasons. First, they provide another example of modern law that would lead to far different outcomes for *The Outsiders* characters if the story were being written realistically today. Second, the interplay of media, political figures, and the public which led to their passage created a condition referred to as moral panic. This is relevant because moral panic is an extreme example of the building of expectations amongst the public for outcomes within the criminal justice system. Third, it is important for the reader to understand that public expectations are better informed than ever, given the fact that most Americans are almost never separated from their media sources via their smart phones, the Internet, the twenty-four-hour news cycle, and social media. Whether their expectations are accurate (much like the crime rate confusion in the early-to-mid 1990s) is another matter: public expectations of outcomes for criminal behavior exist. These expectations respond to input from political and media sources, can cause pressure to be exerted on media and government for answers and remedies, and can be manipulated for gain by both media and politicians.

This is sufficient reason to conclude that it is reasonable to factor in such public expectation of outcomes when weighing whether *The Outsiders* could be written the same today. Within *The Outsiders* universe are several characters (Two-Bit, Dallas, Steve Randle, Tim Shepard) who could theoretically be charged with felonies for their crimes, tried as adults, and become subject to three-strikes-law enhanced sentencing. Those outcomes would probably not seem strange to contemporary readers and would read as more believable than the book ending with several of the characters having no contacts with law enforcement at all.

The Outsiders vs. Private Prisons

One fairly significant change to potential outcomes for *The Outsiders* characters does not directly involve legislation, but rather the type of carceral custody they might find themselves in were they to be processed into the juvenile justice system: the rise of private prisons.

Beginning in 1983, private correctional facilities began to be developed by entrepreneurs Thomas W. Beasley and Doctor R. Crants solely for the purpose of creating an innovative new income stream (Selman and Leighton 55). By 1984, Beasley and Crants' newly formed Corrections Corporation of America had opened its first juvenile facility in Tennessee (Pauly).

Popular with some states because of the potential savings to the state in construction and maintenance costs of facilities and credited by proponents with helping to affordably ease prison overcrowding, CCA has been dogged by controversy and abuse claims throughout its existence, including in 2004, when a U. S. Department of Justice investigation uncovered "physical abuses by staff" among other problems at a CCA juvenile facility in Baltimore (Pauly).

One of the troubling aspects of privately run correctional facilities is that the business model only generates profit when facilities are operating at maximum capacity, which presents a problem for operators and opens the door to political graft on the part of unscrupulous politicians. One well-documented example of incentivized incarceration leading to corruption occurred with two smaller private correctional facility companies in Pennsylvania who paid two judges over $2 million in kickbacks for funneling juveniles to their facilities—sometimes by the use of grossly disproportionate sentences for misbehavior (Urbina and Hamill).

Public awareness of private prisons and correctional facilities may be somewhat less than knowledge of three-strikes laws and minors being tried as adults, and the building of expectation is contingent upon repeated exposure and messaging; therefore, fewer expectations may exist for readers of *The Outsiders* based solely on knowledge of this issue. However, increasing activism on the part of the American Civil Liberties Union and others through the platform of social media has aimed to raise the issue's profile in the public consciousness in recent years as part of a growing demand for accountability in law enforcement and corrections. Thus, public expectation of juvenile justice outcomes that incorporates some knowledge of private prisons may be growing as a part of an overall awareness raised by those social media campaigns.

The Outsiders vs. Wrongful Death (The Surge in American Litigation)

Even if *The Outsiders* were written so that every other character plausibly managed to avoid contact with the juvenile and criminal justice systems, there still might be cause to require a rewrite to depict a more realistic outcome for Ponyboy, based on public familiarity with the existence of wrongful death lawsuits.

Civil suits like wrongful death are separate from criminal proceedings, and a justifiable homicide decision from a judge may not preclude the survivors of a victim, such as Bob Sheldon's parents, from seeking the only legal avenue for outright revenge available to them, after the judge failed to pursue criminal proceedings against Ponyboy (Johnny, by this time, is dead and thus cannot be prosecuted), via a wrongful death lawsuit. The Sheldons could conceivably have sued the Curtis family for failing to adequately supervise Ponyboy, the cost of Bob's burial, and their own suffering due to his loss. It would not have been about the money; it would have been about ruining the Curtis family, and, given the Curtises' hand-to-mouth existence, it wouldn't have taken much of a settlement to do exactly that.

How would the public be aware of the possibilities for civil litigation? Simply by watching an hour's worth of cable television and being subjected to ad after ad for law firms of all types. Since 1977, when the Supreme Court decision in *Bates v. State Bar of Arizona* relaxed rules against lawyers' using television advertising, law firms have steadily increased their advertising spending; in 2017 alone, firms spent over $1 billion for TV ads to reach prospective clients (Li). The litigiousness of American society overall increased right along with it. According to the Bureau of Justice Statistics, there were 25,000 civil trial in 2005, and punitive damages (such as the Sheldons might have pursued) were sought in 12 percent of those cases (Cohen and Harbacek).

It would then be very easy for readers to more readily accept a hypothetical outcome for Ponyboy in which he and his family are sued for Bob's death, can't afford an attorney to represent them, lose the case, and then find they must pay more than they can afford to settle it. Unable to afford an attorney to help them declare bankruptcy, they lose their home and are forced to sell any other valuable goods they own, such as cars, to pay off as much as possible. Perhaps Ponyboy would wind up in foster care as Darry and Sodapop enter the military to avoid homelessness and pay off the debt.

The Outsiders vs. Privilege

Cherry Valance insists to Ponyboy regarding life as a Soc, "We have troubles you've never even heard of . . . things are tough all over," but Ponyboy is far from convinced (S. E. Hinton 31). In the book, Ponyboy has come to accept that while the Socs may be reproached for bad behavior in local newspapers one week, they'll almost certainly be heralded for some civic service the next. He rails against the greasers' collectively getting "all the rough breaks" (S. E. Hinton 38), but whatever travails the Socs have to endure, the threat of jail or "the boy's home" for them never seems to enter Ponyboy's consciousness, and certainly never the text. The greatest fear of the Socs, as voiced by Randy, is being labelled as less-than by their peers: in Randy's case, either a "chicken" or a "punk." (S. E. Hinton 99)

This at least has an anchor in our contemporary reality. Leniency and the defense of an almost mythical "bright future" can be had, even in criminal court, provided the defendant is wealthy, white, and male.

In Texas in 2013, a highly intoxicated sixteen-year-old named Ethan Couch crashed his truck into a small crowd of people, injuring nine and killing four. He was sentenced to ten years of probation supervised through the juvenile justice system. Couch was caught breaking his probation by drinking alcohol again, at which point he and his mother fled to Mexico to avoid the consequences. They were

---

captured and returned to the US, where Couch was ordered to spend a little less than two years in jail for his actions ("Attorneys").

The judge in the case, Wayne Salvant, had ignited controversy with his initial lenient sentence, particularly because Couch's legal team's defense was that Couch was a victim himself, of "affluenza"— that is, not knowing the difference between right and wrong due to overindulgent parents.

In 2016, Brock Turner, who was nineteen at the time of his arrest for sexually assaulting an unconscious woman, received probation and served three months of a six-month jail sentence. In reporting about the sentence, CNN noted a 1997 study that athletes like Turner, a star swimmer at Stanford University, are convicted in only 31 percent of sexual assaults for which they are prosecuted, compared to the 54 percent of convictions of defendants from the general population (Gagnon and Grinberg).

Austin Wilkerson was given probation and ten months in jail, which he was allowed to serve in the form of work release after raping an unconscious woman in 2014. He was twenty-two years old at the time. Judge Patrick Butler stated, "I think we all need to find out whether he truly can or cannot be rehabilitated" (Phillips). Wilkerson was a student at the University of Colorado at the time of the rape and enjoyed opportunity and affluence that Ponyboy and his friends could not aspire to. It would be difficult for readers to picture the greasers' getting that kind of consideration from a judge, but much easier to imagine it for the Socs, who never face arrest, even for their attempted drowning of Ponyboy. Hinton nailed it with the Socs in *The Outsiders*. For all the changes in criminal and juvenile justice outcomes throughout the decades, this theme of privilege appears not to have changed much.

The Outsiders vs. Readers and the Totality of Circumstances

What saves *The Outsiders* for modern audiences is the fact that despite the universality of teen angst and sense of otherness that help adolescents relate to the text, there are dated references to music, slang, typical 60s-era landmarks that would be anachronistic rarities today, like drive-in theaters, that solidly root it in the day and cultural atmosphere in which it was written. These cues to another time and place protect the reader from the challenge to the suspension of their disbelief that might occur if they were forced to attempt to configure the relatively light punishment Ponyboy and his friends incurred (with the notable exception of Dallas) within the context of modern outcomes for delinquency.

In sum, juvenile delinquency and its outcomes within the criminal justice system do not occur in a vacuum, nor is public exposure to them limited to media influence. These interactions occur within our communities and within our schools, and they sometimes involve members of our own families. This is not to say the public at large has expertise in the intricacies of juvenile justice, but the cumulative effect of those repetitive exposures includes the creation of expectations about how young offenders will be dealt with. With this in mind, it is doubtful that an author could write the same sort of outcomes for his or her characters in a book meant to reflect what teens see around them on a daily basis, or that an editor or agent would accept it as such.

S. E. Hinton wrote *The Outsiders* to reflect the world she experienced as a sixteen-year-old, and her voice still comes across as credible, further shielding readers from any disconnect between what happens in the book and outcomes they may have witnessed in real life. It is only in that earnest teenage voice, then, that the book can be said to be realistic in any way, within a modern context wherein teens may face adult punishment for their crimes as a matter of course. The Campaign for Youth Justice notes that the stakes are very high indeed for youth who are tried as adults in particular because the repercussions do not end with their incarceration—they may face unemployment due to the stigma of a felony record and not be able to improve their circumstance through education due to ineligibility for some forms of student assistance ("Key Facts").

This essay began with a quotation from Robert Pruett, who was imprisoned at the age of fifteen for the stabbing death of a neighbor that was committed by his father. Pruett was present when the killing occurred, and according to Texas' "law of parties,"

Pruett was held equally culpable, though he did not strike a blow (Robinson). Pruett was executed after being convicted of killing a corrections officer, despite there being no physical evidence that he was involved in that killing. His story is heartbreaking and grim, but only one of the more recent examples of the serious consequences juveniles may face in the criminal justice system. It is poignant that Pruett recognized something of his own experience in S. E. Hinton's books—possibly even *The Outsiders*. The fact that he did so makes it clear that not only does life imitate art, but that models for art are found in the most hopeless and tragic of events and that the need to ponder and learn from such models is urgent. *The Outsiders* includes an appeal from Hinton, voiced through Ponyboy, for her readers to look more closely at young people from the wrong side of the tracks before forming an opinion about them: "Someone should tell their side of the story, and maybe people would understand then and wouldn't be so quick to judge a boy . . ." (S. E. Hinton 179). It stands to reason that adolescents not only need to be understood, but to understand what it is they might confront if they cross a line and become processed into the criminal justice system.

If *The Outsiders* was the right book to address the grittier experiences of teens in 1967, I would suggest that future novels address juvenile crime, detention, and incarceration with the same unflinching gaze, but with outcomes that reflect what is true of the system as the public would recognize it today. Students deserve literature like *The Outsiders* and future books that will address youth crime and its fallout in way that is meaningful, realistic, and relevant to their own era. To deprive them of it is to consign the issue of engagement with the criminal justice system in literature to dystopian fantasy, which has its own merits, but is unhelpful for opening dialogue, promoting inquiry, and drawing attention to real-life situations in the way one would hope that literature for teens and young adults would do. If formerly incarcerated youth can write true or fictionalized accounts of that experience in their own voices, even better!

While some might criticize this view and question whether it's all right to subject young readers to stories that might disturb them and cause them to question the system in which they live, I would counter that it's more than all right. It's necessary.

Note

1. Quoted from *The Autobiography of Robert Pruett* by Nathan Robinson.

Works Cited

Agnew, Robert, and Timothy Brezina. *Juvenile Delinquency: Causes and Control.* 5th ed., Oxford UP, 2015.

"Attorneys for 'Affluenza' Teen Ethan Couch Ask to Have Him Released." *HuffingtonPost.com*, 1 Sept. 2016, www.huffingtonpost.com/entry/ethan-couch-seeks-release_us_57c818fde4b078581f1128f5/.

Austin, James, and Garry Coventry. *Emerging Issues on Private Prisons.* US Department of Justice, 2001, www.ncjrs.gov/pdffiles1/bja/181249.pdf/.

Bernard, Thomas, and Megan Kurlychek. *The Cycle of Juvenile Justice.* Oxford UP, 2010.

Caldwell, Patrick. "Before He Was America's Wacky Uncle, Joe Biden was a Tough-on-Crime Hardliner." *Mother Jones*, 7 Aug. 2015, www.motherjones.com/politics/2015/08/joe-biden-crime-bill-mass-incarceration/.

Cohen, Thomas, and Kyle Harbacek. "Punitive Damage Awards in State Courts, 2005." *BJS.gov*, 24 Mar. 2011, www.bjs.gov/index.cfm?ty=pbdetail&iid=2376/.

Gagnon, Janette, and Emanuella Grinberg. "Mad about Brock Turner's Sentence? It's Not Uncommon." *CNN.com*, 4 Sept. 2016, www.cnn.com/2016/09/02/us/brock-turner-college-athletes-sentence/index.html/.

Gray, Jerry. "House Passes Bill to Combat Juvenile Crime." *NYTimes.com*, 9 May 1997, www.nytimes.com/1997/05/09/us/house-passes-bill-to-combat-juvenile-crime.html/.

Great Women Writers: *Rita Dove, S. E. Hinton, and Maya Angelou.* Hacienda Productions, 1999.

"H.R. 3355—Violent Crime Control and Law Enforcement Act of 1994." *Congress.gov*, n.d., www.congress.gov/bill/103rd-congress/house-bill/3355/text. Accessed 17 Nov. 2017.

Hinton, Elizabeth. *From the War on Poverty to the War on Crime*. Harvard UP, 2016.

Hinton, S. E. *The Outsiders*. Viking, 1967.

"Juvenile Justice and Delinquency Prevention as amended, Pub. L. No. 93-415 (1974)." *OJJDP.gov*, n.d., www.ojjdp.gov/about/jjdpa2002titlev.pdf/.

"Juvenile Justice Reform Initiatives in the States 1994-1996." *OJJDP.gov*, n.d., www.ojjdp.gov/pubs/reform/ch2_j.html/. Accessed 29 Jan. 2018.

"Juvenile Life Without Parole: An Overview." *SentencingProject.org*, 13 Oct. 2017, www.sentencingproject.org/publications/juvenile-life-without-parole/.

"Key Facts: Youth in the Justice System." *CampaignForYouthJustice.org*, Apr. 2012, www.campaignforyouthjustice.org/documents/KeyYouthCrimeFacts.pdf/.

Kingkade, Tyler. "No Prison for Colorado Student Who Raped Helpless Freshman." *HuffingtonPost.com*, 10 Aug. 2016, www.huffingtonpost.com/entry/austin-wilkerson-boulder-rape-prison_us_57abb86ce4b06e52746f3b22/.

Li, Victor. "Legal Advertising Blows Past $1 Billion and Goes Viral." *ABAJournal.com*, Apr. 2017, www.abajournal.com/magazine/article/legal_advertising_viral_video/.

"1996: Hillary Clinton on 'Superpredators' (C-SPAN)." *Youtube*, uploaded by CSPAN, 25 Feb. 2016, www.youtube.com/watch?v=j0uCrA7ePno/.

"Omnibus Crime Control and Safe Streets." *Transition.fcc.gov*, n.d., transition.fcc.gov/Bureaus/OSEC/library/legislative_histories/1615.pdf/. Accessed 17 Nov. 2017.

Pauly, Madison. "A Brief History of America's Private Prison Industry." *Mother Jones*, July/August 2016, www.motherjones.com/politics/2016/06/history-of-americas-private-prison-industry-timeline/.

Phillips, Noelle. "Boulder Rape Victim, Advocates Say Sentencing Shows too Much Concern for Perpetrator's Future." *Denver Post*, 12 Aug. 2016, www.denverpost.com/2016/08/12/boulder-rape-victim-letter/.

Regoli, Robert, and John Hewitt. *Exploring Criminal Justice*. Jones and Bartlett Learning, 2008.

Robinson, Nathan. "The Autobiography of Robert Pruett." *Currentaffairs. org*, 9 Oct. 2017, www.currentaffairs.org/2017/10/the-autobiography-of-robert-pruett/.

Selman, Donna, and Paul Leighton. *Punishment for Sale: Private Prisons, Big Business, and the Incarceration Binge.* Rowman and Littlefield, 2010.

Smith, Dinitia. "An Outsider out of the Shadows." *New York Times*, 07 Sept. 2005, p. E1. *EBSCOhost*, 0nesearch.ebscohost.com.library. acaweb.org/login.aspx?direct=true&db=f5h&AN=18139141&site= eds-live/.

Urbina, Ian, and Sean Hammill. "Judge Pleads Guilty in Scheme to Jail Youths for Profit." *New York Times*, 12 Feb. 2009, www.nytimes. com/2009/02/13/us/13judge.html/.

Vitiello, Michael. "Criminal Law: Three Strikes: Can We Return to Rationality?" *Journal of Criminal Law and Criminology*, vol. 87, 1 Jan. 1997, p. 395.

Critical Reception: *The Outsiders*_____

M. Katherine Grimes with Lana A. Whited

The Outsiders is probably the best-known book from a pivotal era in literature for adolescent readers, the dawn of young adult literature as a trend. In *Horn Book* in 2003, Patty Campbell writes that *The Outsiders* instigated "a whole new vision of relevance in books for teens" (*"The Outsiders"*). The same publishing era—the 1960s and early '70s—saw the appearance of several novels representing a youth culture fraught with ugly realities not previously confronted directly by adolescent protagonists. Robert Lipsyte's *The Contender* (1967) portrays a black seventeen-year-old high school dropout who lives with his aunt in Harlem and trains as a boxer as an alternative to life on the streets. Ann Head's *Mr. and Mrs. Bo Jo Jones* (1967) depicts young lovers grappling with the life-altering consequences of their sexuality; Paul Zindel's *My Darling, My Hamburger* (1969) also depicts teens confronting the complications of sexual intimacy, including pregnancy, the aftereffects of abortion, and the threat of rape. Bill and Vera Cleaver's *Where the Lilies Bloom* (1969) is about four siblings in western North Carolina attempting to maintain their family and avoid being sent into the foster system in the aftermath of their father's death. Bill Donovan's *I'll Get There. It Better Be Worth the Trip* (1969) is among the first mainstream YA novels about homosexuality, and Beatrice Sparks' *Go Ask Alice* (1971) tells the story of a fifteen-year-old girl who develops a drug addiction and runs away from home. What all these books have in common is their portrayal of teenage characters alienated from adults and facing decisions and circumstances not previously depicted in literature for young readers in a forthright and graphic manner. As Patty Campbell notes, J. D. Salinger's *The Catcher in the Rye* had appeared about fifteen years earlier, but "there was nothing in the literature [prior to 1967] that would suggest a trend" (*"The Outsiders"*).

This same period overlapped with a flush in federal funding for libraries, notes Campbell, who took her first job as a librarian for young adult literature in the Los Angeles Public Library system. Bolstered with money from the Library Services and Construction Act (1962), Title IIB of the Higher Education Act (1965), and the Office of Economic Opportunities, library systems hired more staff and devised new programming designed to attract an increasingly diverse public. Libraries, Campbell says, tried "anything that would bring teens to the library and get books into their hands." The trend in popularity of literature for this age group was enhanced by the fact that baby boomers were teens in the 1960s. According to Campbell, "YA services rode the crest of this population wave, with enthusiasm and federal funding." And authors such as S. E. Hinton were the direct beneficiaries: *The Outsiders*, Campbell says, "hit the target and rang the bell" (*"The Outsiders"*). Soon, the venerable American Library Association, which had previously avoided what it called "junior novels" on its "Best Books" lists, began promoting "Best Books for Young Adults." And librarians specializing in YA literature began congregating at conferences and organizing groups such as the ALA's Young Adult Services Division (YASD), which eventually became the Young Adult Library Services Association (YALSA) in 1991 (Fine). Prior to about 1968, Richard Alm argues, the books offered to young readers were "superficial, often distorted, sometimes completely false representations of adolescence" (qtd. in Campbell, *"The Outsiders"*). S. E. Hinton has said more than once that she was writing *The Outsiders* in part to fill the void left by such bland books. Patty Campbell and several other critics such as Michael Cart believe that Hinton's 1967 novel and a number of essays about literature for adolescents written about the same time "marked the rise of the new realism" (Campbell, "Sand" 373).

The realism of Hinton's first published novel rang true with readers and many critics, but it also offended others. In 1968, respected reviewer Zena Sutherland addressed the controversy arising from the presentation of violence in *The Outsiders*. Sutherland explains that while young people were reading the book with gusto and proclaiming their love for it, parents were expressing concern about the violence, especially violent acts perpetrated by teenagers and not always overtly condemned. The realistic nature of the violence was found to be of particular concern.

A 1970 review in *The [London] Times Literary Supplement* also presumed that parents and their children would react differently to Hinton's novel. The reviewer predicted that adult readers would be unimpressed with the "literary egocentrism" of the novel and the plot that "creaks" and the "wholly factitious" ending. On the other hand, the reviewer thought that young readers would see Ponyboy as both a realistic character and a sort of "folk hero."

The Outsiders was recognized immediately as an important work; the year it was published, 1967, it earned a *New York Herald Tribune*'s best teenage books citation and was named a *Chicago Tribune Book World* Spring Book Festival Honor Book. In the 1970s, the novel won awards from *Media & Methods* and the American Library Association as well as the Massachusetts Children's Book Award. In 1988, S. E. Hinton received the first American Library Association Young Adult Services Division/*School Library Journal* Margaret A. Edwards Award for her work ("S(usan) E(loise) Hinton").

Four decades after the novel's publication, the third generation of readers was beginning to find the novel, some by word of mouth from their friends; others by assignments from their teachers; still others by the recommendations of librarians; and, finally, others by introductions from their parents. The gap between adolescent readers and their parents in regard to the novel no longer existed, for the parents had often read and loved the novel in their youth. In fact, by the fortieth anniversary of the novel's publication, even grandparents and grandchildren were sharing *The Outsiders*.

In a 2006 article in *The English Journal*, published by the National Council of Teachers of English, seventh-grade teacher Joanne S. Gillespie discusses ways she uses *The Outsiders* in her classes to help students understand various aspects of literature, such as characterization. Gillespie recounts incidents in which the novel prompts children to tell stories of their own suffering, especially from bullying. She also notes that one of the most valuable lessons that her students learn is that none of the characters is totally bad or totally good. Developmental psychologist Jean Piaget would cite this observation as evidence of children's beginning to move from the cognitive stage of concrete reasoning to formal reasoning, a stage that shows evidence of more abstract thinking, the ability to think of people and actions as gray instead of black and white, and feeling empathy.

The year 2007 saw numerous articles and essays about the then-forty-year-old novel. One of the most intriguing is an essay in *Children's Literature in Education* by Eric L. Tribunella, who basically refutes the teachers who argue that their students benefit from reading Hinton's book. Reminding readers that Ponyboy Curtis's narrative is written as a make-up project for a class, Tribunella asserts that *The Outsiders* both in content and in its use in schools is really just an academic exercise in the sense that it proposes no real solutions to the problems it describes, either for Ponyboy and his family and friends or for the student readers who are assigned the novel by their teachers. He supports his position with a discussion of the end of the novel, which he claims shows that the only solution Ponyboy has found to the conflicts between the Socs and the greasers and to the hard lives his brothers and friends face is to write about the situations he sees. All the characters from the beginning of the novel are either dead or in about the same situations in which they found themselves before Ponyboy stepped out of the theatre after that Paul Newman movie. Tribunella says that the same is true of the young people who read the novel, as well. While they might feel kinship with Ponyboy, the novel offers them no more practical ways to cope with their lives than it does its narrator.

But numerous teachers disagree with Tribunella. Associate Professor Jennifer Dail explains that her teacher education students are required to read the novel because it focuses on young people's "identity development and finding a place in the world," as well as their distrust of the "system" and desire for "something better" (14).

In a less scholarly look back at Hinton's book forty years after its publication, Dale Peck in *The New York Times* discusses allusions in the novel to books and movies with which the author would have been familiar, such as Shirley Jackson's 1962 novel *We Always Lived in the Castle* and the 1955 film *Rebel without a Cause*, starring James Dean. Peck asserts that Hinton's success came from both her earnestness and the fact that she "wrote to reveal the universality of her Greasers, just as [Richard] Wright and [Ralph] Ellison did for African-Americans, or [Grace] Paley and [Philip] Roth did for Jews."

A few years later, Hinton's fellow Oklahoman Ally Carter wrote about reading the novel with a bunch of her girlfriends when they were teenagers, then learning from her father that Hinton was a woman and that she was from Tulsa, an hour away from Carter's home. Carter writes that reading *The Outsiders* made her see that people other than "dead Europeans" write books. Carter says of *The Outsiders*, "It was the first time I'd realized that *real people* write books. Not only that—I realized that real people who were *like me* wrote books." And so Carter, too, took up the pen, for Hinton "had created this story—pulled it out of thin air and made it come alive." Writing in the *Huffington Post* on *The Outsiders'* fiftieth anniversary, Maddie Crum affirms that Carter's reaction to Hinton's accomplishments is not unusual. Crum asserts that current writers of books for young readers have S. E. Hinton to thank for their success, especially those whose books get made into films, as Hinton's did in 1983.

On the fiftieth anniversary of the novel's publication, Hayley Krischer in the *New York Times* shares Professor Jennifer Buehler's theories as to why the book has endured: the support of librarians and teachers, the characterization, the "universal title and the seemingly genderless author," and "the greasers' . . . need to be seen as human, [which] is similar to what many marginalized groups today are also trying to claim" (Krischer).

After Krischer's article appeared, an article in the *New York Times* reported that it received over 700 responses, generally testimonials to the impact *The Outsiders* had on people's lives. One respondent writes that Hinton's novel is "an incredibly beautiful book about being lost and fighting against stereotypes and poverty" and loved the book enough to skip school to see the movie every day for a week ("Readers"). Another reader pointed out the irony of teachers' assigning to students a novel about teenage rebellion. And one of those teachers explains why he assigns it: "[It d]oesn't matter what the kid's language, culture or race is, they . . . really enjoy it and relate to it" ("Readers").

Many readers testify to the power of S. E. Hinton's book. British novelist Matt Haig writes, "This is not the best written book in the world, . . . but what it has is a powerful feeling of hope coupled with a beautifully sentimental sense of life." Haig notes that it is one of the books that helped him deal with painful depression. He says, "[T]hat American sense of hope was like medicine."

While essays by scholars and articles by journalists give us information about S. E. Hinton's novel and insight about themes, reviews by readers can also be enlightening. Here are a few:

Hemma, a teenaged reviewer for *The Guardian*, attributes the longevity of the book to its "presenting adolescent characters that were the opposite of everything a teenager, by adult standards, should have been." Hemma continues, "We also see through Ponyboy the need felt by most adolescents to fit in and be part of a group, and yet also the need to be an individual and the struggle to figure out who you are within the restrictions set by society, friends, peers and family." Thus, the young reviewer recommends the book to all teenagers.

Dj_bookworm99, also writing in *The Guardian*, asserts that *The Outsiders* is "extremely well written" with scenes that "are always sketched out with extraordinary finesse . . . ." The reviewer finds that *The Outsiders* "sums up perfectly the predicament of the young, not only in the 60s but also in the succeeding years and decades."

Goodreads readers gave the novel an overall rating of 4.07 out of five stars. But many gave it an enthusiastic five-star rating. Here are some of the comments worth noting:

- Emily May writes of *The Outsiders*, "It was quite enjoyable, but I truly do not believe teenage boys in 1960s Oklahoma thought about each other's pretty hair."

- Briynne, who gave the book five stars, writes, "I wish there were more stars to give *The Outsiders*, but five will have to do. I love this book, and have loved it faithfully since I read it in sixth grade—I must have read it a dozen times, and possibly more. I can quote long sections of the book. I was obsessed, and to some degree still am."
- Duane observes, "Occasionally a book is written at the perfect time, with the perfect story, with the perfect group of characters; and it is written with a passion and an insight that make it unique, that distinguishes it from any other book and any other story. And sometimes it defines a generation, or a culture or sub-culture of that generation. That, my friends, is what this book does."
- Kylie gushes, "I think I'm falling in love all over again. This will always be my favorite book and I . . . see myself reading this another 4 times during this year. I believe this is a book that all ages need to read, it's such a life changer and it shows you [how] rough people have it. Rich or poor everybody goes through some sort of hell. It teaches you to respect and appreciate where you are brought up and who you are brought up with. Always choose kindness."
- Chelsea says what many readers feel but don't explain so succinctly: "This book broke my heart."
- And Al leaves us with this: "God I love this book so much I want to marry it and feed it tiny morsels."

Let's check in with *The Outsiders* in about ten years to see what critics and other readers are saying then.

Works Cited

Campbell, Patty. "*The Outsiders*, Fat Freddy, and Me." *Horn Book Magazine*, vol. 79, no. 2, March/April 2003, p. 177. *EBSCO Host, O-search.ebscohost.com.* Accessed 16 Jan. 2018.

_____. "The Sand in the Oyster." *Horn Book Magazine*, vol. 72, no. 3, May/June 1996, pp. 371-76.

Carter, Ally. *NPR Books*, 28 Jan. 2013, www.npr.org/2013/01/28/151966146/ rich-kids-greasers-and-the-life-changing-power-of-the-outsiders/.

Crum, Maddie. "Happy 50th Anniversary to *The Outsiders*, the Book that Created a Genre." *Huffington Post*, 24 Apr. 2017, www. huffingtonpost.com/entry/the-the-outsiders-se-hinton-50th-anniversary_us_58fe3337e4b00fa7de167a54/.

Dail, Jennifer S. "First Opinion: S. E. Hinton's *The Outsiders*: First Look." *First Opinions, Second Reactions*, vol. 7, no. 1, May 2014, pp. 13-15. docs.lib.purdue.edu/cgi/viewcontent. cgi?article=1430&context=fosr/.

Dj_bookworm99. "*The Outsider[s]* by S.E. Hinton—Review." *The Guardian*, 27 Mar. 2014, www.theguardian.com/childrens-books-site/2014/mar/27/review-the-outsider-s-e-hinton/.

Fine, Jana R. "YASD: A Narrative History From 1976 to 1992." *Young Adult Library Services Association*, www.ala.org/yalsa/aboutyalsa/ yalsahandbook/yasdnarrative/. Accessed 17 Jan. 2018.

Gillespie, Joanne S. "Getting Inside S. E. Hinton's *The Outsiders.*" *English Journal*, vol. 95, no. 3, Jan. 2006, pp. 44-48. *JSTOR*, www.jstor.org/ stable/30047043.

Haig, Matt. "*The Outsiders* by S. E. Hinton. Book of a Lifetime: A Powerful Feeling of Hope." *The Independent*, 12 Nov. 2015. www.independent. co.uk/arts-entertainment/books/reviews/the-outsiders-by-se-hinton-book-of-a-lifetime-a-powerful-feeling-of-hope-a6731956.html/.

Hemma (teenaged reviewer). "*The Outsiders* by S.E. Hinton—Review." *The Guardian*, 23 Sept. 2015, www.theguardian.com/childrens-books-site/2015/sep/23/the-outsiders-s-e-hinton-review/.

Krischer, Hayley. "Why *The Outsiders* Lives On: A Teenage Novel Turns 50." *The New York Times*, 12 Mar. 2017, www.nytimes. com/2017/03/12/books/the-outsiders-s-e-hinton-book.html/.

"On the Hook." Review of *The Outsiders* by S. E. Hinton. *The [London] Times Literary Supplement*, 30 Oct. 1970, p. 1258. Rpt. *Contemporary Literary Criticism*, Vol 111, 1999.

Peck, Dale. "*The Outsiders*: 40 Years Later." *New York Times*, 23 Sept. 2007, www.nytimes.com/2007/09/23/books/review/Peck-t.html/.

"Readers Share Their Love for *The Outsiders*." *New York Times Book Review*, 15 Mar. 2017, www.nytimes.com/2017/0315books/ review/readers-share-their-love-for-the-outsiders.html/.

"S(usan) E(loise) Hinton." *Contemporary Authors Online*. Gale, 7 Jan. 2005.

Sutherland, Zena. "The Teen-Ager Speaks." *The Saturday Review*, 27 Jan. 1968, p. 34. Rpt. *Contemporary Literary Criticism*, vol. 111, 1999.

Tribunella, Eric L. "Institutionalizing *The Outsiders*: YA Literature, Social Class, and the American Faith in Education." *Children's Literature in Education*, vol. 38, 2007 (published online 13 Jun. 2006), pp. 87-101. *EBSCO*, doi 10.1007/s10583-006-9016-2.

"You greasers have a different set of values": Othering, Violence, and the Promise of Reconciliation in S.E Hinton's *The Outsiders*____

Jake Brown

After rescuing his younger brother from a brutal beating on the walk home from the movies, Darry Curtis has only one piece of advice for Ponyboy: "if you did have to go by yourself, you should have carried a blade" (Hinton 13). No cops are called; no police reports are filed; no professional medical care is given, all of which would suggest extraordinary circumstances; instead, Darry's advice and the affirmation of his wisdom by his brothers testify to the normality of the violence in the Oklahoma of S. E. Hinton's *The Outsiders.* This violence saturates the novel, culminating in Johnny Cade's killing of Bob, an act itself anticipated by the trauma caused by Johnny's own beating, because he, like Ponyboy, was walking alone, four months before the events of the novel (Hinton 57, 34).

What is at the root of this cycle of violence? Ponyboy links it to the gang warfare between the East-side greasers and the West-side Socs (despite his assertion that there's no gang rivalry in the Southwest), but that's only half true. Bob's death is not the result of the greasers' and the Socs' defending their established boundary lines, but by those lines becoming blurred. In other words, it's not just that Ponyboy tried to pick up Cherry, Bob's Soc girlfriend, but that Cherry was genuinely interested in Ponyboy, in more than just a superficial way, and in a way that clearly threatened the Socs who hunted them down.

Similar to *Romeo and Juliet*'s Montagues and Capulets, *The Outsiders* explores the link between identity and violence, a link that has fascinated philosophers for most of the twentieth century. Poststructuralist philosopher Jacques Derrida, for example, noted that all of reality is typically described in contrasting pairs of words, from basic words such as light/dark, day/night, sun/moon, and white/black, to social words such as Western/Eastern, native/foreign, us/

them, or even Soc/greaser, and that, in each of these cases, the relationship is not stable; one term is always superior to the other, and, in cases where people are involved, situations often turn violent. To Derrida, Ponyboy's story would be an all-too-familiar one, and the conclusions Johnny and Ponyboy reach, that peace can only be attained by un-learning and re-evaluating their identity, are the same that Derrida concludes in *The Other Heading*, after a life dedicated to exploring the relationship between identity and violence.

Jacques Derrida was born in 1930 in El Biar, Algeria, but moved to Paris at age nineteen to attend school and lived in Paris until his death in 2004. He was a major philosophical force in the mid-to-late twentieth century and a major influence for later philosophers, historians, and literary critics, primarily due to his two reading techniques, deconstruction and différance, which influenced all of his further ideas. These ideas are excruciatingly nuanced and very complicated, but can be defined as follows: deconstruction is an unmasking; it is based on the premise that no text (and by text, Derrida means pretty much anything) is stable, but only pretends to be; therefore, a careful reader or observer can unmask and expose what a piece of writing (or other medium, up to and including real-time events) is trying to be; each text contains within it, by its nature, the seeds of its own unmaking.

Différance refers to what Derrida thought was a natural (but not obvious) human tendency: that of identifying things according to what they are not, instead of what they are. As an example, when do we find it acceptable to use the word "car" when referring to a vehicle? A car has four wheels! Yes, but so do a limousine and an ATV; are those cars? But cars carry families around on roads to complete everyday middle-class activities, unlike limousines (which are for special occasions or rich people) or ATVs (which don't belong on roads). But so do SUVs. So what is a car? Derrida thinks we naturally define terms by what they are not. Instead of trying to define what a car is, which we can never really do, we usually explain that it is not an SUV, an ATV, or a limousine; we define it with just enough context to establish it as a car and move on with our narrative.

To be clear, Derrida would not say that something has a core essence, or that it essentially *is* something, a contrary position called Essentialism, but we find it convenient to define it against what it is not; he would say something is *only* what it is not, without being ever fully able to be pinned down. In his view, it is impossible to define anything without context, because nothing exists without context. This applies to all reality, and therefore exists in all languages; it is impossible to discuss anything without a consideration of what it is not, and, therefore, words can be written in terms of their opposites, in binary pairs such as light/dark, day/night, sun/moon. It is not possible to have any true, unadulterated meaning, outside of context (Derrida and Bass 43).

So what happens when these binaries, such as day/night, break down? Violence. According to Derrida, it is not possible for these binary pairs to be neutral. Instead, we always privilege one over the other, and this is because the words we use come from a tradition stretching back thousands of years, to the ancient Greeks ("Violence and Metaphysics" 102-104). To use his term, each binary exists in a "violent hierarchy" with each term trying to "govern" the other (Derrida and Bass 41). The term "light" wants to define itself as different from, and better than, "dark," and we usually let it. In science class, we learn that darkness is the absence of light, but we could just as easily think outside the box and define light as the absence of darkness, and the fact that we don't testifies to the ancient privileging of the term light over dark, a privileging that is inherited today. To pick up on our car metaphor from earlier, the car would try to define itself against the SUV. It would prioritize its fuel efficiency, agility, and lack of road noise, while downplaying its lack of off-road capabilities. It would probably claim that a vehicle, by its nature, shouldn't stray from the road, and the fact the SUV does so is vulgar. The car would tend to define itself by its best attributes; its worst belong to the SUV.

Of course, vehicles can't think or talk this way. But people can. Derrida links egocentrism with the attempt to define ourselves like the car and the SUV, with our highlighting our best attributes and hiding our worst, often by casting them on others. When these clean definitions break down, as they invariably do because of the inability to define ourselves securely (because, remember, for Derrida, nothing written or spoken is ever stable or secure, but only pretends to be), this violence occurs. As he says,

> Hope, fear, and trembling are commensurate with the signs that are coming to us from everywhere in Europe, where, precisely in the name of identity, be it cultural or not, the worst violences, those that we recognize all too well without yet having thought them through, the crimes of xenophobia, racism, anti-Semitism, religious or nationalist fanaticism, are being unleashed, mixed up, mixed up with each other, but also, and there is nothing fortuitous in this, mixed in with the breath, with the respiration, with the very "spirit" of the promise. (Derrida, *Other Heading* 6)

Two important considerations should be extracted from this passage. The first is that when Derrida says that "the worst violences" are committed "in the name of identity," he is referring to his earlier works, in which he suggests that when The Other slips out of the boxes in which we try to place them in order to feel better about ourselves, we often resort to violence against them. We need to place them back in the box we created for them, so that we can remain confident in our understanding of ourselves. And if we can't do so, and use The Other's presence to feel better about ourselves, then their presence is not useful to us, and we try to destroy them (Derrida, "Violence" 156-158). The second consideration is the promise to which Derrida refers. This promise is his conclusion that a face-to-face confrontation with other humans is a major obstacle to overcome and, as he says, often leads to violence. However, if we can use them as a benign mirror, as a way to honestly critique ourselves while simultaneously recognizing that they, too, are undergoing the same difficult process, then we can grow more secure in our identity while gaining respect for The Other (which, like all other terms, means less and less, and more and more its opposite, as we get more acquainted with it).

Confused? Let's return to *The Outsiders.* S. E. Hinton's city environment is a perfect case study for Derrida's philosophy. Split into two social groups based on geography and class, the Socs, or Socials, described as "the jet set, the West-side rich kids," and greasers, a term "which is used to class all . . . boys on the East Side," are perpetually at war. The novel opens with a look into the reality of this war, as four Socs jump the main character, Ponyboy. Their language makes two things perfectly clear: their animosity for Ponyboy, and the fact that this animosity springs from his identity in general and his hair, as a symbol of that identity, in particular. They open by asking if he needs a haircut, "greaser," before pinning him down, putting a blade to his throat, and sneering: "how'd you like that haircut to begin just below the chin?" As Ponyboy believes they could kill him, he panics and thrashes around until he is rescued (Hinton 6). Despite his later assertion that the Socials jump greasers just for "kicks," the potentiality for murder in this opening scene suggests otherwise, and the Socs' obsession with Ponyboy's hair and his label as a greaser suggest that his identity plays no small part in the animosity they display towards him (38).

From this opening scene onward, the violence between the greasers and the Socs only intensifies, and almost every character in the novel is assigned to one of these two categories, creating a sharp bifurcation between the two groups. Each group is further divided based on physical, territorial boundaries. As previously noted, the greasers are from the East Side of town, while the western half belongs to the Socs, but each side also has its own drive-ins: the Socs go to the Way Out and to Rusty's; the greasers go to The Dingo and to Jay's (The Nightly Double, where Ponyboy meets Cherry, is left ambiguous) (Hinton 20). Both sides express a vested interest in maintaining their boundaries, including using violence if needed.

In addition to geographical boundaries, there are other physical characteristics that mark a greaser a greaser and a Soc a Soc. Socs wear "[b]lue madras" shirts and smell like "English Leather shaving lotion and stale tobacco" (Hinton 5). In other passages, they're associated with the smell of whiskey, Chevrolet Corvairs, and "striped or checkered shirts with light red or tan-colored jackets or madras ski jackets" (54, 71,141). They drive a "blue Mustang" and the rings they wear on their fingers are "what cut Johnny up so badly"

(33). The greasers, on the other hand, have their leather jackets; black T-shirts; and, of course, their hair. The hair is the "trademark," which is why the Socs target Ponyboy's hair in the opening scene. As he explains, it is "the one thing we were proud of. Maybe we couldn't have Corvairs or madras shirts, but we could have hair" (71). Ponyboy continues to explain the differences between the Socs and the greasers:

> We're poorer than the Socs and the middle class. I reckon we're wilder, too. Not like the Socs, who jump greasers and wreck houses and throw beer blasts for kicks, and get editorials in the paper for being a public disgrace one day and an asset to society the next. Greasers are almost like hoods; we steal things and drive old souped-up cars and hold up gas stations and have a gang fight once in a while. I don't mean I do things like that . . . . I only mean that most greasers do things like that, just like we wear our hair long and dress in blue jeans and T-shirts, or leave our shirttails out and wear leather jackets and tennis shoes or boots. I'm not saying that either Socs or greasers are better; that's just the way things are. (Hinton 1, 2-3)

Notice that Ponyboy defines neither the greasers nor the Socs independently, but in opposition to the other. Speaking to the reader, he sets up his definitions as us versus them: "we're poorer than [they are]"; we wear this, they wear that; we act like this, they act like that.

The Socs, too, define themselves against the concept of the greaser. After Ponyboy meets Cherry, she offers a companion speech to his, in which she explores what it means to be a Soc, instead of and in contrast to a greaser:

> It's not just money. Part of it is, but not all. You greasers have a different set of values. You're more emotional. We're sophisticated— cool to the point of not feeling anything. Nothing is real with us. You know, sometimes I'll catch myself talking to a girl-friend, and realize I don't mean half of what I'm saying. I don't really think a beer blast on the river bottom is super-cool, but I'll rave about one to a girl-friend just to be saying something . . . . Rat race is a perfect name for it . . . . We're always going and going and going, and never asking where. Did you ever hear of having more than you wanted?

So that you couldn't want anything else and then started looking for something else to want? It seems like we're always searching for something to satisfy us, and never finding it. Maybe if we could lose our cool, we could. (Hinton 33)

Cherry's speech, spoken to Ponyboy, offers us a different vantage point from Ponyboy's, which is directed solely to the reader. By directing it at the opposing force, the greaser, Cherry slips into a second-person binary phraseology: You're x, we're y, clearly indicating that, while her analysis is less fashion-focused then Ponyboy's (which may be explained by the "haves" being less materially focused than the "have-nots" in general), it nevertheless demonstrates that the Socs possess, fundamentally, the same worldview as the greasers: there are two kinds of people and only two, and those two kinds are perpetually at odds with one another.

What is not overtly discussed is how much each of these other kinds of people relies on the other to forge themselves against. The greasers' leather jackets would not mark them as such without the Socs' madras shirts and khaki jackets; the greasers' long hair would not mark them as such if the Socs had long hair too. Remember Derrida's assertion, that we can only define ourselves by having something to define ourselves against, and that this difference exists at our very core, at the "origin" of being (Derrida and Bass 43). The greasers' defining characteristics only define them because the Socs do not possess these same characteristics and, actually, precisely because the Socs do not possess them. But Ponyboy's observations are only based on fashion, or skin-deep. Let's assume, for a moment, that in the opening scene, the Socs had robbed Ponyboy, worn his clothing, and grown out their hair. Would they be greasers? No, because, presumably, they would still return home at nights to their wealthy homes on the West Side of town, and they would still be from affluent families. If they ran away from home to the East Side and lived in the vacant lot sacred to the greasers, would they be greasers then?

According to Cherry's speech, presumably not, because the differences are more than simply fashion or wealth, reflected in their attitudes as well. After Cherry explains that their cold disposition is a key factor which differentiates Socs from greasers, Ponyboy realizes "that was the truth." He recalls a "social-club rumbler" in which the Socs fought each other "coldly and practically and impersonally." He sees Cherry's point that the core difference between the two groups is not the money or its materialistic manifestations, but the intensity of feeling the greasers' experience and the Socs' absolute lack of it (Hinton 34).

Cherry and Ponyboy's realization has shifted the conversation slightly. No longer are we dealing in the realm of superficial symbols, such as clothing or geographical and biological accident (after all, people can't help where or to whom they're born), but now we are discussing core personality attributes. Two-Bit continues this discussion when he defines the greasers against the Socs in his explanation to Cherry of Dally's behavior at the Nightly Double drive-in after Dally has left the group to look for a fight:

> "A fair fight isn't rough," Two-Bit said. "Blades are rough. So are chains and heaters and pool sticks and rumbles. Skin fighting isn't rough. It blows off steam better than anything. There's nothing wrong with throwing a few punches. Socs are rough. They gang up on one or two, or they rumble each other with their social clubs. Us greasers usually stick together, but when we do fight among ourselves, it's a fair fight between two. (Hinton 29)

Two-Bit, like Cherry, also pivots from fashion alone to define moral discrepancies between the two groups and, like Cherry, shifts the argument; it is not just clothes and cash that separate greaser from Soc; it is the wild, unprincipled violence of the Socs, in contrast to the rules-governed violence of the greasers. Of course, the male Socs would probably say the opposite. It doesn't matter whether any differences exist, only that each group believes they do. If these differences are more than skin deep, then there is little possibility of reconciliation. Both the greasers and Socs exist in a tenuous relationship with each other, relying on their respective boundaries, and the violence that reinforces them, to define their own sense of identity and being.

Cherry and Ponyboy's brief moment together marks another milestone. It is the first instance of a nonviolent confrontation with the social Other, and as part of it, Ponyboy learns something about himself that he possesses, by virtue of being a greaser, an intensity of feeling foreign to others. He doesn't seem particularly offended by this revelation, the way he does when other Socs identify him by his greaser characteristics; instead, it allows him to open himself up to Cherry more, telling her about Soda's horse, which he had "never told anyone about" because it underscored Soda's vulnerability, and thus, humanized him as different from his public identity (Hinton 34).

As Ponyboy, Cherry, Two-Bit, Marcia, and Johnny walk home from the Nightly Double, greaser and Soc briefly cohabit the city in peace. This connection is indicative of how Derrida believes a face-to-face encounter with The Other can lead to living a good life, but it does not last. Ponyboy is not ready to admit that the Socs are just people like him, although he is willing to make an exception for Cherry. In fact, after speaking with her, he only halfway fulfills Derrida's observation. Remember, Derrida believed a face-to-face encounter with The Other could lead to a mutually-beneficial relationship in which both sides develop a greater understanding of themselves and respect the individuality and humanity of The Other. Cherry seems to understand both premises, but Ponyboy only recognizes the former, not the latter. Cherry flips the dynamic when she says,

> "I'll bet you think the Socs have it made. The rich kids, the West-side Socs. I'll tell you something, Ponyboy, and it may come as a surprise. We have troubles you've never even heard of. You want to know something?" She looked me straight in the eye. "Things are rough all over." (Hinton 31)

Ponyboy claims to believe her, but ends the conversation abruptly. However, later, he uses her final line in an outburst of his own:

> "It ain't fair!" I cried passionately. "It ain't fair that we have all the rough breaks!" I didn't know exactly what I meant, but I was

thinking about Johnny's father being a drunk and his mother a selfish slob, and Two-Bit's mother being a barmaid to support him and his kid sister after their father ran out on them, and Dally—wild, cunning Dally—turning into a hoodlum because he'd die if he didn't, and Steve—his hatred for his father coming out in his soft, bitter voice and the violence of his temper. Sodapop . . . a dropout so he could get a job and keep me in school, and Darry, getting old before his time trying to run a family and hold on to two jobs and never having any fun—while the Socs had so much spare time and money that they jumped us and each other for kicks, had beer blasts and river-bottom parties because they didn't know what else to do. Things were rough all over, all right. All over the East Side. It just didn't seem right to me. (Hinton 37)

Notice how Ponyboy lumps all the Socs together into a group, but speaks about the plight of each of his greaser friends individually, while simultaneously dismissing Cherry's notion that any of the Socs had it rough too. Also notice that Ponyboy can't just tell us what his friends' problems are; he has to use the Socs as a foil to define their troubles against. In other words, the chance meeting between Cherry and Ponyboy actually affects Cherry much more positively after their one conversation; she begins the evening afraid of the greasers, but ends it by realizing their struggles were the same as her own. This is why she helps them later as the "war" between the Socs and greasers grows (Hinton 72). Ponyboy, however, still has not learned this lesson.

The violence in the novel escalates quickly after Ponyboy and Cherry connect at the Nightly Double. Late in the night, Ponyboy sees a car tailing his greaser friends and himself, and asks Johnny of the Socs following them, "What do they want? This is our territory. What are Socs doing this far east?" Johnny replies, "I don't know. But I bet they're looking for us. We picked up their girls." Bob quickly confirms Johnny's theory; when Johnny says he better "watch it" because he is in greaser territory, Bob responds that it's the greasers who need to be careful, and that next time they want to pick up girls they should "pick up [their] own kind—dirt" (Hinton 54-55).

Bob's threat refers to another kind of boundary between the greasers and Socs: women. Ponyboy recognizes that romancing Cherry would cross this boundary when he first sees her and Marcia, using Bob's phrase by noting "those two girls weren't our kind," as opposed to when he was discussing Soda's girlfriend Sandy, saying that she "was our kind—greaser—but she was a real nice girl" (Hinton 19,13-14). The same phrase is used by Dally when he blames Cherry for the escalating violence after Bob's death: "Man, next time I want a broad I'll pick up my own kind . . . [Cherry] said she felt that the whole mess was her fault, which it is." As Dally tells it, Cherry, too, recognizes her role in causing "all-out warfare all over the city" (71).

Thus, as we've seen before, both various Socs and greasers recognize that going after members of the other group's opposite sex violates the rules of engagement in the delicate social contract between the groups by threatening interbreeding and, thus, threatening each group's self-identification (would the babies be greaser or Soc)? It's not something that Bob can let go unpunished.

Of course, those words would be some of Bob's last. Before he is killed, however, he and Ponyboy have a surprisingly astute exchange, although neither of them realizes its importance:

> "You know what a greaser is?" Bob asked. "White trash with long hair." I felt the blood draining from my face. I've been cussed out and sworn at, but nothing ever hit me like that did . . . . "You know what a Soc is?" I said, my voice shaking with rage. "White trash with Mustangs and madras." (Hinton 55)

Neither Bob nor Ponyboy is entirely incorrect; both the greasers and Socs share aspects of "white trash"; they drink and fight and rob and steal; both groups engage in acts of violence, and both are quick to carry blades and other weapons in case of a fight. In his rage, Ponyboy realizes, although not consciously, that the groups are not wholly different from one another. As the barriers break down, the violence escalates correlatively, resulting in Bob's death and Ponyboy and Johnny's flight from the city.

After hiding out in the country for a few days, Johnny and Ponyboy are visited by Dally, who tells them that Bob's death has resulted in "all out warfare all over the city," introducing the escalation of violence as Derrida predicted. Dally then tells them that the greasers have a spy in the war: "Cherry what's-her-name," to which both Johnny and Ponyboy react with extreme surprise. As Ponyboy relates, "Johnny gagged and I almost dropped my hot fudge sundae. 'Cherry?' we both said at the same time. 'The Soc?'" (Hinton 72).

Hinton is masterful in showing how little Ponyboy has learned from his first encounter with Cherry. While she grew from the encounter enough to recognize that Socs and greasers were not wholly different and works to reconcile both groups, Ponyboy reacts to her aid the exact same way Johnny—who was not privy to their "things are rough all over" conversation—does: by reducing her once again from her personhood to simply "The Soc."

After his initial reaction, Ponyboy does clarify to himself that "it wasn't Cherry the Soc who was helping us, it was Cherry the dreamer who watched sunsets and couldn't stand fights" but still concludes that "it was hard to believe a Soc would help us, even a Soc that dug sunsets," proving that he is not ready to see Cherry as independent from her label, nor is he ready to see beyond the Soc/greaser divide that defines the city (Hinton 73).

It is not until right before the final "rumble" between the Socs and the greasers that Ponyboy has an encounter with a Soc that truly changes his mind. He and the greasers stop at the Tasty Freeze to rest before the big fight, but the blue Mustang pulls up and unloads a number of Socs, including Randy Adderson, who pulls Ponyboy away from the group because he "would never have believed a greaser could pull something like [running into the burning barn to save the country children]" (Hinton 97). Their subsequent exchange gets close to fulfilling Derrida's "promise." Ponyboy replies that "'Greaser' didn't have anything to do with it. My buddy over there wouldn't have done it. Maybe you would have done the same thing, maybe a friend of yours wouldn't have. It's the individual," to which Randy replies: "I'm sick of all this. Sick and tired. Bob was a good guy. He was the best buddy a guy ever had. I mean, he was a good fighter and tuff and everything, but he was a real person too. . . ." Randy senses that the greasers don't view the Socs as real people and tries to impress upon Ponyboy the humanity of their group by sharing Bob's less-than-desirable interactions with his parents, who gave him everything he wanted and nothing that he needed (97).

Randy continues, in a speech reminiscent of Ponyboy and Cherry's first encounter:

> I don't know why I'm telling you this. I couldn't tell anyone else. My friends—they'd think I was off my rocker or turning soft. Maybe I am. I just know that I'm sick of this whole mess . . . . And tonight . . . people get hurt in rumbles, maybe killed. I'm sick of it because it doesn't do any good. You can't win, you know that, don't you . . . . You can't win, even if you whip us. You'll still be where you were before—at the bottom. And we'll still be the lucky ones with all the breaks. So it doesn't do any good, the fighting and the killing. It doesn't prove a thing. We'll forget it if you win, or if you don't. Greasers will still be greasers and Socs will still be Socs." (Hinton 97-99)

Randy's effortless effusion to Ponyboy, and his realization that he couldn't speak as easily to his own friends, directly parallels Ponyboy and Cherry's first encounter and invites us to realize that Ponyboy and Randy's encounter marks the second, and final, face-to-face confrontation with The Other. Like the first, this encounter also leads to one side, Ponyboy, understanding the shared humanity between greasers and Socs. Although Randy believes that nothing matters and the social strata are incapable of change, Ponyboy understands, finally, that "things are rough all over" (Hinton 99).

Ponyboy offers his name, and then calls Randy by his, before returning to his greaser friends. When Two-Bit asks "what'd Mr. Super-Soc have to say?" Ponyboy pauses for a moment before replying: "He ain't a Soc . . . he's just a guy. He just wanted to talk," before concluding to himself, "Things were rough all over, but it was better that way. That way you could tell the other guy was human too" (Hinton 97-100).

Cherry and Randy offer Ponyboy two face-to-face interactions in *The Outsiders*. While Cherry recognizes Ponyboy's value as a person after their initial encounter—enough to defect and spy for the greasers—Ponyboy is stubborn in his ways and needs a little more time to recognize an ideal ethical encounter with The Other.

The Outsiders provides an excellent example of Derrida's philosophy of Othering through its thorough construction and subsequent breakdown of the Soc/greaser binary and Ponyboy and Cherry's understanding of their own humanity through each other. That it was published simultaneously with Derrida's ideas is either mere coincidence, or a testimony to their veracity.

Works Cited

Derrida, Jacques. "Violence and Metaphysics: An Essay on the Thought of Emmanuel Levinas." *Writing and Difference*. 1967. U of Chicago P, 2017, pp. 97–192.

_____, and Alan Bass. *Positions*. U Chicago P, 1998.

Derrida, Jacques, et al. *The Other Heading: Reflections on Today's Europe*. 1992. Indiana UP, 2010.

Hinton, S. E. *The Outsiders*. 1967. Speak Publishing, 2006.

"Things are rough all over" Indeed: Suffering and Salvation in James Baldwin's "Sonny's Blues" and S. E. Hinton's *The Outsiders*_____

Julia Hayes

In "Sonny's Blues," James Baldwin writes, "For, while the tale of how we suffer, and how we are delighted, and how we may triumph is never new, it always must be heard. There isn't any other tale to tell, it's the only light we've got in all this darkness" (57). Set in Harlem in the 1950s, "Sonny's Blues" is a short story about the suffering of Sonny, a young African American musician and heroin addict, and his brother, a high school math teacher and the unnamed narrator of the story. Like Sonny, Ponyboy Curtis, the narrator and protagonist of S. E. Hinton's novel *The Outsiders* (published ten years after "Sonny's Blues"), experiences suffering and a need to "be heard." Sonny's suffering and Ponyboy's have similar causes: violence, substance abuse, discrimination, social and economic disadvantages, loved ones' deaths, neglect, and their brothers' struggles to "find a way to listen" (Baldwin 54).

Certainly violence permeates *The Outsiders* in a form unfamiliar to modern readers. Even Ponyboy, who lives the violence and to some extent enjoys it, concludes, "There isn't any real good reason for fighting except for self-defense" (Hinton 137). And when tough greaser Dally tells Ponyboy's dying friend Johnny that the greasers "beat the Socs" in the rumble, "Johnny [doesn't] even try to grin at him" before he replies, "Useless . . . fighting's no good . . ." (Hinton 148). But indulging in a cause of suffering as a means to cope with suffering, thereby perpetuating the misery, is human nature. As William Faulkner says in "A Rose for Emily" after Miss Emily refuses to give up her dead father for burial, people "have to cling to that which had robbed [them], as people will" (316).

In "Sonny's Blues," Sonny is robbed by his heroin addiction. Sonny tells his brother, "*Everybody* tries not to [suffer]," so perhaps "it's better to do something to give [suffering] a reason, *any* reason"

(Baldwin 53). Sonny's description of "what heroin feels like sometimes" courageously explores the appeal of drugs to people with unbearable suffering. Sonny describes his habit to his brother this way: "[Heroin] makes you feel—in control. Sometimes you've got to have that feeling" (Baldwin 52).

Perhaps needing to feel in control is a reason that, throughout *The Outsiders*, Ponyboy clings to the violence that robs him of the time and health that he needs to succeed in high school, where he is a "good runner" on the track team (Hinton 108), a decent artist who "could get [Dally's] personality down in a few lines" (Hinton 10), and a promising student who had been "put up a year in grade school" (Hinton 23). Fighting the Socs with the greasers even jeopardizes Ponyboy's ability to stay in his home with his brothers. As his brother Darry reminds him frequently, Ponyboy is at risk of being removed from his home, maybe even ending up in reform school like Curly Shepherd, the younger brother of Tim, a greaser who had been a high school athlete.

The violence in "Sonny's Blues" occurs in a flashback that does not involve Sonny or his brother. However, its cause is sinister, and its effects far-reaching. The last time the narrator talks to his mother, she implores him to look out for Sonny. When the narrator reminds her that Sonny is "a good boy [with] good sense," his mother replies, "It ain't only the bad ones, nor yet the dumb ones that gets sucked under" (Baldwin 43). Then she tells her son the story of his uncle's death on a moonlit Saturday night after a dance. A carload of drunk white men saw the narrator's father and uncle walking down the road, then "let out a great whoop and holler and . . . aimed the car straight at [the uncle]. They was having fun, they just wanted to scare him, the way they do sometimes, you know." But when the narrator's father reached his brother, he "weren't nothing but blood and pulp." The far-reaching effects of that killing are evident when the narrator's mother says of his father, "Till the day he died he weren't sure but that every white man he saw was the man that killed his brother" (Baldwin 44). The white man who killed the black man is nameless and faceless, so he becomes, to the narrator's father, every white man he sees.

The perpetrators of violence on the greasers in *The Outsiders* are neither nameless nor faceless. However, until Ponyboy connects with Cherry, and later with Randy, the Socs are all alike, members of what Two-Bit calls the "socially elite checkered-shirt set" (Hinton 41). Unlike the seemingly random, possibly accidental killing in "Sonny's Blues," the violence between the greasers and the Socs in *The Outsiders* is deliberate and mutual, with parties' agreeing on the time, location, and rules.

One violent act in *The Outsiders* is Johnny's killing Bob because Bob ordered Dave to hold Ponyboy's head under the water in the park fountain. Ponyboy does not witness the killing. Hinton describes its aftermath:

> "I killed him," [Johnny] said slowly. "I killed that boy."
>
> Bob, the handsome Soc, was lying in the moonlight, doubled up and still. A dark pool was growing from him, spreading slowly over the blue-white cement. I looked at Johnny's hand. He was clutching his switchblade, and it was dark to the hilt. My stomach gave a violent jump and my blood turned icy. (Hinton 56)

Although Bob encouraged Dave to drown Ponyboy, Hinton portrays Johnny's killing of Bob as an act of self-defense. The reader accepts that view because we know by the rings Bob wears that he was the perpetrator of the beating that left Johnny "jumpier than ever," a boy who "would kill the next person who jumped him" because the Socs "had scared him that much" (Hinton 34).

Violence is a more obvious cause of suffering in *The Outsiders* than in "Sonny's Blues." It is also a choice. As Two-Bit tells Ponyboy, "Shoot, everybody fights." Before the rumble, the greasers celebrate their reputation in the community. After doing cartwheels and other acrobatics off the front porch of Ponyboy's house, the greasers boast about their behavior:

> "I am a greaser," Sodapop chanted. "I am a JD and a hood. I blacken the name of our fair city. I beat up people. I rob gas stations. I am a menace to society. Man, do I have fun!"

"Greaser . . . greaser . . . greaser . . ." Steve singsonged. "O victim of environment, underprivileged, rotten, no-count hood!"

"Juvenile delinquent, you're no good!" Darry shouted. (Hinton 136)

Why, Ponyboy wonders, do the greasers fight? He concludes that "Soda fought for fun, Steve for hatred, Darry for pride, and Two-Bit for conformity" (Hinton 137). Though the characters mock the idea that greasers are victims, Hinton's characters are clearly affected by setting and circumstances. Soda dropped out of school to work to help Darry pay bills after their parents died. Steve hates the Socs, who intimidate and harass the greasers. Darry, a head of household at twenty who should be in college instead of working construction, fights to show the Socs, the greasers, and even himself that he *is* somebody. Ponyboy realizes that Two-Bit, who has little going for him except his personality, fights to fit in. Ponyboy himself fights to please Darry, his father figure. Finally, Johnny, victimized by his father's brutality and his mother's neglect, fights *back*.

Baldwin, too, believes that environment can marginalize, and thereby victimize, individuals and groups of people. In his fiction and essays, he is a teacher in that school of thought and a preacher in that church. In "Sonny's Blues," the environment is rife with systemic racism and its concomitant suffering. White people's injuring and killing black people with impunity was common in America before and during the 1950s. In fact, in 1951, the Civil Rights Congress filed a petition titled "We Charge Genocide" with the United Nations, providing evidence of "killings by police, killings by incited gangs, killings at night by masked men, killings always on the basis of 'race,' [and] killings by the Ku Klux Klan." The petitioners added that "the majority of Negro murders are never recorded, [so the] evidence, though voluminous, is scanty when compared to the actuality" ("We Charge Genocide").

And in Baldwin's America, segregation was the law of the land. When "Sonny's Blues" was published in 1957, the ruling in *Brown v. the Board of Education*, which proclaimed that public schools would be integrated, was three years old and on a long, bloody road to many states' compliance. The narrator of "Sonny's Blues" realizes that his Harlem high school students "are filled with rage" because "they were growing up in a rush and their heads bumped abruptly against the low ceiling of their actual possibilities" (Baldwin 36). In his book *Notes of a Native Son*, Baldwin writes, "I imagine one of the reasons people cling to their hates so stubbornly is because they sense, once hate is gone, they will be forced to deal with pain" (91). Sonny grew up under that same ceiling, in that same "darkness" in which the narrator's algebra students "might, every one of them for all [he] knew, be popping off needles every time they went to the [bathroom]," a habit that might do "more for them than algebra ever could" (Baldwin 36).

Like the students at the Harlem high school in "Sonny's Blues," characters in *The Outsiders* "cling to their rage" because they "cling to that which [robs them]" (Faulkner 316). So, yes, as Cherry Valance says to Ponyboy, "Things are rough all over" (Hinton 35). African American history readers may be inclined to smile, even roll their eyes, when Cherry says that to Ponyboy. Later in the novel, after she declines to visit Johnny in the hospital, Ponyboy scolds Cherry: "I wouldn't want you to see him. You're a traitor to your own kind and not loyal to us. Do you think your spying for us makes up for the fact that you're sitting there in a Corvette while my brother [Soda] drops out of school to get a job?" (Hinton 129). Ponyboy could be speaking for the students in Baldwin's narrator's algebra class.

But the Socs and the greasers live in Oklahoma, a state still *studying* desegregation in 1976. In fact,

> During the early part of February 1976, the Oklahoma Advisory Committee, as part of the Commission's national school desegregation project, conducted extensive field investigations in Tulsa, Oklahoma, to secure information on that community's efforts to desegregate its public schools. ("School Desegregation")

The report was published in August 1977, the same month I turned sixteen and had attended integrated schools in North Carolina for ten years, twenty-three years after *Brown vs. the Board of*

Education, which ruled that "state-sanctioned segregation of public schools was a violation of the 14th amendment and was therefore unconstitutional" (*Brown v. Board of Education*).

The discriminatory environments drive the characters in "Sonny's Blues" and *The Outsiders* to alcohol and other drugs to dull their pain. Sonny's heroin addiction is both a distraction from and a cause of his suffering. Seeking discipline from his parents, Bob Sheldon drinks liquor. Ponyboy, at fourteen, does not use alcohol or harder drugs, but he is addicted to nicotine. On the fifth day in the abandoned church building, where Ponyboy and Johnny hide after Bob's death, Ponyboy says, "I had smoked two packs of Camels, and . . . got sick. I hadn't eaten anything all day; and smoking on an empty stomach doesn't make you feel real great. I curled up in a corner to sleep off the smoke" (Hinton 79).

After the church fire, Ponyboy talks with Jerry, the man who rode to the hospital in the ambulance with him. Jerry says, "You shouldn't be smoking." Ponyboy asks, "How come?" to which Jerry replies, "Why, uh . . ., you're too young" (Hinton 97).

Fourteen-year-old Ponyboy is a very young smoker. But "[e]veryone in [his] neighborhood, even the girls, smoked" (Hinton 97). How did these teenagers procure cigarettes? According to "Minimum Ages of Legal Access for Tobacco in the United States from 1863 to 2015," "In the 1950s, tobacco companies were openly marketing to children" (Apallonio and Glanz). Although laws against selling cigarettes were in place, maybe 1950s Oklahoma was like Oxford, North Carolina, in 1970, where one of young Tim Tyson's friends says of store owner Robert Teel, "*For 35 cents, he'd sell the baby Jesus a pack of smokes*" (*Blood Done Sign My Name*).

In *The Outsiders*, the greasers are heavy smokers; the Socs are hard drinkers. While Two-Bit drinks frequently, the character who pays the highest price for drinking is Bob. According to *What were the 1960s like in Oklahoma?,*

> Legislators wrote a *referendum* for a Liquor Control Act. They suggested an Alcoholic Beverage Control Board could license liquor stores. On April 7, 1959, the question went to the people in an election . . . [and] added the Twenty-seventh Amendment to the

Oklahoma Constitution. The first package (liquor) stores opened on September 1, 1959.

Certainly a high-schooler, even a Soc, should not have been able to purchase alcohol. In addition to blaming Bob for his own death, Cherry blames the people who made alcohol available to him. She asks, "Why do people sell liquor to boys? Why? I know there's a law against it, but kids get it anyway" (Hinton 129).

Cherry also believes that Bob's parents contributed to his death. She tells Ponyboy, "They spoiled him rotten . . . . One time he came home drunker than anything . . . . They thought it was their fault— that they'd failed him and driven him to it or something." She thinks they should have "[laid] down the law, set the limits, [given] him something solid to stand on" (Hinton 116). Cherry adds: "If his old man had just belted him—just once—[Bob] might still be alive" (Hinton 116).

Cherry's observations are ironic. When Bob and five other Socs confront Ponyboy, Johnny, and Two-Bit, who are walking Cherry and Marcia home from the drive-in, Two-Bit breaks off the top of a bottle for Ponyboy and opens his switchblade. To prevent a fight, Cherry agrees to ride home with Bob, "[shuddering] and saying 'I can't stand fights . . . I can't stand them . . .'" (Hinton 45). The irony is that Cherry cannot abide the fighting between the Socs and greasers, but she says that Bob's father might have saved his son's life by beating him. Bob, who had beaten Johnny almost to death, is killed by Johnny, whose father beat him regularly.

The role of parents, those present and absent, is important in both "Sonny's Blues" and *The Outsiders*. Darry is raising Sodapop and Ponyboy because their parents died in a car crash approximately eight months before the novel opens (Hinton 48). This loss may be Ponyboy's first realization that the Robert Frost poem he quotes reveals a painful truth: "Nothing gold can stay" (Hinton 77). As Ponyboy and Johnny are lying in the lot looking at the stars, Ponyboy reminisces about his parents and fantasizes about what life would be like if they were alive. He remembers that "[his] mother was golden and beautiful" (Hinton 48). Ponyboy believes that, if their parents had lived, Darry would be in college, Sodapop would be in high school, and Ponyboy would have two loving parents raising him instead of Darry, who struggles to keep the three of them together.

The sorrow of the spiritual "The Motherless Child," captured by brothers James Weldon Johnson and John Rosamond Johnson, permeates African American literature. In "Sonny's Blues," the mother of the narrator and Sonny dies while the narrator is in the army and Sonny is in high school. Sonny wants to join the service so he can "get out of Harlem," but he is too young. He tells his brother, "I want to join the army. Or the navy. . . . If I say I'm old enough, they'll believe me" (Baldwin 48).

Although Ponyboy's mother, had she lived, might have been able to protect her boys, Sonny's mother was unable to protect her sons from "the killing streets of [their] childhood" (Baldwin 41). Baldwin describes a memory from his youth, "when the old folks were talking after the big Sunday dinner" (42). The adults sit and talk while "the night is creeping up outside . . . and every face is darkening . . . [for they are] looking at something a child can't see" (Baldwin 42-43). The children wish for the scene to last; however, "something deep and watchful in the child knows that [soon] someone will . . . turn on the light. Then the old folks . . . won't talk anymore that day." Baldwin acknowledges that "they won't talk anymore because if [the child] knows too much about what's happened to *them*, he'll know too much too soon, about what's going to happen to *him*" (42-43).

The narrator understands that darkness upon the heartbreaking death of his daughter. Baldwin writes,

> Little Grace died in the fall [of the year]. She was a beautiful little girl. But she only lived a little over two years. She died of polio and she suffered. She had a slight fever for a couple of days, but it didn't seem like anything and we just kept her in bed. And we would certainly have called [the doctor], but the fever dropped, she seemed to be all right. . . .Then, one day, . . .[Isabel] heard her fall down in the living room. . . . Grace was quiet . . . . And [Isabel] ran to the living room and there was little Grace on the floor, all twisted up, and the reason she hadn't screamed was that she couldn't get her breath.

And when she did scream, it was the worst sound, Isabel says, that she'd ever heard in all her life, and she stills hears it sometimes in her dreams. (Baldwin 50)

According to "Polio Elimination," published by the Center for Disease Control and Prevention, "In the early 1950s, . . . polio outbreaks caused more than 15,000 cases of paralysis each year in the United States." The first vaccine was introduced in 1955, and the number of polio cases fell by 85 to 90 percent to under 6,000 in 1957 ("This Day in History"), the year "Sonny's Blues" was published. However, Grace was not protected from the disease, and her death brings darkness to the narrator, Isabel, their sons, and Sonny.

Baldwin's narrator's account of Grace's death begins, "I read about Sonny's trouble in the spring." It concludes, "I think I may have written Sonny the very day that little Grace was buried. I was sitting in the living room in the dark, by myself, and I suddenly thought of Sonny. My trouble made his real" (Baldwin 50).

Later, while Sonny and his brother are looking out the narrator's window, Sonny observes, "All that hatred down there, . . . all that hatred and misery and love. It's a wonder it doesn't blow the avenue apart" (Baldwin, "Sonny's" 55). In *The Outsiders*, Hinton's language is similar. For example, Ponyboy describes Sodapop and Steve as having "too much energy, too much feeling, with no way to blow it off" (16). While Ponyboy and Johnny lie in the park looking at the sky, Ponyboy "felt the tension growing inside of [himself] and . . . knew something had to happen or [he] would explode" (47). Ponyboy says when he visits Johnny in the hospital: "Years of living on the East Side teaches you how to shut off your emotions. If you didn't, you would explode. You learn to cool it" (Hinton 122).

The coolest greaser is Dally. Ponyboy says, "It would be a miracle if Dally loved anything. The fight for self-preservation had hardened him beyond caring" (Hinton 59). But Dally loves Johnny. Although Dally "would not tolerate anyone's trying to [tell] him what to do," when Johnny defends Cherry and Marcia at the drive-in, "Dally [just] got up and stalked off, his fists jammed in his pockets and a frown on his face" (Hinton 24-25). However, when Dally sees

Johnny die, Two-Bit observes, "even Dally has a breaking point" (Hinton 152). Dally

> slammed back against the wall. His face contracted in agony, and sweat streamed down his face.
>
> "Damnit, Johnny . . ." he begged, slamming one fist against the wall, hammering it to make it obey his will. "O, damnit, Johnny, don't die, please don't die . . . ."
>
> He suddenly bolted through the door and down the hall. (Hinton 149)

Ponyboy returns home, where Steve, Darry, Two-Bit, and Soda, all injured, are resting after the rumble. Ponyboy informs them that "Dallas is gone . . . . He ran out like the devil was after him. He's gonna blow up. He couldn't take it'" (Hinton 152). His friends locate Dally in the vacant lot, where the police arrive and Dally draws his gun, a "heater" that is not loaded but "sure does help a bluff" (Hinton 153). Dally commits suicide-by-cop, dying "with a look of grim triumph on his face . . . dead before he hit the ground." Ponyboy "knew he would be dead, because Dally Winston wanted to be dead and he always got what he wanted" (Hinton 154).

After Dally's death, Ponyboy receives a letter from Johnny, who had written, "There's still lots of good in the world. Tell Dally. I don't think he knows." Ponyboy knows it is "too late to tell Dally" and wonders if "[he would] have listened" (Hinton 179). In Pony's grief, he recognizes what made Johnny special: "I guess [Johnny] had listened to more beefs and more problems from more people than any of us. A guy that will really listen to you, listen and care about what you are saying, is something rare" (Hinton 178).

As Pony tells Cherry, the group members "stick together, make like brothers" (Hinton 26). Unlike Johnny, Ponyboy complains, Darry does not "really listen to [him]" (Hinton 178). But Ponyboy does not listen to his brothers either. When Darry says that Sodapop had received a letter back "unopened" from his pregnant girlfriend Sandy, Ponyboy thinks, "So that was what had been bugging Soda all afternoon. And I hadn't even bothered to find out. And while I was thinking about it, I realized that I never paid much attention to

Soda's problems. Darry and I just took it for granted that he didn't have any." Darry says that Soda had learned that he was not the father of Sandy's baby and asks Ponyboy, "Why didn't he tell you? . . . I thought he told you everything." Ponyboy replies, "Maybe he tried." He then asks himself, "How many times had Soda tried to tell me something, only to find I was daydreaming or stuck in a book? He would always listen to me, no matter what he was doing" (Hinton 174).

Brotherly love, or lack thereof, is a tale as old as time. Probably the most familiar story of fraternal conflict is that of Cain and Abel. After Cain kills Abel, the Lord says to Cain, "'Where is your brother Abel?' [Cain] said, 'I do not know; am I my brother's keeper?' And the Lord said, 'What have you done? Listen; your brother's blood is crying out to me from the ground!'" (Gen. 4. 8-11). Clearly, God's answer is that yes, we are our brothers' keepers. Even Dally acts as Ponyboy's keeper when he lends him his jacket. After the fire, Ponyboy learns why he "didn't feel it" when "his back was in flames." As Jerry, the man in the ambulance with Ponyboy, explains, "We put [the flames] out before you got burned. That jacket saved you from a bad burning, maybe even saved your life." Trying to put out the fire on Ponyboy, Dally had hit him (Hinton 94). Furthermore, Dally is burned "trying to drag [Johnny] out the window" (Hinton 95).

Jerry tells Ponyboy, "Mrs. O'Briant and I think you [and Johnny and Dally] were sent straight from heaven." Ponyboy replies, "Johnny is wanted for murder, and Dallas has a record with the fuzz a mile long" (Hinton 95). Nevertheless, each greaser acted as his brother's keeper, even at the risk of death.

Another example of the brother's keeper theme is the relationship between Darry and Ponyboy. Throughout the book, Darry scolds Ponyboy for not "[using his] head." Once after Darry shouts at Sodapop, leading to Pony's yelling at Darry, Darry "wheeled around and slapped [Ponyboy] so hard that it knocked him against the door" (Hinton 51). This "slap" drives Ponyboy out into the park and the deadly encounter with the Socs.

Near the end of the novel, Darry and Ponyboy are arguing again. Sodapop, "the middleman," reminds them, "If we don't have each other, we don't have anything . . . Please . . . don't fight anymore" (Hinton 176). Ponyboy notes,

Darry looked real worried. I suddenly realized that Darry was only twenty, that he wasn't so much older that he couldn't feel scared or hurt and as lost as the rest of us. I saw that I had expected Darry to do all the understanding without even trying to understand him. And he *had* given up a lot for Soda and me. (Hinton 176)

In *The Outsiders*, since the Curtis boys' parents were killed suddenly, Darry had the responsibility for his brothers thrust upon him. In "Sonny's Blues," however, the narrator and Sonny have time to develop their relationship. Before the narrator's mother tells him about his uncle's death, she says, "I want to talk to you about your brother . . . If anything happens to me he ain't going to have nobody to look out for him." She tells the narrator, "I'm telling you [the story of your uncle] because you got a brother. And the world ain't changed" (Baldwin 43).

The narrator's mother makes her request explicit: "You got to hold onto your brother . . . and don't let him ever fall, no matter what it looks like is happening to him and no matter how evil you gets with him. You going to be evil with him many a time. But don't you forget what I told you, you hear?" When the narrator promises, "I won't forget . . . . I won't let nothing happen to Sonny," his mother replies, "You may not be able to stop nothing from happening. But you got to let him know you's *there*" (Baldwin 45).

Throughout the story, however, the narrator shows an inability, perhaps an unwillingness, to honor his promise to his mother. The narrator knows he has failed his brother. When Sonny's friend speaks to the narrator about Sonny's drug arrest, the narrator "hated him [and] couldn't stand the way he looked at [the narrator]" (Baldwin 37). The friend pushes Sonny's brother for answers:

"What're you going to do? . . . I mean about Sonny?"

"Look. I haven't seen Sonny for over a year. I'm not sure I'm going to do anything. Anyway, what the hell *can* I do?"

"That's right, . . . ain't nothing you can do. Can't much help Sonny no more, I guess."

It was what I was thinking[,] so it seemed . . . he had no right to say it. (Baldwin 37-38)

In a flashback, Sonny and his brother are "alone in [their mother's] empty kitchen," and the narrator asks Sonny, "What do you want to be?" Sonny tells his brother he wants to be a musician who plays piano, surprising the narrator, who realizes that he had hardly "ever *asked* Sonny a damn thing" (Baldwin 45). Later in the conversation, when Sonny tells his brother that he wants to play jazz like Charlie "Bird" Parker, that playing jazz "[is] the only thing [he wants] to do," the narrator realizes that he "didn't know [Sonny] at all" (Baldwin 46-47).

Sonny's explanation of his own darkness reinforces the necessity of listening. Sonny tells his brother,

You walk these streets, black and funky and cold, and there's not really a living ass to talk to, and there's nothing shaking, and there's no way of getting it out—that storm inside. You can't talk it and you can't make love with it, and when you finally try to get with it and play it, you realize *nobody's* listening. So *you've* got to listen. You got to find a way to listen. (Baldwin 54)

Baldwin's illustration of the "brother's keeper" theme is an obvious allusion to the biblical first brothers. Hinton might or might not have had Cain and Abel in mind while creating the Curtis brothers. Neither author, however, drew characters who benefited from church or religion. Ponyboy had attended church with his parents and, after their deaths, with the greasers but was too embarrassed to return after Steve and Johnny made a scene during a service. Ponyboy describes the church building in which he and Johnny seek sanctuary: "It was a small church, real old and spooky and spiderwebby" (Hinton 66). Inside the church, Ponyboy had "a kind of creepy feeling. What do you call it? Premonition?"

(Hinton 67). Later Ponyboy lies "on the cold rock floor, wrapped up in Dally's jacket" (Hinton 69). Whereas the church building itself provides no comfort, Ponyboy is kept warm by his buddy's jacket, which Ponyboy later gives to Johnny (Hinton 73).

In the church, Ponyboy and Johnny's diet includes a "week's supply of baloney" (Hinton 70) and discussions about "the Southern gentlemen—their manners and charm" in *Gone with the Wind*. Johnny "didn't know anything about the Civil War" (Hinton 75). Furthermore, in 1960s Oklahoma, perhaps most readers had not yet learned that books and movies romanticizing the Civil War were also full of "baloney."

In addition to reading *Gone with the Wind*, Ponyboy and Johnny discuss Robert Frost's poem "Nothing Gold Can Stay." Although Frost is often referred to as a nature poet, many Frost scholars believe he looks to the natural world for answers about human experience, God's existence, and the relationship between people and their Creator. Frost himself even quipped, "I am not a nature poet. There is almost always a person in my poems" (Seltzer). Ponyboy recites the poem to Johnny and admits that he "always remembered it because [he] never quite got what [Frost] meant by it" (Hinton 78). Without the poem's sixth line, the poem describes the shortness of spring, the inevitability of winter, and the sunrise's brief time before "dawn goes down to day" (Hinton 77). Johnny shows that he understands the poem's metaphor for human mutability in the letter he writes Pony before he dies: ". . . [Y]ou're gold when you're a kid, like green. When you're a kid, everything's new, dawn . . . [When] you get used to everything [,] it's day" (Hinton 178).

For Ponyboy and Johnny, "gold" and "golden" are descriptors for people who are beautiful, gentle, and kind. Ponyboy says his mother was "golden," and Johnny's last words to Pony are "Stay gold, Ponyboy. Stay gold . . ." (Hinton 148). Hinton illustrates that Pony will "stay gold" when Ponyboy picks up glass from a bottle he broke because he "didn't want anyone to get a flat tire" (172).

Understandably, neither Ponyboy nor Johnny acknowledges the sixth line of "Nothing Gold Can Stay": "*So Eden sank to grief . . .*" (qtd. in Hinton 77). So although they recognize the mutability theme, they overlook the allusion to the Adam and Eve story, "The Fall of Man" and the first couple's banishment from the Garden of Eden so they will not attain immortality from the "tree of life" (Gen. 3). Pony and Johnny fail to grasp the mortality theme in Frost's poem which is obvious in the poem's last line, *"Nothing gold can stay"* (qtd. in Hinton 77). No loss in the novel makes Frost's point better than Johnny's injury in the fire. Ponyboy reflects, "[Even] if Johnny did live he'd be crippled and never play football or help us out in a rumble again. He'd have to stay in that house he hated, where he wasn't wanted, and things could never be like they used to be" (Hinton 103). Johnny's life ended in the church fire.

In "Sonny's Blues," religion plays a larger role, and the brothers deliberately refuse to embrace it. As the narrator watches a street revival outside his window, he realizes that, "though [he] had watched these street meetings all [his] life, . . .[it] was strange, suddenly, to watch" (Baldwin 51). A quartet sings *"Tis the old ship of Zion. . ., it has rescued many a thousand!"* Baldwin writes, "Not a soul under the sound of their voices was hearing this song for the first time, not one of them had been rescued. Nor had they seen much in the way of rescue work being done around them" (51).

Sonny writes explicitly about his lack of faith after Gracie's death, saying to his brother,

> Give my love to Isabel and the kids and I was sure sorry to hear about little Gracie. I wish I could be like Mama and say the Lord's will be done, but I don't know it seems to me that trouble is the one thing that never does get stopped and I don't know what good it does to blame it on the Lord. But maybe it does some good if you believe it. (Baldwin 40)

The characters in "Sonny's Blues" and *The Outsiders* attempt to alleviate their suffering in various ways, but religion is not among them. After the relationships with their brothers are healed through love and communication, however, both Ponyboy and Sonny are ready to seek the road to salvation. For both characters, that road is laid by their own creations—Pony's story and Sonny's music.

Ponyboy's story originates with his English teacher, Mr. Syme, who tells Pony that if he will "come up with a good semester theme," Mr. Syme will "pass [him] with a C grade" (Hinton 169), and the essay can be "as long as [Ponyboy wants] it" (Hinton 179). So *The Outsiders* is created, beginning and ending with the same lines: "When I stepped out into the bright sunlight from the darkness of the movie house, I had only two things on my mind: Paul Newman and a ride home" (Hinton 1, 180).

Baldwin concludes "Sonny's Blues" with Sonny's playing piano at a nightclub. The narrator, who has come to *listen* to his brother play, describes the experience as occurring in Sonny's "kingdom," where "his veins bore royal blood" (Baldwin 56). As the band plays "Am I Blue," Sonny's friend and band member Creole "seemed to be saying, listen. Now these are Sonny's blues" (Baldwin 57). Both Ponyboy's "theme" about his experience as a greaser and Sonny's interpretation of the blues song on piano illustrate the characters' salvation from suffering through the creation of art.

However, as Baldwin's narrator observes at the end of Sonny's performance, "I was aware that this was only a moment, that the world waited outside, as hungry as a tiger, and trouble stretched above us, longer than the sky" (58). Similarly, Ponyboy acknowledges the world's darkness:

I could picture hundreds and hundreds of boys living on the wrong sides of cities, boys with black eyes who jumped at their own shadows. Hundreds of boys who maybe watched sunsets and looked at stars and ached for something better. I could see boys going down under street lights because they were mean and tough and hated the world, and it was too late to tell them that there was still good in it, and they probably wouldn't believe you if you did. (Hinton 179)

Ponyboy, clearly the voice for Hinton here, continues: "There should be some help, someone should tell [people] before it [is] too late. Someone should tell their side of the story, and maybe people would understand then . . ." (179). So S. E. Hinton tells their story, just as Baldwin tells "the tale of how we suffer, and how we are delighted, and how we may triumph . . . ." After all, in 2018, timeless stories may feel like "the only light we've got in all this darkness" (Baldwin 57).

Works Cited

Apollonio, Dorie E., and Stanton A. Glantz. "Minimum Ages of Legal Access for Tobacco in the United States from 1863 to 2015." *American Journal of Public Health*, vol. 106, no. 7, July 2016, pp. 1200-1207. *PMC*, www.ncbi.nlm.nih.gov/pmc/articles/PMC4902755/.

Baldwin, James. *Notes of a Native Son.* Dial, 1949.

_____. "Sonny's Blues." 1957. *The Story and Its Writer: An Introduction to Short Fiction*, edited by Ann Charters, compact 8th ed., Bedford/Saint Martin's, 2011, pp. 36-58.

The Bible. New Revised Standard Version, HarperCollins, 2007.

Blood Done Sign My Name. Directed by Jeb Stuart, Real Folk Productions, 2010.

Brown v. Board of Education of Topeka, Opinion, Records of the Supreme Court of the United States; Record Group 267. National Archives, 17 May 1954, www.ourdocuments.gov/.

Faulkner, William. "A Rose for Emily." 1931. *The Story and Its Writer: An Introduction to Short Fiction*, edited by Ann Charters, compact 8th ed., Bedford/St. Martin's, 2011, pp. 314-20.

Hinton, S. E. *The Outsiders.* 1967. 50th anniversary ed., Penguin, 2017.

"Polio Elimination in the United States." *Global Health*, Centers for Disease Control and Prevention, 28 Nov. 2017, www.cdc.gov/polio/us/.

"Salk Announces Polio Vaccine." *This Day in History—March 26.* History, 2010, www.history.com/this-day-in-history/salk-announces-polio-vaccine/. Accessed 8 Jan. 2018.

"School Desegregation in Tulsa, Oklahoma: A report prepared by the Oklahoma Advisory Committee to the United States Commission on Civil Rights, August 1977." *Thurgood Marshall Law Library*, U of Maryland School of Law, www.law.umaryland.edu/marshall/usccr/documents/cr12d4522.pdf/. Accessed 18 Nov. 2017.

Selzer, Barbara. "'I Am Not a Nature Poet': Why Robert Frost Is So Misunderstood." *Flavorwire*, 26 Mar. 2015, flavorwire.com/511378/i-am-not-a-nature-poet-why-robert-frost-is-so-misunderstood/.

"We Charge Genocide: The Historic Petition to the United Nations for Relief from a Crime of The United States Government against the Negro People (1951)." *BlackPast.org*, 2017, www.blackpast.org/we-charge-genocide-historic-petition-united-nations-relief-crime-united-states-government-against/.

"What Were the 1960s like in Oklahoma?" *Oklahoma Uniquely American*, n.d., oklahomauniquelyamerican.com/materials/Book%20PDF/Chapter%2016.pdf/. Accessed 18 Nov. 2017.

CRITICAL READINGS

S. E. Hinton on *The Outsiders*: A Compendium of Interviews_____

Robert C. Evans

Although S. E. Hinton, the author of *The Outsiders*, has often been described as reclusive and "publicity-shy," she has granted numerous interviews, especially in the last fifteen years. This is a "compendium" of her published interviews. Hinton has been asked many of the same questions repeatedly, and her answers have also often been almost identical. But there is some interesting variety in her responses. The interviews give a strong sense of how and why the book was written, how it was received, and why its popularity has continued to grow. The interviews also reveal Hinton herself as tough, plain-spoken, good-humored, and genuinely warm.

Biographical Background and Sources
Readers unfamiliar with Hinton's biography may be surprised to learn the details of her home life as a girl. According to one interviewer, her father, "Grady, was a door-to-door salesman, her mother, Lillian, an assembly-line worker. 'My mother was physically and emotionally abusive,' Ms. Hinton said. 'My father was an extremely cold man.'" Her family, she noted, attended a "fundamentalist, hellfire and brimstone" church that "turned [her] off religion" (Smith). Hinton says frequently in interviews that she was a tomboy, telling one reporter that she was

> happiest at her grandmother's farm, where her aunt had a horse. She
> longed for her own horse, and escaped into reading and writing books.
> ... "When I was writing [my mother would] come into my room, grab
> my hair and throw me in front of the TV, [and say] 'You're part of
> this family—now act like it.' I hate TV now." [One time] her mother
> threw her manuscripts in the trash burner, but allowed her to rescue
> them. "I would tell myself, 'It'll get better. . . . Hang on.'" When she
> was 15, her father developed a brain tumor. As he was dying, she

wrote "The Outsiders," [which] was inspired, she said, by injustices perpetrated against her Greaser friends by the Socs. (Smith)

When one reporter asked to see her childhood home, in a poor section of Tulsa, Oklahoma, Hinton "curtly" replied, "I don't want to revisit it. . . ." Hinton told another interviewer, "My goal from being a child was to have a happy home life" (Smith).

Asked to explain the genesis of *The Outsiders*, Hinton replied that "the act of reading was my biggest inspiration. That is still the case today" (Jensen). She told one journalist,

I loved to read, and as soon as I learned how I was reading everything I could get my hands on. I was a horse nut, and *Peanuts the Pony* was the first book I ever checked out of the library. I still remember that book. The act of reading was so pleasurable for me. For an introverted kid, it's a means of communication, because you interact with the author even if you aren't sitting there conversing with her. (*Outsiders* Fanclub)

"The major influence on my writing," she told another interviewer, "has been my reading. When I was young, I read everything, including cereal boxes and coffee labels. Reading taught me sentence structure, paragraphing, how to build a chapter. Strangely enough, it never taught me spelling" (*Outsiders* Fanclub). She often jokes about how poor her spelling was and how it actually caused one teacher to give her a "D" in creative writing. In fact, she has said that she was "flunking a writing class while [she] was writing" her most famous book:

It was like *The Outsiders* ate my homework. But it was creative writing. . . . I hate that this is the most well-known anecdote about a teacher, because I had great English teachers who were very encouraging. But all I can think of is this woman who counted off for spelling, which publishers don't. [In a recent interview] the interviewer said, "Weren't you just devastated?" I said, "No, I was sitting there, thinking, 'Woman, you're gonna feel like such an idiot.'" (Ihnat)

Asked what prompted her to write *The Outsiders*, Hinton replied,

A few reasons. The first is I just like to write. I've been writing practically since I learned to read. So by the time I wrote *The Outsiders*, I'd been writing for about eight years. It wasn't like, "Oh, all of a sudden I'm 15 years old and started writing a book." It was actually the third book I'd written. It's just the first one I ever tried to get published. (Biendenharn)

Explaining why the book features so many male characters, she said,

Well, I grew up with guys as friends. My cousin, Jimmy, who *The Outsiders* is dedicated to, he and I, we're not quite a year apart and we were raised more like brother and sister than cousins. And I hung around with his friends. I couldn't identify with anything in the female culture then. You got your status from what kind of car your boyfriend drove. I didn't care about my boyfriend or didn't even have one for a long time. I wanted the cool car myself. . . . And to this day my close male friends outnumber my close female friends. . . . I've got twice as many close guy friends as I do close female friends. I like hanging out with guys. There's no undercurrent of—I don't know. There's so many things about the female culture I don't get . . .—but you know guys are quite a bit less complicated. (Sheridan)

Asked if any characters in *The Outsiders* were based on people she actually knew, Hinton replied,

Loosely based. I couldn't say, "This is who such-and-such is based on," because I fictionalized everybody, mixed up their looks and personalities and so forth. But yeah, I knew the situation, being in a greaser neighborhood and hanging out with guy friends like that. It kills me when people say it's a gang book. It's not a gang book. I have no idea how organized gangs work, but I'm very aware of the social class warfare that was going on in my school. (Ihnat)

Hinton herself was, she has said,

> a tomboy—I played football, my close friends were guys. Fortunately, I was born without the need-to-belong gene, the gene that says you have to be in a little group to feel secure.
>
> I never wanted to be classified as anything, nor did I ever join anything for fear of losing my individuality. I didn't even realize that these guys, who were my good friends, were greasers until one day we were walking down the street and some guys came and yelled, "Greaser!" It's funny to look back at people you've known your whole life, to suddenly see them as everyone else sees them, with their slicked-back hair and cigarettes hanging out of their mouths and their black leather jackets, and respond, "My God, they're hoods." You knew them and they're not hoods, but they just look like hoods. I had friends on the rich side of town, too, and saw that they had their share of problems, also. (*Outsiders* Fanclub)

Hinton explains how relevant *The Outsiders* was to her own experiences and the experiences of her friends:

> I was upset about the social warfare that was happening between the cliques in my high school. The two extremes were the Socs and Greasers, but I could have written an encyclopedia to include everybody: the artsy-crafty people, the theater people, the jocks. I grew up in a Greaser neighborhood, but I was placed in college-track classes with a lot of Socs, so I could see both sides. I was kind of just an observer. But when [a] friend got beat up, that was when I got mad and wrote a short story about a kid who was beaten up on his way home from the movies. (Loerke)

"That story," she says, "turned out to be about 40 pages long, single-spaced type. And I just kept going back over it and adding more details and flashbacks and so forth. The draft the publisher saw was about the third draft I'd done" (Biederharn). As she told another interviewer, "I didn't have any grand design. I just sat down and started writing it. I look back and I think it was totally written in my subconscious or something" (*Outsiders* Fan Club). To still another reporter she explained that in the beginning the book "was just something to let off steam" (*Outsiders* Fan Club).

Ponyboy's gang, she has said elsewhere, "was inspired by a true-life gang, the members of which were very dear to me. Later, all the gang members I hung out with were sure they were in the book— but they aren't. I guess it's because these characters are really kind of universal without losing their individuality" (*Outsiders* Fanclub). But often she comments that *The Outsiders* isn't really about "gangs" *per se*: "They weren't gangs, it was social class warfare" (Korfhage).

Recalling her own high school experiences, Hinton has said,

> I got put in, nowadays what would be called AP classes. They called them college track in those days. So I was in a different group of kids when I was in high school. So I got to see both sides. I refused to identify with either one of them. I've always been an observer. There's people who do things and people who watch, and I'm a watcher. I was very well aware of what was going on.
>
> I went to a huge high school, baby boomer. The senior class that I graduated with was 1,000 kids. That was the smallest class in the school. The bell rings and this mass of humanity, you have to try to find your way through to get to your next class. But you couldn't have a lot of friends. You got there, and you decided what group you were in, or somebody decided what group you were in for you, and then you didn't have any friends outside of the group. And I was watching these people obey all these rules—nobody said, "Where do these rules come from? Why do we have to do this? Why can't we have friends in any group we want to?" And I just thought the whole damn thing was stupid. So I just was watching it. (Ihnat)

In a series of points Hinton has made repeatedly to various interviewers, she has explained that "another reason why I wrote [*The Outsiders*] is that I wanted to read it. There was nothing realistic being written for teens at that time. It was all, like, 'Mary Jane Goes to the Prom.' And I'd been to a few proms, and that was not what was happening. I really wanted to read a book that dealt realistically with teenage life as I was seeing it" (Biederharn). As she has said elsewhere,

When I was in high school, there was nothing being written for the teenagers except Mary Jane goes to the prom and she wants to go with the football hero, but she ends up with the quiet boy next door, and has a good time anyway. Well, I'd been to a couple of proms by then and the big plot was, who got killed in the parking lot? The subplot was who brought the booze and how did they get it in? So I just couldn't find anything that dealt realistically with what I saw teenage life was like in high school. (Sheridan)

The high school years, she has said, are "a rough time of life." If her book has a message, she has commented, it is simply that "it will get better" (Staino). She has noted that she closely identified— and still does—with the sensitive Ponyboy:

A lot of Ponyboy's thoughts are my thoughts. He's probably the closest I've come to putting myself into a character. He has a lot of freedom, true-blue friends, people he loves and who love him; the things that are important to him are the things that are important to me. I think Ponyboy and Soda and Darry come out better than the rest of them because they have their love for one another. (*Outsiders* Fanclub)

Elsewhere she has said of Ponyboy that he is

a lot like I was at that age. Any character you write—I don't care if you think you're basing it off your best friend—has some aspect of yourself, because you're the filter they have to go through to get on the page. That's all I can say. Some part of me was a lot like Dallas, too, or I wouldn't be able to write him. (Blynn)

Writing *The Outsiders*
Commenting on her general approach to writing, Hinton has said,

Writing is easy for me because I never begin to write unless I have something to say. I'm a character writer. Some writers are plot writers .... I have to begin with people. I always knew my characters, exactly what they look like, their birthdays, what they like for breakfast. It doesn't matter if these things appear in the book. I still have to know. I get ideas for characters from real people, but overall they are fictional; my characters exist only in my head. (*Outsiders* Fanclub)

She tends to focus on male characters, she has explained,

> just because it was easiest as a tomboy, most of my close friends were boys, and I figured nobody would believe a girl would know anything about my subject matter. I have kept on using male characters because (1) boys have fewer books written for them (2) girls will read boys' books, boys usually won't read girls', and (3) it is still the easiest for me. (Graham)

All of her closest friends, she has said repeatedly, "were guys. To this day, most of my closest friends are guys. I couldn't identify with anything the female culture was doing at that time. I was playing football and going to rodeos. I thought, well, if I wrote this and said a girl was doing this, nobody would believe it" (Blynn). She could not, she has said,

> find anything in the female culture to identify with. What girls got to do was stand in the john, outline their eyes in black, and do their hair and brag about their boyfriend's car. I didn't want that. I wanted my own damn car. Even today, my men friends outnumber my women friends. So I think maybe my mind—I'm not saying I have a masculine mind, because god knows my husband does, and I have no idea how that works—but it's just that I don't find a lot of female characters as interesting. And, it's the easiest voice for me. . . . It was very easy for me to switch over to the persona of a boy, and I've written from a male point of view ever since, just because it's easy and I'm lazy. (Ihnat)

The actual composition of the book began, she has said, "when I was 15. . . . The year I was 16, my junior year of high school, was the year I really put the work in. I went back and put in more details, flashbacks, new little asides. I always say 16 was the year I wrote it" (Blynn). Asked how and why she invented such creative names as Ponyboy, Sodapop, and so on, she replied, "People ask me that all the time, and I say, 'I don't remember how I came up with those names, but I do know I wasn't drinking at the time'" (Biederharn). Elsewhere she has said, "I do remember at that age everyone wishing they were named something else, probably part of establishing an identity other than the one your parents have for you. The strange names seemed to fit the characters, though, so I left them" (Graham).

Another question she is often asked is why she chose to allude to Robert Frost's famous poem "Nothing Gold Can Stay." To one interviewer she replied,

> When I was writing *The Outsiders*, I would just pick up bits and pieces around school and write them into the book. In my much-maligned creative writing class, I just picked up a magazine and read that poem, and thought, "Oh, this is what I'm trying to say with *The Outsiders*." I couldn't define it, but I went in and wrote it into the book. And of course, that phrase "stay gold." I just hit a penny. (Ihnat)

Hinton often jokes that she wishes she had copyrighted the phrase, which has become enormously popular (although often misquoted as "stay golden"). She told another interviewer, "[A]s you know, Ponyboy's a reader. I don't think it would be totally unheard of for him to have come across that poem and remembered it, because . . . when he first recited it to Johnny, he said, I never forgot it because I couldn't quite figure out what he meant. But it stayed with me, haunted me or something. And that's the way I felt about the poem" (Sheridan).

Hinton has often said that she could not have written *The Outsiders* "four years later" than she did: "I couldn't have been that idealistic. And that's what the kids [i.e., her young readers] relate to, those true feelings I had at that time." As she explained to a reporter,

> [W]hen I was 16, that was the year I was doing my major work on *The Outsiders*. I wasn't thinking about any kind of audience for it. I wasn't thinking about a whole lot of stuff that, you know, of course, afterwards you kind of have to think about. An adult writer I think [would say], "Gosh, it's emotionally over-the-top. It's so dramatic." But that's the way you feel when you're that age. And that's one

reason why it's stayed so long—people are like, "Yes, I felt like this!" I could never do that again. It's one of the reasons I'll never write a sequel. (Biederharn)

The Publication Process
Having written the book, Hinton had no special plans to publish it. After all, she had written two previous novels and had not sought publication. But one day Hinton was talking to one of her friends, who said,

> "My mom writes children's books," and I said, "Oh, I write!" She said, "Oh really, let my mom read it," which she did, and she gave it to a friend of hers, who was also a published writer, but she had an agent, and she said, "Here's my agent, send it to them." I had no idea what was the difference between an agent and an editor. I had a name and an address. So I did send it to her. Marilyn Marlow of Curtis Brown did call me my senior year and said, "I've sold it to Viking. It was the second publisher that saw it, and it's going to come out in a year." Of course, I was just dumbfounded, and of course, excited. I got a contract on graduation day, which just blew graduation out of the water. (Ihnat)

Marlow, Hinton has said,

> was the first "professional" to read *The Outsiders*. I still have her first letter to me, saying she thought I had "captured a certain spirit" and would try to find a home for it. My age and inexperience did not seem to matter (although I am sure my spelling horrified her). She sold it to the second publisher who saw it, and I remained with her until her death.
>
> Marilyn looked out for me. She was there to meet the plane when my fifteen-year-old sister and I (eighteen) came to New York for the first time. I think in a lot of ways, she always thought of me as a child needing protection[;] she certainly was the last person to think that way, and I loved it. I had to look out for myself and other people at an early age, so it was a great relief that I had Marilyn to deal with the business side of things, who was a tough lady (and I emphasize "lady" because she always conducted herself as such) and a very thorough agent. Nothing got by her. (Bransford)

Hinton has also said that she had "great rapport" with her early editors. She explains, "Nobody changed a word I wrote. They asked me to cut descriptions once in a while. They corrected my spelling, thank god. And [they gave] the most helpful editorial comments I'd ever had, or have ever had since" (Biederharn).

Hinton continues,

> My first editor was Velma Varner of Viking Press, another legend I got to work with. And her notes were so great. She sent me about three pages. And they were very specific, which is like, page such and such. All of a sudden, Dallas has a gun. Can we put it in earlier that he has a gun so we're not all surprised he has a gun? Yeah. And it was mostly like, you do not need to describe these guys every couple of pages. You've done that real well. Just leave out descriptions. And on page such and such, this doesn't tie in with this. I mean, very, very easy. It was three pages of notes. But they were easy to follow, easy for me to correct. It wasn't rewriting me. Some people go, oh well, her teachers must have wrote [*sic*] that book for her. There's not a word in *The Outsiders* that I didn't write and none of my editors have written a line in my books. (Sheridan)

Viking paid one thousand dollars for the book (Smith), choosing to publish it using Hinton's initials rather than her full name, Susan Eloise, because the company was "afraid that the reviewers would assume a girl couldn't write a book like *The Outsiders*. Later," Hinton said, "when my books became popular, I found I liked the privacy of having a 'public' name and a private one, so it has worked out fine" (Graham).

Initial Reception

Commenting on initial reactions to the novel, Hinton has said that she did not experience "overnight fame and fortune." She explains, "I went to New York and did some media. They weren't celebrity crazy in those days . . . I wasn't on YouTube" (Cluff). Sales of the book "built slowly . . . It wasn't like an overnight success. . . . My first royalty check was 10 dollars." That amount, she continued, "could get you a tank of gas in Tulsa at that time. There was no big fan base and no big money. [The novel] grew to be part of my life. Now, it is hard to remember a time without it" (Graham). Asked how she responded when some readers at first seemed shocked by the book's realism, she replied,

> I was pleased that people were shocked . . . . One of my reasons for writing it was that I wanted something realistic to be written about teenagers. At that time realistic teenage fiction didn't exist. If you didn't want to read Mary Jane Goes to the Prom and you were through with horse books, there was nothing to read. I just wanted to write something that dealt with what I saw kids really doing. (*Outsiders* Fan Club)

Before the publication of *The Outsiders*, she has said, reading matter was divided into "childrens' books and adult books" (Jensen), leading many to credit Hinton and her novel with creating the whole genre of "young adult" fiction. Hinton herself agrees with that claim: "It's basically true. There'd certainly been books before that were written [from the perspective of] teenage protagonists—*Huckleberry Finn*, *The Catcher in the Rye*, *A Tree Grows in Brooklyn*. Great books, but they were all published as adult books" (Biederharn). When *The Outsiders* was issued

> in paperback, that's how the young adult genre started. It came out as a drugstore paperback, like Mickey Spillane. It didn't sell. It came back from those places in droves. Publishers were gonna let it go out of print. But they realized in certain places it was selling real well. It turned out teachers were using it in classrooms for reluctant readers by word of mouth. (Korfhage)

At first, she has said, "sometimes it was banned—just from parents seeing the book's cover and not reading the book" (Korfhage). But then "teachers said to students, 'Take the book home and read it.' Nowadays," she reports, "grandparents share it with their grandchildren" (Korfhage). Asked in 2017 how the book was received in her own home town, she replied,

Oh, well the Greasers loved it. Absolutely loved it. And a lot of the Socs took a second look at themselves. I remember I was doing a screening of the "complete novel" edition of the DVD in Tulsa, and Ralph Macchio [who played Johnny] and Tommy Howell [who played Ponyboy] were there with me. We had a question and answer thing going on afterward, and this guy gets up and he looks like he's about 65 or something, my age, and says, "This is the way it was, and this is the truth. I was there." And he'd been a Greaser. (Biederharn)

Reasons for the Novel's Popularity

Hinton explains the book's enduring popularity in various ways. "Everyone," she has said, "identifies with being an outsider," and sometimes "even within their own group they don't feel like they can be themselves. They're still kind of putting on a mask to fit in" (Cluff). Moreover,

> every teenager feels that adults have no idea what's going on. That's exactly the way I felt when I wrote *The Outsiders*. Even today, the concept of the in-group and the out-group remains the same. The kids [today] say, "Okay, this is like the Preppies and the Punks," or whatever they call themselves. The uniforms change, and the names of the groups change, but kids really grasp how similar their situations are to Ponyboy's. (*Outsiders* Fanclub)

In fact, Hinton has said,

> everyone everywhere can identify with the in group and the out group and even feel like an outsider in their own group. . . . In Ponyboy's group, no one liked to read books or see movies by themselves like he did. The character Cherry felt the same way, but she couldn't tell her friends how she felt because it wouldn't be cool. Teens still identify with those emotions. That and raging against injustice. That's just the way you feel at the age. (Blynn)

Interestingly, Hinton has commented that "the world's biggest fans" of the novel "first of all, are girls . . . . And I think at the age they're reading it—they're seventh and eighth grade girls—and they're reading 'The Outsiders' and they're going, 'Oh, so this is what boys are really like'" (Altschul). In fact, the book now sells better than it ever did because "readers still identify with it very strongly" (Jensen). Although the novel is set in a midwestern town distant from most of the country's population, Hinton has argued that "Tulsa's a pretty universal city. . . . It doesn't have the definition that either New York or LA has, so more people can envision [a story set there] happening to them" (Seiler).

But Hinton thinks *The Outsiders* has also proved popular because it lends itself well to classroom use. She has noted that it

> gained more and more followers, mostly from word of mouth and from teachers, bless their hearts, who found they could get nonreaders to read with it. And it's a great book for teaching. It's got themes. It's got characters. It's got dialogue. It's got foreshadowing. . . . But it's on a simple enough level that any kid can grasp what's there. So teachers love it. Thank God they did. I tried teaching. I couldn't do it. I don't have the nerves for it. So anything I could do to help teachers. They're my heroes. I'm glad it worked out for both of us. (Sheridan)

Aftermath of the Novel's Publication

Ironically, the very success of *The Outsiders* created problems for Hinton as she contemplated working on her next book. Her first novel was not immediately profitable—"My first royalty check was for 10 dollars. So I wasn't thinking, 'Oh, I've got it made for the rest of my life.'" But as the book's popularity grew, Hinton felt "overwhelmed" by . . . the realization that there was an audience out there"—a fact that "gave [her] writer's block for four years" (Biederharn). In fact, she has elsewhere said that the "writer's block" was either the result or cause of "an intense depression" (Smith).

> I had never had it before, and I never had it since. I have had people say that there's no such thing. Yeah, there is such a thing. I had had times where I couldn't think of anything to say, didn't want to say anything, didn't feel like writing. After the publication of *The Outsiders*, it was the first and only time I experienced a block, and it was extremely depressing. (Staino)

Part of the problem, she has said, resulted from the fact that she "had never thought about the audience before." She explains,

> When I wrote *The Outsiders*, I was totally unaware of an audience, since getting published wasn't my big deal. My big deal was getting the book right. I mean, I wrote it through different drafts before the publishers saw it. All of a sudden, I'm aware of the audience, and everybody's expecting me to do a masterpiece. I didn't have a masterpiece in me. I was in college, and I was reading some good writers. And of course, when I reread *The Outsiders*, I magnified all those faults. (Ihnat)

She thus faced a dilemma common to many a successful first-time novelist: how would she "top" (or even equal) her initial success? But in a way she didn't need to: in writing *The Outsiders* she had written a book that would never be forgotten and that would only grow in popularity over the years.

The Novel's Lasting Impact on Readers

Hinton is obviously pleased by the fact that *The Outsiders* has "never gone out of print. It sells better every year" (Ihnat). Its popularity has proven to be "multigenerational: Grandparents are sharing it with their grandkids. I began writing it," she notes, "when I was 15, and it's never been out of print. *The Outsiders* has been part of my life as long as just about anything." (Loerke). Asked to describe her "most memorable letters from fans," Hinton replied,

> Well, they're the ones that I'm most protective of because, you know, I get them from prison. I get them from all over the world. I get them from people who grew up in circumstances like *The Outsiders* boys did. I get them from . . . Indonesia, which you think would have no corresponding society to identify with, but they do. It's the ones that say you changed my life. It's overwhelming. I mean, I'm going, "I didn't change your life, the book changed your life." (Sheridan)

Fifty years after the book was first published, she still gets the same letters, the same responses. I get so many letters from people saying, "You changed my life." That scares me. I love getting letters saying, "I never liked to read, but I read your book, and now I'm going on to read other books." But the "You changed my life" stuff is scary, because who am I to change anybody's life? But I've learned to deal with it by thinking, *The Outsiders* was meant to be written, and I got chosen to write it. The rest of 'em [her other novels], I just wrote, but *The Outsiders* was supposed to be there. (Biederharn)

Readers have often informed Hinton directly of the impact the book has had on their lives. She said, once a person "told me she was contemplating suicide when she first read it, and it made her have hope" (Korfhage). More humorously, she recalls,

I used to work in a shoe store. My husband and I opened the first Earth shoe store in Tulsa, and we sold some other brands, too. I worked in there, measured feet and all that stuff. These big kids in their 20s came in to buy some construction boots and stuff. My husband went by and said, "Did you guys ever read *The Outsiders*?" This kid I was fitting, he said to him, "This is her." He looked at me and said, "You made me cry on the school bus." (Ihnat)

Hinton has said that "it's usually the young kids that burst into tears. I've had some older ones, too, teachers that have used it for a long time in school, kids that want to be writers and say I'm an inspiration to them" (Seiler). She believes that "there is no one 'right' way to read a book" and asserts, "since I think I am not alone in writing from my subconscious, I don't even think [reading to determine] 'writer's intent' is high on the list of ways to read a book. A reader will always bring their own experiences, thoughts, feelings to the mind-meld that is reading" (Jensen).

Although she says she was "very surprised" that the book was still in print after its first twenty years, she says, "after that, I wasn't surprised at all" (Biederharn). By 2015, the book had "sold more than 15 million copies" and had "been translated into 30 languages" (Blynn)—evidence of its impact on readers around the world.

The First Film

By the early 1980s, *The Outsiders* had proved so popular that Francis Ford Coppola—then one of the most esteemed American directors—decided to film both this book and *Rumble Fish*, another of Hinton's novels. Coppola hoped that films of the Hinton books would help his company (Zoetrope Studios) recover from some financial setbacks. He had actually received letters from a class of California students who had read *The Outsiders* asking him to film it. Hinton has explained that at first the novel

> was bought just for a property, for Zoetrope to be developed for the studio. On an airplane, Francis read it himself and decided he wanted to do it himself. And came to Tulsa and I met him. We scouted locations together and auditioned some actors together and . . . really, really hit it off. And he said, well, I'm going to shoot it here and can you help me with stuff and I said, sure. So I helped him scout locations, with wardrobe. I had my finger in about every piece of pie there was on that. (Sheridan)

In fact, Hinton has noted that she and Coppola jointly wrote "the screenplay for *The Outsiders*, no matter whose name you see on the credits." She explains that another person

> had done a screenplay based on *The Outsiders* sort of, but the only thing that they had in common with the book was the names of the characters. Francis loved it when he read the book, and he decided he wanted to write a screenplay. He came to Tulsa, and I showed him around to different locations, the neighborhoods and stuff like that, and he said, "Oh, I love this. We're going to shoot it here, and you can help me with everything." And he said, "You want to help me write a screenplay?" I said, "Sure." And he took out all the pages of the book in the paperback: He outlined the narration in one color, the action in one color, and dialogue in another color, and cut them up, and put them roughly on a screenplay form, pasted it on copy paper, handed it to somebody, and they came back with it typed up in kind of a screenplay format. He handed it to me and said, "Susie, you want to cut it for me?" I said, "Sure." . . .

So I was pretty ruthless. I knew you couldn't slow things down on the screen. You can't give people big speeches. I'm [at that time] in my 30s, and I come across some dialogue, and I think, "Ugh." So I rewrote it, gave it back to Francis. He was fine with all the cuts, because I'm good at that, I'm good at editing. And he goes, "Susie, this line isn't the same as it is in the book." I said, "No, Francis, it's better." He said, "We're making it for the kids. We want to use the dialogue word for word." So that was my big problem with working with the man—he wanted to be true to the book. (Ihnat)

Unfortunately, although Coppola essentially filmed the entire novel closely following the book's plot, by the time the film was actually released much of it had been cut from the final product—a fact that bothered both Hinton and Coppola. "We shot the whole book," Hinton has said,

but the film had to be cut drastically. It cut out the heart of the book, which for me is the bond between the brothers. It was disappointing in that we had shot the whole book, and then something happened in the editing room—I don't know what it was—but so much of it was just cut to ribbons. All of Rob [Lowe]'s good scenes. And he told me, it cracked him up because he thought he was so bad he had to be taken out. Which was not the case. (Ihnat)

Lowe and many other of the young and mostly unknown actors who starred in the film went on to become major celebrities, and Hinton often speaks of how much she loved working with him and the other "boys," for whom she functioned as a kind of substitute mother or big sister.

The "Second" Film: *The Outsiders: The Complete Novel*
In 2005, twenty-two years after the film version of *The Outsiders* appeared, Coppola released a version on DVD that was twenty-two minutes longer than the original film; it restored many of the scenes cut from the 1983 release. As Hinton explained to one interviewer, Coppola

dug out footage that had been deleted and scrambled them back into another version, and then he later came out with that version. It's called *The Outsiders: The Complete Novel*. It has all those scenes in it, including one of the ones I liked best, the opening scene when Ponyboy gets jumped and all his friends from the neighborhood come to rescue him. It's the only time in the book or the movie you see them all together. Each of the actors had a minute, two lines, to establish their characters, and they did it so, so well. I was so glad to see that. And of course, Rob [Lowe]'s good scenes. So [Coppola is] the only director I ever heard of that recut a movie because fans of the book asked him to. (Ihnat)

Coppola also, Hinton notes, "restored a scene in which Sodapop comforts his brother, Ponyboy, in bed. It was cut because, though innocent, early audiences snickered" (Smith). One of the most significant changes in the DVD release is a generally new soundtrack, this time featuring popular 1960s music rather than the symphonic track written for the original film by Coppola's father (who had since died). The 2005 version prompted many reporters to interview Hinton. One asked if there would ever be a remake of the film. "Not if I can help it," Hinton replied. "But more importantly, Francis owns the rights, and he doesn't want a remake either. Where are we going to get a cast like that? What makes the movie so good is those boys were so close to the age of the characters. They couldn't find kids that could be that talented, including Diane Lane." In a remake, she said, "they'd probably cast a bunch of 25-year-olds" (Seiler).

A Sequel to the Novel?
Hinton has also rejected the idea of writing a sequel to the novel. Asked if she would ever consider doing so, she replied,

Oh, no! Even by the time I wrote this I knew it was the end. I could not write a sequel. I could remember what it was like to be 16, but I'm not 16. I could not re-come up with those emotions. Besides that, the story ends where it's supposed to end. Where, for about two weeks in Ponyboy's life, he learned to look at life completely differently. To me, that's where the story ends. I didn't want to go on to Ponyboy Visits Hawaii or something. (Blynn)

Although she has said that she still has dreams about the novel's characters and thinks it would be "a piece of cake" to revive Ponyboy, she has also said that she "couldn't capture the intensity. It would be a letdown" (Italie), commenting further that "the intensity of the feelings at that age—the awareness of injustices, the emotional responses, I felt like that at sixteen and the readers realize they are not alone in that. I couldn't have written it four years later. And that's why I will never attempt" a sequel (Jensen). Hinton noted that she *has* "worked on the TV pilot. I worked on the play version. I'm *Outsiders*'d out. I don't need to read it again" (Blynn).

Hinton's Present Assessment of *The Outsiders*

When Hinton looks back on the book that made her famous, she responds with a mixture of pride and chagrin. Now, as a more experienced writer, she can perceive various flaws in her first novel, but she can also see its strengths, especially its appeal to young readers. She told one interviewer that "at the age of 20, when I re-read *The Outsiders*, I was very, very critical of it. Now I've learned to love it for what it is. But at that time I was going, oh, god. So [in her later writing] I was trying to correct every mistake I made in *The Outsiders*" (Sheridan). When the interviewer expressed surprise that Hinton considered her first book imperfect, Hinton replied,

> As an adult writer, I see tons of things wrong with it. But I wrote it at the right time. That's why I get so frustrated with people nagging me to do a sequel. I couldn't—even by the time I wrote *That Was Then* [published in 1971], I couldn't have written *The Outsiders*. I wrote it at the right time in my life. I wasn't expecting anybody to read it. I wrote with the emotions of a teenager, you know, the absolutely naive, idealistic frame of mind that they all have. . . . I've talked to some of the toughest schools in America, and I haven't found one yet that didn't have some glimmer of idealism, which is one of the main characteristics of *The Outsiders*. So I'm glad I wrote it when I did.

I'm very proud of the effect it's had, not just on America, but all over the world. (Sheridan)

When Hinton looks at the novel from her present perspective, she calls it "overemotional, over the top, [and] melodramatic," but she also thinks that "its vices were its virtues, because kids feel that way" (Italie). There are, she says, "parts that make me cringe as an adult writer. I could never be that un-self-conscious again. It was involving to teenagers, how emotionally over the top it is. At the time I didn't know anybody else felt this way" (Korfhage). But despite some present misgivings, she has also said,

> I can think of parts I'm very proud of. Man, I used to be smart. The opening paragraph where Ponyboy declares himself a person who's half imagination, half in the practical world? How he wanted to look like Paul Newman but wishes he had a ride home? I'm also very proud of the ending because it makes people go back and read it again. (Korfhage)

Asked if she would change anything in the novel, Hinton responded:

> No! Sometimes kids write me, "Why did you kill Johnny?!" and I usually say, "Because I'm a stone-cold bitch." But to me, that was the story that came to me. I never sit down and write a book and decide this person won't live. I have a story that comes to me and I write it. If part of the story is that somebody dies then they die. But there's still a hopeful ending. (Blynn)

Hinton's Advice to Young Writers

Hinton once replied to a question about advice for beginning authors, "You should only worry about how good your writing is. You have to read and practice, read and practice. That's all I did to develop my writing skills: read and practice. You don't have to take lessons in creative writing" (Loerke). About her own writing method, she has said, "The only thing I am sure of is that it involves a lot of staring out the window. . . . Write for yourself first. Don't study the market, it will change before you can get a book done. The writing is the thing to concentrate on. If you don't want to read it, nobody will" (Bransford). Similarly she tells young beginning writers, "Worry about the writing, not the publishing. Don't try to please an audience, please yourself. Ignore things like word count, get spell check. If you really don't have anything to say, don't say anything" (Jensen).

Works Cited

Altschul, Serena. "S.E. Hinton's *The Outsiders*, a Teen Classic, Turns 50." *CBS News*, 23 Apr. 2017, www.cbsnews.com/news/the-outsiders-se-hinton-a-teen-classic-turns-50/.

Biederharn, Isabella. "S.E. Hinton on *The Outsiders*' success: 'It gave me writer's block for four years.'" *Entertainment Weekly*, 24 Apr. 2017, ew.com/books/2017/04/24/the-outsiders-anniversary-s-e-hinton/.

Blynn, Jamie. "*The Outsiders*' Author S.E. Hinton Celebrates the Novel's 50th Anniversary: I Hope Ponyboy 'Isn't Bald.'" *US Magazine*, 13 Apr. 2017, www.usmagazine.com/entertainment/news/se-hinton-looks-back-on-the-outsiders-for-50th-anniversary-w476427/.

Bransford, Nathan. Interview with S. E. Hinton. 14 May 2009, blog. nathanbransford.com/2009/05/interview-with-se-hinton/.

Cluff, Rick. "Author S.E. Hinton on the 50th anniversary of *The Outsiders*." *CBC News*, 1 Apr. 2017, www.cbc.ca/news/canada/british-columbia/author-s-e-hinton-on-the-50th-anniversary-of-the-outsiders-1.4049621/.

Sheridan, Dana. "The Bibliofiles: S. E. Hinton." *The Bibliofiles*, n.d., www.princeton.edu/cotsen/gallery-programs/bibliofiles/se-hinton. pdf/. Accessed 10 Jan. 2018.

Graham, Ginnie. "Forever an Outsider: Tulsa author S.E. Hinton looks back 50 years to her first book." *Tulsa World*, 5 May 2017, www. tulsaworld.com/scene/twm/forever-an-outsider-tulsa-author-s-e-hinton-looks-back/article_ce9a7027-c470-50f3-82f0-3a993cd2f768. html/.

Ihnat, Gwen. "Interview: *Outsiders* author S.E. Hinton is still gold after 50 years." *The AV Club*, 16 May 2017, film.avclub.com/outsiders-author-s-e-hinton-is-still-gold-after-50-yea-1798262219/.

Italie, Hillel. "S.E. Hinton Reflects on *The Outsiders.*" *NewsOK*, 29 Sept. 2007, newsok.com/article/3136960.

Jensen, Kelly. "*The Outsiders*—and YA Lit—at 50: An Interview with SE Hinton." *Book Riot*, 24 Apr. 2017, bookriot.com/2017/04/24/outsiders-ya-lit-50-interview-se-hinton.

Korfhage, Matthew. "*Outsiders* Author S.E. Hinton Talks Matt Dillon, and Why Everybody Keeps Showing Her Their Tattoos." *Willamette Week*, 17 May 2017, www.wweek.com/uncategorized/2017/05/16/outsiders-author-s-e-hinton-talks-matt-dillon-and-why-everybody-keeps-showing-her-their-tattos/.

Loerke, Liz. "S. E. Hinton Reflects on the 50th Anniversary of *The Outsiders.*" *Real Simple*, 3 Apr. 2017, www.realsimple.com/work-life/entertainment/se-hinton-interview-outsiders-50th-anniversary/.

The Outsiders Fan Club. Excerpts from Interviews with S. E. Hinton. *Theoutsidersfanclub*, n.d., theoutsidersfanclub.weebly.com/exclusive-interview-with-se-hinton.html/. Accessed 10 Jan. 2017.

Seiler, Margaret. "Staying Gold: S. E. Hinton on *The Outsiders* at 50." *Portland Monthly*, 11 May 2017, www.pdxmonthly.com/articles/2017/5/11/staying-gold-s-e-hinton-on-the-outsiders-at-50/.

Smith, Dinitia. "An Outsider, Out of the Shadows." *The New York Times*, 7 Sept. 2005, www.nytimes.com/2005/09/07/movies/MoviesFeatures/an-outsider-out-of-the-shadows.html/.

Staino, Rocco. "SLJ Talks to S.E. Hinton on 'The Outsiders' Turning 45." *School Library Journal*, 26 Jun. 2012, www.slj.com/2012/06/industry-news/slj-talks-to-s-e-hinton-on-the-outsiders-turning-45/.

Taylor, Elizabeth. "An Interview with S. E. Hinton." *Chicago Tribune*, 31 May 2008, articles.chicagotribune.com/2008-05-31/entertainment/0805300368_1_hinton-outsiders-gender/.

A Portrait of the Artist as a Young Greaser:
The Outsiders as Künstlerroman_____

Lana A. Whited

In her note to the reader at the start of *The Outsiders*, author S. E. Hinton explains that she wrote the novel because of a dearth of realistic fiction for adolescent readers. Hinton, who was sixteen when she began the novel, writes that she "desperately wanted something to read that dealt realistically with teenage life." Much about Hinton's novel fits that bill: her protagonist, his brothers, and his friends are adolescents from "the wrong side of the tracks"; they are East-side boys, as opposed to the West-side "socials" or "Socs." Their families are working class, and the boys are much more influenced by one another than by any adult authority figures, including parents. The Curtis brothers—Darrel, Soda Pop, and Ponyboy—are raising themselves due to their parents' deaths in a car accident. Most of the boys view education as an experience to be endured or abandoned. They pride themselves on the greasy hair that is the source of their gang name. Some, like Dallas "Dally" Winston, already have records of juvenile delinquency. They smoke cigarettes, steal hubcaps, and get into fights, using not only their fists but also knives and broken bottles. Dally has "dangerous mood[s]" that suggest "a hatred of the whole world" (Hinton 10); he was formerly a member of a New York City gang and has spent time in jail, which he says "hardened" him (90). It is difficult to believe the "greasers" made famous by the teenage author, Hinton, emerged from a decade when many youngsters still grew up reading The Hardy Boys and Nancy Drew.

Fourteen-year-old Ponyboy Curtis may appear to be a modern-day Huckleberry Finn, enjoying a freedom caused by his separation from adult authority figures and his gang's general disregard for conventional adolescent behavior. Nevertheless, the protagonist of *The Outsiders* is not a prototypical bad boy. When a reader first encounters Hinton's protagonist, he is on his way out of a movie theatre, thinking of Paul Newman and wishing he looked more like the movie idol. Throughout Hinton's novel, Ponyboy narrates the confrontations between "greasers" and "Socs" or "socials" with the artistic sensibility of a novice author. During the course of the narrative, he mentions two novels, Charles Dickens' *Great Expectations* and Margaret Mitchell's *Gone with the Wind*. In a scene central to the novel's theme, he recites Robert Frost's poem "Nothing Gold Can Stay" to his friend Johnny. "Stay gold," an allusion to the Frost poem, is the last thing sixteen-year-old Johnny says to Ponyboy before dying. Early in the novel, when Ponyboy encounters a Soc girl, Cherry Valance, at a drive-in movie theatre, she recognizes that he is different from most "greasers." In their first encounter, after dismissing Dallas Winston as a "hood," Cherry says to Ponyboy, "you don't look the type" (to annoy her and her friends) when he has said no more to her than "no" (Hinton 22). In only the second paragraph, Ponyboy twice refers to himself as "different." After his physical appearance, his sense of himself as a loner is the first aspect of his identity that he describes. He likes to watch movies alone, he says, noting "I'm different that way" (2). He doesn't like anyone looking over his shoulder while he reads, adding that his reading habit also distinguishes him from his brothers and friends. "I'm not like them. And nobody in our gang digs movies and books the way I do. For a while there, I thought I was the only person in the world that did. So I loned it" (2).

Hinton uses Ponyboy's literary allusions and poetic sensibility as the primary means of differentiating him from other teenaged boys of his social milieu. His sensitive, artistic perspective softens the characterization of a fourteen-year-old orphan being raised by two older brothers who have assumed their places in a Realistic world to which, at least at fourteen, Ponyboy is still an outsider. In the novel's denouement, it is implied that the entire text of *The Outsiders* was written by Ponyboy for an English class assignment. Upon this revelation, the reader recognizes Hinton's novel for what it is: not merely a coming-of-age story but a *Künstlerroman*, the story of the romantic and artistic sensibility that helps to insulate

Ponyboy and to distinguish him from his rougher, more Realistic companions. It is a portrait of the artist as a young greaser.

The Realism of Hinton's novel is largely responsible for the book's reputation as controversial. It has held a spot on the American Library Association Office of Intellectual Freedom's list of banned or challenged books as long as the OIF has maintained that list (it is on the 1990–1999 list, the earliest available on the ALA web site). R. Wolf Baldassarro writes that the novel "is ranked #43 on the American Library Association's Top 100 Most Challenged Books of 1990–2000 and has been banned from some schools and libraries because of its portrayal of gang violence, underage smoking and drinking, strong language, slang usage, and exposé on family dysfunction." Francis Ford Coppola's 1983 film adaptation was also controversial, not surprising for a movie that was assigned a PG rating despite the fact that a major character is shot to death in a police confrontation at the end. However, analysis of the film's suitability for young viewers was colored by its receiving the PG rating in the last year before the PG-13 rating was introduced. *The Outsiders* film was released on March 25, 1983, while the PG-13 rating was first assigned to *Red Dawn*, released on Aug. 10, 1984, which coincidentally also starred Patrick Swayze (Pallotta). The Common Sense Media panel of experts recommends age twelve for readers of Hinton's book and fourteen for watching the film. According to *Goodreads* and many other sources of book recommendations, teachers and librarians tend not to suggest the book to prospective readers before middle school. But the book's literary reputation has outpaced its notoriety: as of this writing, *The Outsiders* was number six on the list "Top-100 Middle School Must-Reads" compiled by *Goodreads* book club members.

The fictional universe of *The Outsiders* reflects the attributes of Realism, a literary movement which was the dominant mode in American literature between the Civil War and the end of the nineteenth century. To say that the novel is Realistic means that it is an accurate portrayal of the lives of boys like the Curtis brothers living in the Midwest of the mid-1960s: the story is life-like; the characters could be real boys, and the plot is believable. Ponyboy wears jeans and t-shirts, drinks Cokes, sees movies, and has homework assignments. If he stays up too late or has been in a fight, he may have a headache. He wants to emulate his older brothers and be involved in the activities of their extended group of friends. These are the clothes, the actions, and the feelings of real boys. In this sense, *The Outsiders* is a realistic story.

A hallmark of realistic literature is the presentation of characters speaking everyday language (including slang), not the idealized language of the Romantic literature that preceded realism. Huckleberry Finn, one of the first realistic characters in American literature, introduces himself to the reader just as a contemporary boy in rural Mississippi might:

> You don't know about me, without you have read a book by Mr. Mark Twain called "The Adventures of Tom Sawyer," but that ain't no matter. That book was made by Mr. Mark Twain, and he told the truth, mainly. There was things which he stretched, but mainly he told the truth. That is nothing. I never seen anybody but lied, one time or another. . . . (Clemens 7)

The use of dialects is so important to Twain's novel that he addresses it in a preface, declaring that he felt it necessary to emphasize that "without it many readers would suppose that all these characters were trying to sound alike but not succeeding" (Clemens 2). Ponyboy's language, too, is peppered with the slang of his social milieu. His friends are *greasers*, so named from their habit of overdoing it with their hair dressing, and their rivals are Socs or Socials. To really understand another person is to "dig."

It is not just the language of *Huckleberry Finn* that marked a departure from the fiction that immediately preceded it, as its plot also includes developments and themes that have caused some adults to view it as inappropriate for young readers: Huck's father drinks heavily and neglects his son, leaving Huck under the well-meaning but naïve eyes of two elderly ladies. Huck has disdain for two social institutions generally viewed by adults as good for children—school and church—and instead runs away to the river. Before long, the boy encounters a runaway slave, Jim, and faces the decision to aid or report him, a serious dilemma with legal consequences in the mid-1800s. The slave, Jim, eventually finds Huck's father dead in a houseboat, apparently shot to death. Huck and Jim share a portion of their journey on the Mississippi with the Duke and the King, petty crooks and shysters. And then there is Twain's repeated use of the word "nigger," which has historically been the source of the most vehement critics' objections, including a crusade led in the 1950s by the NAACP ("Mark Twain").[1] Twain's stark departure from the more nuanced depiction of conflict and the standardized or homogenous character speech of Romantic literature led Ernest Hemingway to write half a century later, "All modern American literature comes from one novel by Mark Twain called *Huckleberry Finn*" ("Mark Twain").

Despite the differing historical contexts, Huck Finn and Ponyboy Curtis have much in common. Both protagonists find themselves orphaned (or practically orphaned, in Huck's case) and under the supervision of guardians by age fourteen. Both boys are members of a gang (in Huck's case, Tom Sawyer's robbers gang), and each gang struggles with matters of reputation; just as the older greasers view Ponyboy and Johnny as novices still in need of protection and training, Huck Finn is the recipient of Tom's regular lectures about respectability. Each boy escapes from a scene involving violence to become a fugitive: in Ponyboy's case, he and Johnny leave for the countryside after Johnny kills the Soc Bob Sheldon, and Huck kills a pig to fake his own death and escape from his abusive father, who has kidnapped him. Each boy's experience while on the lam is essentially about figuring out who he is apart from society: for Ponyboy, the society in which working-class boys and middle-class boys live on opposite sides of the tracks, and for Huck, the social divide between white and black Southerners. Each boy must figure out his own place in a culture that insists that everyone belongs on one side or the other, and each eventually realizes there is another choice. Each protagonist performs a heroic act: Huck saves Jim, and Ponyboy, with Johnny, saves the children from the burning church. Clearly, each of these actions involves sacrifice: for Ponyboy, his injuries and the ultimate loss of Johnny, and for Huck, his potential loss of reputation and his own freedom for hiding a runaway slave and, moreover, the (perceived) loss of his immortal soul. From departure to return, Ponyboy and Huck come to insight about themselves that will ultimately enable them to move forward toward an adulthood not characterized by the social divide that created their predicaments.

A final similarity between *The Outsiders* and *Adventures of Huckleberry Finn* is the revelation at the end of each story that the protagonist has been functioning in the role of artist. *The Outsiders* is revealed to be a long narrative that Ponyboy wrote as an assignment for English class. Huck Finn declares after the episodes at Tom Sawyer's aunt and uncle's farm that he is finished with authorship: "there ain't nothin' more to write about, and I am rotten glad of it, because if I'd knowed what a trouble it was to make a book, I wouldn't a tackled it, and ain't a-going to no more" (Clemens 229). Ironically, of course, until Ponyboy and Huck step forward near the end of their narratives to claim authorship, the reader has viewed them all along as the creation of a third party outside the narrative proper. The youthful protagonist clarifies, in the end, that the experience he has just recounted is the one that formed his identity as artist, and this construct is where Ponyboy Curtis and Huckleberry Finn part ways: Huck has reached the end of his career as storyteller, but Ponyboy is only beginning. This is the distinction most useful to explaining Ponyboy's development as the Romantic protagonist of a Realistic novel.

The *Künstlerroman*, or story of the artist's psychological and moral development, is fundamentally a Romantic subtype of literature. The word is a portmanteau or compound of *Künstler*, the German word for artist, and *roman*, the word for novel. Thus, the *Künstlerroman* is the artist-novel. Although novels falling within this category represent artists at every stage of life, the most common is a blend of the *Künstlerroman* with the bildungsroman or "coming-of-age" novel. The *Künstlerroman* became popular in German literature in the late eighteenth century, continuing into the nineteenth century, "a period when the artist . . . was held in high esteem, and the man of genius became an exalted figure. . . . Fictitious artists were often favoured central figures" ("*Künstlerroman*"). Johann Wolfgang von Goethe, Hermann Hesse, Rainer Maria Rilke, and Thomas Mann are well-known German practitioners of the type. Goethe's *Wilhelm Meister's Apprenticeship* (1795–96) is usually identified as the first example.

The prototype for the *Künstlerroman* in modern literature is James Joyce's *A Portrait of the Artist as a Young Man,* first published in 1916, which was heralded by H. G. Wells as "the most living and convincing picture that exists of an Irish Catholic upbringing." *Portrait* was Joyce's first novel. Just as *The Outsiders* is presented (in the end) as Ponyboy's first extended work of narrative prose, most critics view Joyce's novel as accounting for the author's own artistic development. Joyce's novel focuses on the growth of Stephen Dedalus's intellectual and religious identity from his earliest literary memories—his father telling him nursery stories—through his home-leaving, or launch into the adult world. Most critics view Stephen as Joyce's literary alter ego; for example, Dedalus also appears in Joyce's novel *Ulysses* (1922), wherein the protagonist, Leopold Bloom, notes Stephen's pleasant tenor singing voice, a talent shared by his creator. Joyce's biographers have written at length about similarities between Stephen's youth and that of his creator, who also attended Clongowes School and signed some of his early work using Stephen Dedalus's name (Bowker 219).

Stephen has much in common with Ponyboy Curtis, despite the fact that Stephen is Roman Catholic with a Jesuit education, whereas Ponyboy's development focuses more on general morality than a specific denomination or religion. (As a slightly older protagonist for the majority of the narrative, Stephen is also far more aware of girls.) Both Stephen and Ponyboy are top students, although Stephen is more overtly focused on his academic achievements. Ponyboy accepts but does not dwell on his good grades, an achievement he shares with his oldest brother, Darry, who was headed to college on a football scholarship before the parents' death and his decision to go to work and support his younger brothers. When Stephen has his hand hit with the pandybat for breaking his glasses, his sense of injustice is increased by his awareness that his work is generally superior: "he always got the card for first or second" (Joyce 52). His moral outrage and sense of himself as a good student propel him to the rector's office, where he is received respectfully and rewarded with a promise that the rector will speak on Stephen's behalf to the prefect of studies. Stephen's assertiveness enhances his leadership ability, and his classmates recognize that he has challenged injustice by shouldering him through the schoolyard, cheering. (Stephen, meanwhile, feels that he must get loose from their grasp.) Stephen's confidence increases, and by the time he changes to Belvedere College due to his father's financial trouble, he and his friend Heron are "during the year the virtual heads of the school" (Joyce 76).

For both protagonists, the transformation from boy to artist is fueled by avid reading. Stephen does not mind when the illness that sends him to the Clongowes School infirmary is extended: "it would be nice getting better slowly. You could get a book then" (Joyce 26). After Ponyboy is released from the hospital to recover from the concussion he suffered in the fire, he recuperates in a bedroom cluttered with books. Stephen and his classmates at Belvedere often discuss literature and what books are in their fathers' libraries. Ponyboy claims he has "read everything in the house about fifty million times" (Hinton 177). He has even read Darry's copy of Harold Robbins' 1961 novel *The Carpetbaggers*, although he agrees with his brother Darry that he (Ponyboy) "wasn't old enough to read it" (Hinton 177).

Not only are Stephen and Ponyboy both avid readers, but both seem to have cultivated a preference for Romantic texts and authors. During Stephen's summer in Blackrock, he spends his days with his father and his granduncle, but "[h]is evenings were his own; and he pored over a ragged translation of *The Count of Monte Cristo*" (Joyce 62). Alexander Dumas' novel tells the story of a man wrongfully imprisoned who sets out to achieve vengeance against those responsible for his imprisonment. Primarily a historical adventure novel, it was first published in 1844, toward the end of the Romantic period, and Dumas is generally regarded as a major figure of French Romanticism. Stephen reads the novel and imagines himself as the lover of the beautiful and highly desirable Mercédès, whom the protagonist, Edmond Dantès, is prohibited from marrying due to the allegations against him.

Despite the apparent bleakness of the Oklahoma landscape against which *The Outsiders* is set, Ponyboy also prefers Romantic fiction. Oddly, the novel most present in the pages of S. E. Hinton's story is *Gone with the Wind*, a novel of the American Civil War and the Reconstruction period, written by Margaret Mitchell and published in 1936. After Ponyboy and Johnny run away to the abandoned church building in the countryside, when Johnny finally ventures out for supplies, he returns with sandwich makings, cigarettes, peroxide (to bleach the boys' hair), and a copy of Mitchell's novel. Ponyboy is overjoyed to see the book, exclaiming, "A paperback copy of *Gone with the Wind*! How'd you know I always wanted one?" (Hinton 71). Johnny reminds him that they saw the movie together, and over the next few days, the runaways pass long hours reading aloud to each other from the 1,024-page book. Five days after Johnny brings the novel, the boys have read to the siege of Atlanta, which comes around a third of the way through (Hinton 79). The focus of the boys' discussion is the gallantry of the Confederate soldiers, which Johnny compares to Dally Winston's coolness in "taking the rap" for something Two-Bit actually did. Ponyboy's immersion in the story is a textbook example of his vivid inner life:

> I had almost decided that I had dreamed the outside world and there was nothing real but baloney sandwiches and the Civil War and the old church and the mist in the valley. It seemed to me that I had always lived in the church, or maybe lived during the Civil War and had somehow got transplanted. (Hinton 79)

In the aftermath of the fire in the church building, when he and Johnny are loaded into ambulances, Ponyboy thinks regretfully of what the boys lost in the fiery explosion: their gun and their copy of *Gone with the Wind* (Hinton 96). In the hospital, when Two-Bit asks if Johnny can think of anything he wants besides hair grease, Johnny replies, "'The book'—he looked at [Ponyboy]—'can you get another one?'" (Hinton 120).

One cannot help but guess that Ponyboy (and Johnny) would also love to read *The Count of Monte Cristo*.

Where poetry is concerned, Stephen Dedalus champions George Gordon, Lord Byron, and, when he begins writing his own poetry, imitates Byron's habit of writing a dedication to a woman at the beginning of the poem: "To E—C—" (Joyce 70). Stephen even becomes engaged in a fistfight with his classmates Heron and Boland, who defend Alfred, Lord Tennyson as "the best poet" (Joyce 80). By contrast, Stephen considers Tennyson "only a rhymester!" (Joyce 80). Tennyson, the most popular poet of his era, was a Victorian, while Byron was a Romantic.

Ponyboy, too, is characterized by the Romantic imagination that he keeps largely to himself, sharing it only with Johnny and perhaps allowing Cherry Valance to glimpse it. Stephen's difference from his schoolmates is emphasized early, when he watches the other boys playing ball but does not participate himself. Ponyboy clearly prefers the interior, intellectual life, devoting much of his free time to movies and books. This theme of the artist's quasi-separation from the world around him and his more intense perception of beauty in all forms is developed throughout *Portrait*, beginning with Stephen's early appreciation of language and culminating in chapter five when Stephen's dean asks him directly (after Stephen has failed the mundane task of lighting a fire), "You are an artist, are you not, Mr. Dedalus? . . . The object of the artist is the creation of the beautiful. What the beautiful is is another question. . . . Can you solve that question now?" (Joyce 185).

It is coincidental, in regard to this point about the artistic temperament, that Stephen and Ponyboy's aesthetic nature is revealed in both narratives in important scenes involving their appreciation of clouds. In *Portrait*, Stephen's description of the clouds above Dollymount Strand became one of the most famous passages written by Joyce:

He drew forth a phrase from his treasure and spoke it softly to himself:—A day of dappled seaborne clouds. The phrase and the day and the scene harmonized in a chord. Words. Was it their colours? He allowed them to glow and fade, hue after hue: sunrise gold, the russet and green of apple orchards, azure of waves, the grey-fringed fleece of clouds. No, it was not their colours: it was the poise and balance of the period itself. Did he then love the rhythmic rise and fall of words better than their associations of legend and colour? Or was it that, being as weak of sight as he was shy of mind, he drew less pleasure from the reflection of the glowing sensible world through the prism of a language many-coloured and richly storied than from the contemplation of an inner world of individual emotions mirrored perfectly in a lucid supple periodic prose? (Joyce 166-67)

After stepping off the bridge which Joyce describes, in a projection of Stephen's own state, as "trembling," Stephen recognizes two of his friends coming out of the waves, thinks briefly of the story of Dedalus and Icarus, and subsequently experiences his epiphany: observing a girl standing in the surf and gazing out to sea, Stephen exclaims "Heavenly God!"; the narrator notes that this utterance originates in Stephen's soul (Joyce 167). He realizes, in the formative scene, that he will reject the invitation to join the Jesuit order and become instead the artificer of the "profane joy" of mortal beauty which the narrator says he experiences (Joyce 171). It is clear in the passage that Joyce intends this epiphany as the transitional event between Stephen's childhood and youth: "His soul had arisen from the grave of boyhood, spurning her grave-clothes. Yes! Yes! Yes! He would create proudly out of the freedom and power of his soul, as the great artificer whose name he bore, a living thing, new and soaring and beautiful, impalpable, imperishable" (Joyce 169-70).

Ponyboy's taste in poetry may not specifically include the Romantic, but his meditations on Robert Frost's poem "Nothing Gold Can Stay" reflect his essentially philosophical temperament, his interest in beauty and the beautiful. Discussing that poem with Johnny in the church building, Ponyboy articulates his aesthetic philosophy, much as Stephen discloses his own to his friend Cranly. The scene in which Ponyboy describes the sunrise and landscape is remarkably similar to Stephen Dedalus's epiphany on the Dollymount Strand. Both boys are looking out across a natural landscape through the eyes of the novice artist.

Hiding out in the old church, Ponyboy and Johnny cannot watch sunsets because that would require them to be on the side of the barn where they might be seen from the road. But one morning Ponyboy wakes up in time to see the sun rise and describes it in remarkably poetic language:

All the lower valley was covered with mist, and sometimes little pieces of it broke off and floated away in small clouds. The sky was lighter in the east, and the horizon was a thin golden line. The clouds changed from gray to pink, and the mist was touched with gold. There was a silent moment when everything held its breath, and then the sun rose. It was beautiful. (Hinton 77)

Ponyboy wishes he could paint the scene, and then Johnny is at his side, admiring the gold and silver mist. When Johnny observes, "Too bad it can't stay like that all the time," Ponyboy remembers and recites the Frost poem, which begins and ends with the line "Nothing gold can stay," and Johnny declares that this sentiment is "what I mean" (Hinton 77). Ponyboy says that the meaning Frost intended has "eluded" him, and Johnny replies that he never noticed the beauty of the physical world until Ponyboy started to point it out to him. After a pause, Johnny remarks on Darry and Soda's similarities with Ponyboy's parents, ending, "And you don't act like either one" (78).

Ponyboy's identity as outsider is reinforced in Johnny's observations, and he immediately points out that he is comfortable exposing that self to Johnny and Sodapop "[a]nd maybe Cherry Valance" because "you ain't like any of the gang" (Hinton 78). When Johnny affirms the idea that Ponyboy is different, Ponyboy blows "a perfect smoke ring" and declares, thinking of the other members of their gang—those to whom he would not admire the beauty of the sunrise in poetic terms—"maybe *they* are" (Hinton 78). This conversation underscores another potential meaning for Hinton's title, suggesting not the gang members' status as social outsiders but their remoteness from the artistic temperament which Ponyboy illustrates and Johnny at least glimpses. In this sense, Ponyboy and

Cherry Valance are *outsiders* to the habit of conventional thoughts and behaviors in the world they inhabit.

Stephen Dedalus is also an outsider in this sense. For example, Stephen's school uses red and white roses (for the houses of Lancaster and York in the War of the Roses) for scholastic competition, just as students at Hogwarts can earn house points for correct answers. Stephen admires these colors but thinks of a song he has heard "about the wild rose blossoms on the little green place" and wonders "why you could not have a green rose. But perhaps somewhere in the world you could" (Joyce 13). These musings (which perhaps also, in Stephen's color choice, foreshadow the campaign for Irish independence) reflect Stephen's tendency to adopt a mindset apart from conventional ideas.

Late in *A Portrait of the Artist as a Young Man*, Stephen expresses his desire to escape convention: "When the soul of a man is born in this country there are nets flung at it to hold it back from flight. You talk to me of nationality, language, religion. I shall try to fly by those nets" (Joyce 203). At this point, Joyce evokes most obviously the classical myth from which Stephen derives his name: the story of Dedalus and Icarus, a myth that resonates in Stephen's story. The labyrinth designed by Dedalus might be viewed as a metaphor for Stephen's journey to adulthood and the formation of his artistic identity. Like Dedalus, Stephen will be an artificer, and the primary medium of his art will be his own soul. In order to shape that soul, he must escape the conventional realm of Irish politics and Roman Catholicism and venture, like Dedalus and Icarus, away from the familiar. During his "formative" years, he has acquired the materials for the great work of the adult artist, saving only the one element which he needs in greater quantity: "I go to encounter for the millionth time the reality of experience and to forge in the smithy of my soul the uncreated conscience of my race" (Joyce 253).

Unlike Stephen, Ponyboy does not choose to go away, but toward the end of *The Outsiders*, he reveals a more mature and objective view of the conflict that has dominated his brothers' adolescence. He talks with Randy about the futility of the fighting, listening as Randy explains, "people get hurt in rumbles, maybe killed. I'm sick of it because it doesn't do any good. You can't win, you know that, don't you?" (Hinton 117). Randy says he's thought of leaving town, although he knows that wouldn't help, and ultimately concluding, "I don't know what to do" (Hinton 117). Finally, he and Ponyboy use each other's names instead of calling the other "greaser" or "Soc," and when Ponyboy realizes that Randy "ain't a Soc . . . he's just a guy," he demonstrates his own ability to transcend social categories and see instead the essence of things (Hinton 118). This is the sort of perception that has connected him with Cherry Valance, a connection sealed by their eventual agreement that a person can see the sunset equally well from both the East and West parts of town (Hinton 129-30), whereas most of their friends would prefer the view from their side of town, or would not bother to admire sunsets at all.

Ponyboy Curtis is the remnant of Romanticism in the overtly Realistic world of *The Outsiders*. Johnny has urged him to "stay Gold," meaning to remain for as long as possible in that state that parallels dawn holding its breath before emerging onto the landscape. What he is encouraging Ponyboy to do—whether or not he could articulate it—is to stay in that state of innocence and purity associated with childhood, an innocence of spirit that the Romantic writers prized and that Ponyboy has not completely left behind, although the experience he describes in his narrative certainly propels him forward. Johnny's death is the symbolic death of innocence, the death of the smallest member of the gang, the one who served as the gang's pet. His loss represents the end of Ponyboy's childhood, which, at least in Johnny's view, was "gold." And it heralds Pony's new identity as no longer a young greaser, but a young man who will be the smithy of his own soul.

Note

1. The controversy surrounding Twain's novel is the subject of a ninety-minute PBS documentary called *Born to Trouble:* Adventures of Huck Finn (2000), the first installment in a four-part series called *Culture Shock.*

Works Cited

American Library Association Office for Intellectual Freedom. "Frequently Challenged Young Adult Books." *Banned and Challenged Books*, August 2016, www.ala.org/advocacy/bbooks/frequentlychallengedbooks/YAbooks/.

Baldassarro, R. Wolf. "Banned Book Awareness: *The Outsiders.*" *World. edu: World Education Network*, 8 May 2011, world.edu/banned-books-awareness-outsiders/.

"Born to Trouble: *Adventures of Huck Finn.*" *Culture Shock: The TV Series and Beyond. Blue Ridge Public Television*, n.d., www.pbs.org/wgbh/cultureshock/beyond/huck.html/. Accessed 3 Feb. 2018.

Bowker, Gordon. *James Joyce: A New Biography*. Farrar, Straus and Giroux, 2011.

Campbell, Patty. "*The Outsiders*, Fat Freddy, and Me." *Horn Book Magazine*, vol. 79, no. 2, March/April 2003, p. 177. *EBSCOhost*, 0-search.ebscohost.com/.

Clemens, Samuel Langhorne (Mark Twain). *Adventures of Huckleberry Finn*. 1885. Edited by Scully Bradley, et al. Norton Critical Ed., 2nd ed., Norton, 1977.

Fine, Jana R. "YASD: A Narrative History From 1976 to 1992." *Young Adult Library Services Association*, n.d., www.ala.org/yalsa/aboutyalsa/yalsahandbook/yasdnarrative/. Accessed 17 Jan. 2018.

Hinton, S. E. *The Outsiders*. Penguin, 1967.

Joyce, James. *A Portrait of the Artist as a Young Man*. 1916. Penguin, 1976.

Kocurek, Carly. "*The Outsiders.*" Review of *The Outsiders* (film). *Common Sense Media*, n.d., www.commonsensemedia.org/movie-reviews/the-outsiders/. Accessed 17 Jan. 2018.

"*Künstlerroman.*" *Blackwell Reference Online*, Blackwell Publishing, n.d., www.blackwellreference.com/public/tocnode?id=g9781444333275_chunk_g978144433327512_ss1-27/. Accessed 3 Feb. 2018.

Lawrence, Karen. "Gender and Narrative Voice in *Jacob's Room* and *A Portrait of the Artist as a Young Man.*" *James Joyce: The Centennial Symposium*, edited by Morris Beja et al., U of Illinois P, 1986, pp. 29-38. Rpt. *A Portrait of the Artist as a Young Man* by James Joyce, edited by John Paul Riquelme, Norton Critical Ed., Norton, 2007, pp. 381-89.

Lynch, Robert. "American Realism: A Webliography and E-Anthology: 1865–1900." *Dr. Robert Lynch. Longwood University*, n.d., www.longwood.edu/staff/lynchrl/English%20336/american_realism.htm, Accessed 23 Jan. 2018.

"Mark Twain's *Adventures of Huckleberry Finn.*" *Blue Ridge PBS*, n.d., www.pbs.org/wgbh/cultureshock/flashpoints/literature/huck.html/. Accessed 3 Feb. 2018.

Mitchell, Margaret. *Gone with the Wind*. 1936. Avon, 1973.

Pallotta, Frank. "How 'Indiana Jones' Finally Forced Hollywood To Create The PG-13 Rating." *Business Insider*, 24 Apr. 2014, www.businessinsider.com/indiana-jones-and-the-temple-of-doom-created-pg-13-rating-2014-4/. Accessed 22 Feb. 2018.

"Top 100 Middle School Must-Reads." *Goodreads*, n.d., www.goodreads.com/list/show/1606.Top_100_Middle_School_Must_Reads/. Accessed 23 Jan. 2018.

Wells, H. G. "James Joyce." Review of *A Portrait of the Artist as a Young Man* by James Joyce. *New Republic*, 9 Mar. 1917, newrepublic.com/article/91729/james-joyce/. Accessed 22 Feb. 2018.

Wyatt, Monica. "*The Outsiders.*" Review of *The Outsiders* by S. E. Hinton. *Common Sense Media*, n.d., www.commonsensemedia.org/book-reviews/the-outsiders/. Accessed 17 Jan. 2018.

"It's like being in a Halloween costume we can't get out of": Identity and Authenticity in S. E. Hinton's *The Outsiders*

Jake Brown

"Stay Gold." A quick Google search confirms that Johnny's dying words still resonate today, fifty years after S. E. Hinton published *The Outsiders* (Google "Still Gold tattoos" if you're feeling adventurous). They're the pivotal moment of the novel, the two culminating words of wisdom that justify all of Johnny and Ponyboys' trauma and act as the catalyst for Ponyboy to tell Johnny's story. In this way, *The Outsiders* is a bildungsroman, a novel focused on a young adult or teenager coming of age and the experiences and moral development he must undergo to make a successful transition to adulthood.

For Ponyboy, this transition can be linked to the command "Stay Gold," but what does this even mean, and why should we accept the words of the novel's most violent offender (Johnny, after all, is the only person who actually kills anyone else) as its moral lesson? Perhaps it is precisely because he has committed the most violent act that we should accept his wisdom. In Ponyboy and Johnny's Oklahoma, violence and morality are always linked. The interactions between the Socs and the greasers are always violent, always carry the threat of death, and are always justified by self-defense ("it occurred to me then that they could kill me"), boundary crossing ("This is our territory"), or by identity politics at play ("A fair fight ain't rough . . . Socs are rough") (Hinton 5, 54, 29). No one holds himself responsible for his violence; like Montagues and Capulets or Hatfields and McCoys, the violence is inextricably bound up in group identity and, therefore, never the responsibility of the individual person.

When Johnny kills Bob, he realizes it is not the greasers who have to hide in a rural church; it is Johnny himself. It is not the greasers for whom the police search; it is Johnny. And it is ultimately not the greasers who must accept responsibility for Bob's death; it is Johnny. By killing Bob, Johnny learns what it means to Stay Gold in S. E. Hinton's Oklahoma: it means to rediscover the simple fact that his individual identity is not his group affiliation, in a world that raises him to think both are the same. This is what Johnny means when he says that "you're gold when you're a kid," meaning before the individual identity and group affiliation become confused (178). Therefore, *The Outsiders* is a Romantic bildungsroman, touching on a central theme of British Romanticism and its American counterpart, Transcendentalism: society is a corrupting force that obscures our inner divinity, and one that we must cast aside to return to recover our true selves. This is true of Ponyboy's journey to adulthood as well. *The Outsiders* is not so much his quest to stay gold, but rather to become gold once again, by also learning Johnny's lesson, through Johnny's experiences and his own, and untangling these two threads that became one harmful knot of violence.

Ponyboy's journey begins in the opening pages, as he proclaims "I am a greaser," before describing what that means in the larger social scene of Hinton's novel. Greasers are the poorest group in town, poorer than both the Socs and the middle class, and are likened to "hoods" in that they steal, rob gas stations, and hold gang fights. They drive "souped-up cars" and can be identified by their outfits: jeans; t-shirts; boots or tennis shoes; leather jackets; and, of course, their namesake, the long greasy hair (1-3).

Socs, meanwhile, wear blue madras shirts, or otherwise "striped or checkered shirts with light red or tan-colored jackets or madras ski jackets," and smell like "English Leather shaving lotion," "stale tobacco," and whiskey (5). In other passages, Ponyboy also associates them with "tuff" cars, the Chevrolet Corvair and Ford Mustang (54, 71,141).

Ponyboy clearly splits his society into greaser and Soc, and he assigns people to either one category or the other based on two attributes: by physical characteristics and fashion, such as long hair, leather jackets, and untucked shirts, and by their actions: Socs throw parties; greasers hold up gas stations.

Ponyboy is not the only character to organize people into groups this way. At the drive-in, Two-Bit explains to Cherry that greasers are more principled in their fights among themselves than are the Socs and are less rough overall because they use their fists and are less willing to use weapons than the Socs (29). When a Mustang drives by while Ponyboy and the other greasers are walking with Cherry and Marcia, Ponyboy suggests it's not the Socs, but of course it is, as Cherry quickly confirms, "it's Randy and Bob," to which Two-Bit adds "and . . . a few other of the socially elite checkered-shirt set" (41). Two-Bit's quick quip shows that he and the rest of the greasers share Ponyboy's social view.

What about the Socs? They, too, buy into a deterministic view of group identity. We can't forget the opening scene of the novel, in which Ponyboy is jumped by five Socs who claim they're going to "do [him] a favor . . . [they're] gonna cut all that long greasy hair off" before uttering a far more violent suggestion: "How'd you like that haircut to begin just below the chin?" (4). Both the greasers and the Socs recognize the importance of hair to the greasers, which is why the Socs are able to classify greasers as greasers, precisely because the greasers themselves identify as such. A similar phenomenon occurs during Cherry and Ponyboy's first meeting, in which Cherry does not recognize Ponyboy as a greaser, but asks him why he is with the "trash" Dally, to which Ponyboy replies that he's "a grease, same as Dally. He's my buddy" (23). By uttering this reply, Ponyboy forfeits an opportunity to meet Cherry outside of the established identity paradigm, instead firmly reestablishing his own position within it. But he never really had a choice; he has not yet learned that he has an identity independent of the greaser identity that he and his family and friends share.

After some initial conversation, Cherry explains to Ponyboy what it means to her to be a Soc. To Cherry, it means weekends of attending parties she does not really wish to attend and otherwise participating in the "rat race" of the upper-middle-class social scene. It means taking a cool and calculated approach to life, as opposed to what she believes is the emotionally-driven one of the greasers (33). It's clear she shares a similar world view as the greasers: there are two groups at odds with each other; the members of those groups inherit the group personality; and the groups, along with their constituent members, are perpetually at odds with one another, with little possibility of reconciliation.

But Ponyboy and Cherry's brief connection suggests that reconciliation is possible; in fact, their connection seems deeper than any they have within their own social classes. After knowing each other for only a short while, Ponyboy shares an intimate moment with Cherry. He tells her about his brother Sodapop's horse, a story that outlines Soda's vulnerability and is therefore considered "personal" (39). Cherry, likewise, reveals something personal about herself, that she likes sunsets and dreams of escaping Oklahoma. Their intimate moment doesn't last, however. Cherry concludes her story by saying "if I see you in the hall at school or someplace and don't say hi, well, it's not personal or anything" (45). Instantly, the budding illusion of a teenage romance is shattered by the barrier between greaser and Soc, once again erected, and Ponyboy can only reply "I know" (45).

Before continuing, it's worth addressing an important question this exchange raises: Why would Cherry and Ponyboy, or the Socs and the greasers in general, attend the same school? Ponyboy, Two-Bit, and Cherry's speeches show that they all understand the other group to be radically different and violent, so why would their parents or the adult world at large want the two groups to be together in the same environment, thus endangering their children?

The answer is simple: they don't get it. When riding in the ambulance, Jerry, the adult who was with the children who were pulled from the fire, asks Ponyboy, Johnny, and Dallas if they're "professional heroes," to which Ponyboy incredulously replies "'No, we're greasers'" (95). Jerry replies, "You're what?" He's clearly not used to the Soc and greaser terminology that pervades the novel up until this point.

Later, when Ponyboy is smoking in the hospital waiting room, Jerry stares at him before commenting that he shouldn't be smoking. Perplexed, Ponyboy looks around for No Smoking signs, but can't find any, so he simply asks "How come?" to which Jerry replies: "you're too young" (97). Johnny asks, "I am?" and his following internal monologue is telling:

I had never thought about it. Everyone in our neighborhood, even the girls, smoked. Except for Darry, who was too proud of his athletic health to risk a cigarette, we had all started smoking at an early age. Johnny had been smoking since he was nine; Steve started at eleven. So no one thought it unusual when I started. (97)

When he is questioned, Ponyboy lapses into his groupthink: "all greasers smoke," another over-generalization like the ones that pervade the early part of the novel. More than that, though, by cataloging each character and his age, Ponyboy reminds the reader of the sheer lack of adults in his world after both of his parents died in a car crash before he turned fourteen.

The reader may have missed, and would have to be forgiven for doing so, that Jerry is the first adult character given a voice in the novel (we're not told exactly how old Jerry is, but we know he wears a wedding ring, which is a clear symbol of adulthood) (93). Ponyboy meets "a farmer" while in the country, but he only gives Ponyboy directions before offering a bromide so trite that Ponyboy finds him simple. The greasers' adult parents are likewise mentioned in passing: Two-Bit's mother is a barmaid, and his father ran out on them; Steve hates his father, who tells him to "about once a week to get out and never come back"; and Johnny's father is physically abusive, besides being "a drunk and his mother a selfish slob" (43, 77). Labeling these adults in short stereotypes testifies to their absence from the action, again creating a feeling that the greaser children are on their own, which would also imply the adults know little, if anything, of the boundaries and conflict between greaser and Soc. Jerry, certainly, is oblivious, and if he is a stand-in for the rest of the adults in the novel, it's obvious why the greasers and Socs share a school with a hallway in which Cherry would ignore Johnny, and Johnny would know why. The adults' ignorance also shows that greaser and Soc are not transcendent identifiers or immutable characteristics shackled to babies at birth, but instead a loose group affiliation that has no meaning in the adult world.

But Ponyboy is not yet a member of this adult world, and, in his adolescent world, as he bids farewell to Cherry after their encounter at the nightly double, the group identity politics between greaser and Soc are still real. Ponyboy and Cherry might not realize it in the moment, but they destabilized both the barriers between grease and Soc, some of which they were not even aware existed, simply by recognizing each other as human beings.

The boundary lines of the physical territory are never very clearly defined in the novel; we know that "the lot" is safe for the greasers, as well as eastern territory, and the further east the better. Ponyboy and Cherry's meeting renders the physical barriers irrelevant; as Ponyboy asks of the Socs following them, "What do they want? This is our territory. What are Socs doing this far east?" Johnny replies "I don't know. But I bet they're looking for us. We picked up their girls." Bob quickly confirms Johnny's theory; when Johnny says he better "watch it" because he is "outta [his] territory," Bob responds: "Nup, pal, yer the ones who'd better watch it. Next time you want a broad, pick up yer own kind—dirt" (54-55).

Of course, those words would be some of Bob's last. Before he is killed, however, he and Ponyboy have a surprisingly astute exchange, although neither of them realizes its importance. Each boy calls the other "white trash," pointing out that the only difference between them is superficial: long greased hair on the one hand and fancy cars and clothes on the other (55).

It is true that both groups share characteristics of "white trash;" they commit violence and other crimes, especially status crimes such as underage drinking and smoking. In his rage, Ponyboy realizes, although not consciously, that the groups are not wholly different from one another, and it is this realization that begins Ponyboy's slow transformation throughout the second act of the novel, in which Johnny and Ponyboy escape to the country.

Ponyboy's time in exile is a way for him to realize a world without greaser or Soc. The countryside has always represented a space for self-exploration in American literature, and *The Outsiders* is no different. Both Johnny and Ponyboy have crossed the barriers erected and violated the social contract between the greasers and the Socs, and thus both have to flee the violent but relatively structured society of the city for the vast expanse of farmland beyond, where they can unlearn the group identity thrust upon them at birth in favor of an authentic self.

The process is not immediate. Ponyboy briefly recognizes the opportunity of the countryside for a space for self-exploration, realizing "this is the country, I thought, half asleep. My dream's come true and I'm in the country" (55). The dream to which he refers is expressed earlier in the novel, when Johnny and he fall asleep in the park. Johnny has just noted that there had to be "someplace without greaser or Socs, with just people. Plain ordinary people," when Ponyboy responds, "Out of the big towns . . . . In the country . . ." before drifting off:

> In the country. . . . I loved the country. I wanted to be out of towns and away from excitement. I only wanted to lie on my back under a tree and read a book or draw a picture, and not worry about being jumped or carrying a blade or ending up married to some scatterbrained broad with no sense. The country would be like that. (42)

Johnny's phrase "[p]lain ordinary people," especially uttered in his desire to be free of the greaser/Soc dichotomy, implies a yearning not for a different identity, but for no identity. "Plain" and "ordinary" are words that suggest not an identity construct, but the absence of one. The country was destined to represent the fulfillment of this absence and a blank space upon which to forge his own identity; however, Ponyboy can't let go of his greaser identity easily. When he encounters strangers in the country his first thought is

> I don't look like a farm boy. . . . I suddenly thought of my long hair, combed back, and the slouching stride I used from habit. I looked at Johnny. He didn't look like any farm boy to me. He still reminded me of a lost puppy who had been kicked too often, but for the first time I saw him as a stranger might see him. He looked hard and tough, because of his black T-shirt and his blue jeans and jacket, and because his hair was heavily greased and so long. I saw how his hair curled behind his ears and I thought: We both need a haircut and some decent clothes. I looked down at my worn, faded blue jeans, my too-big shirt, and Dally's worn-out jacket. They'll know we're hoods the minute they see us, I thought. (55-56)

Ponyboy's slouching stride is not his only bad habit! Even in the country, far away from his past, Ponyboy can't help but describe himself as a greaser, and, in the absence of any Socs, he defines, in his own mind, another identity, the "farm boy," with which to contrast the greaser. Note that, like the Soc, Ponyboy sees the "farm boy" persona that he just came up with in his own head as superior to the greaser, betraying his own feelings of inferiority, feelings he and the other greasers constantly battle in a society that clearly privileges Socs, an observation to which Ponboy alludes in the final rumble:

> [The Socs] looked like they were all cut from the same piece of cloth: clean shaven with semi-Beatle haircuts, wearing striped or checkered shirts with light red or tan-colored jackets or madras ski jackets. They could just as easily have been going to the movies as to a rumble. That's why people don't ever think to blame the Socs and are always ready to jump on us. We look hoody and they look decent . . . [and] people usually go by looks. (120)

As for the greasers' conception of their place within society, a telling exchange occurs on the way to this same rumble. While walking along, Sodapop announces: "I am a greaser . . . . I am a JD and a hood. I blacken the name of our fair city. I beat up people. I rob gas stations. I am a menace to society. Man, do I have fun" to which Steve sings "greaser . . . greaser . . . greaser . . . O victim of environment, underprivileged, rotten, no-count hood," and Darry adds: "juvenile delinquent, you're no good!" and Darry shouts: "Get thee hence, white trash" (116). This is the identity that Ponyboy has been trying to legitimatize.

However, the fact that this identity is subordinated to that of the "farm boy" that he created extemporaneously shows that he clearly has not yet legitimatized it in his own mind. He still feels trapped within this greaser identity, which he still feels is an immutable identity stamped upon him at birth; even in the countryside to which he dreamed to escape because it knew no such thing as greasers, Ponyboy curses himself for bringing his greaser identity with him.

Well, it won't remain with him for long. Being on the run, Johnny has the idea to change their appearance—with peroxide: "We're gonna cut our hair, and you're gonna bleach yours." Ponyboy reacts with horror: "'Oh, no!' My hand flew to my hair. 'No, Johnny, not my hair!'" he exclaims, before explaining,

> It was my pride. It was long and silky, just like Soda's, only a little redder. Our hair was tuff—we didn't have to use much grease on it. Our hair labeled us greasers, too—it was our trademark. The one thing we were proud of. Maybe we couldn't have Corvairs or madras shirts, but we could have hair. (61)

The hair is part and parcel of the greaser identity, and to remove it is to violate the subject's identity and disorient him; it is not unlike trimming a cat's whiskers, which it uses to remain in balance and carefully navigate the world around it.

Ponyboy describes the haircut as if he's being scalped: "Johnny flipped out the razor-edge of his switch, took hold of my hair, and started sawing on it." The scene is not unlike the one that opened the novel, in which a group of Socs threatened to cut off his hair with a switchblade, the same instrument Johnny uses to complete the task.

After it is done, Ponyboy looks at himself in a cracked mirror with short, blonde hair. His reaction? "I look like a blasted pansy. I was miserable" (62). Like the farm boy persona, Ponyboy now creates a new one, the pansy, by which to judge himself, which introduces a complicated question. If Ponyboy really saw his identity as a greaser as innate, how is he so quick to be miserable over a haircut? If he really feels himself to be a greaser, and if being a greaser is a prescribed social position that can't be changed, then the haircut shouldn't change this fact. Johnny recognizes this, saying "it's just hair," to which Ponyboy replies, "It took me a long time to get that hair just the way I wanted it. And besides, this just ain't us. It's like being in a Halloween costume we can't get out of" (63). But Ponyboy is exactly wrong in using this metaphor. A Halloween costume is an external façade used for a specific purpose; the person who wears it knows this, and he knows that the external costume that he presents to the world is separate, distinct, and apart from he who is inside it. This is the approach Johnny is taking; his "it's just hair comment" testifies to it.

It's the approach Ponyboy wants to take, but just can't. When Johnny realizes how much losing his hair affected Ponyboy, he apologizes for cutting it off, to which Ponyboy replies: "Oh, it ain't that . . . . I really don't know what's the matter. I'm just mixed up" (63). To return to the cat whisker metaphor, losing his hair has taken away Ponyboy's "feelers," his innate and automatic method for perceiving the world around him and his place within it, a tool upon which he has relied, if we recognize the hair as a metonymy, a stand-in for the greaser identity, since birth. He recognizes that, while he may have occasionally been at odds with his identity as a greaser, he nevertheless used it as a safety net to feel like he belonged to the world and to society, even if it was in a less-than-desirable role.

In cutting and bleaching his hair, Ponyboy demonstrates the true significance of the Halloween metaphor. The short-bleached hair is not the Halloween costume that hides his greaser self, as Ponyboy assumes and as is the literal case with Johnny; the greaser identity itself is a Halloween costume Ponyboy has been wearing his whole life, forgetting the essence of himself that lies underneath. Remembering this is Ponyboy's transformational moment, and it plants the seeds in his psyche that allow him to return to the city with a new perspective. His transformation is not immediate; when he first returns to the city, he temporarily lapses back into his groupthink in his interactions with Jerry at the hospital, but this can be explained by the stress of the situation and the initial jolt of reintegrating to the city. Nevertheless, it is clear that Ponyboy has grown by the conclusion of the novel. Consider his meditation when the other greasers and he are getting ready for the final rumble with the Socs:

> Soda and Steve and I had put on more hair oil than was necessary, but we wanted to show that we were greasers. Tonight we could be proud of it. Greasers may not have much, but they have a rep. That and long hair. (What kind of world is it where all I have to be proud of is a reputation for being a hood, and greasy hair? I don't want to be a hood, but even if I don't steal things and mug people and get boozed

up, I'm marked lousy. Why should I be proud of it? Why should I even pretend to be proud of it?) (112)

The parenthesis indicates Ponyboy's double-voice, or, rather, his underlying voice that he discovered in the countryside. The first part of the passage reads like any one of the group-identity passages that litter the opening pages of the novel ("A fair fight isn't rough . . . Socs are rough," "greasers . . . steal things . . . and have a gang fight once in a while") but his inner monologue is commenting on these words even as he proclaims them (27, 4). He now recognizes that if he doesn't want to live this role anymore, he doesn't have to; when walking with the greasers to the final rumble, he is inside his Halloween costume, but it does not define him.

He is like the countryside now, a blank slate upon which to forge a new identity. This is what the countryside had always represented to him in his dreams, and now he fully realizes it. It won't be easy; it's never easy to discard a path that others have laid out for you since birth and take the first steps down a new one, but it is a pivotal moment in transitioning from the adolescent dichotomies of greaser and Soc to a more nuanced adulthood where his concept of society and his place within it are his own to create, with, of course, one brief piece of advice to guide him: "Stay Gold."

Work Cited

Hinton, S. E. *The Outsiders*. 1967. Speak, 2006.

"I'm going to look just like him": S. E. Hinton's Young Adult Novels and the Fraternal Lens____

Sarah E. Whitney

The tough and tuff boys at the heart of S. E. Hinton's five young adult novels live a rough and tumble existence of knife fights, gun battles, and violence. Some have little interest in formal education; most have little use for the friendship of girls. Society views them as beasts or aliens, boys who couldn't "write a compound sentence," in one middle-class character's dismissive tone (Hinton, *Taming the Star Runner* 85). In fact, Ponyboy Curtis and his literary brethren sound like just the sort of cautionary tales about boys that waft through contemporary parenting books and internet memes. In particular, the phrase "Boy Crisis," which depicts American boys in freefall, experiencing high rates of suicide, violence, and poor health at the hands of social and educational institutions that do not suit their boisterous needs, has been percolating through popular culture, psychology, and education since the 2000s.

The term "Boy Crisis" has its critics; some would dispute its existence by pointing to the continued influence of patriarchal power in most American institutions. Others, meanwhile, take exception to the idea of a universally experienced adolescent male crisis, reminding us that there are significant differences *between* boys. Yet both skeptics and supporters of Boy Crisis rhetoric would agree that in a globalized and postindustrial world, expectations for today's boys are rapidly changing. While feminism has, write Shannon R. Wooden and Ken Gillam, provided a "rich and complex ongoing cultural discourse" to help girls and their allies "think through the films, fashions, and other artifacts that colored [their] world," boys face a comparatively barren theoretical landscape (xi). As the field of boyhood studies develops, one resource for studying adolescent male development might be found in an unexpected source—the rich Tulsa soil of S. E. Hinton's narratives.

114

Through the course of five young adult novels, Hinton investigates how fraternal relationships, both genetic and self-chosen, acts as a key touchstone in boys' moral development. Despite its tough exterior, *The Outsiders* creates a textured world where brothers positively shape a young man's sense of empathy and connection to others. Hinton's next two novels, *That Was Then, This is Now* and *Rumble Fish*, mine darker territory, interrogating the *negative* impacts of coercive or unhealthy fraternal influences. Her final two novels represent increasingly nuanced positions. The redemptive *Tex* demonstrates the endurance of brotherly bonds despite the changes wrought by adulthood, while Hinton's final YA, *Taming the Star Runner,* transposes her work on fraternity to a masculinized *girl*. Frequently employing visual fraternal resemblance motifs (such as eye or hair color) that are easy for young readers to grasp, Hinton interrogates boys' sense of themselves within families. Such evocations of male domesticity and fraternal affection may complicate traditional readings of S. E. Hinton's work as gruff realism. Yet they can also contribute to our growing understanding of the diverse ways boys attain emotional literacy.

The Outsiders: To Whom Do I Belong?

When *The Outsiders'* iconic character Ponyboy Curtis steps into the novel from "the darkness of the movie house," he is both alone and placed within a community of male peers. In meandering prose, Ponyboy differentiates his own intellectual self from his brother Sodapop, who "never cracks a book at all"; his other brother Darrel, too busy working to enjoy cultural activities; and his fellow gang members, who don't appreciate "movies and books the way" he does (Hinton, *Outsiders* 5). Ponyboy further describes his hair through contrast, deeming it "longer than a lot of boys wear theirs" in a neighborhood that "rarely bothers to get a haircut" (5). Within the novel's first two pages, Hinton has neatly framed two sets of outsiders. Ponyboy belongs to a stigmatized teen male greaser subculture; he also feels, in typical adolescent style, adrift *within* this group.

Ponyboy and his friends form a family reliant upon one another for literal and emotional sustenance in *The Outsiders*. Hinton uses visual and haptic (touch-centered) motifs to emphasize her characters' longing for comfort. Throughout the book Ponyboy reads faces, sorting physical resemblances and attempting to classify typologies. When he discusses the "gold" of his parents or scans a boy's eye color to determine his viciousness, Ponyboy attempts to make the ephemeral connections between people materialize; he wants to hang on to something in his orphaned world. Yet *real* belonging in his world is not discerned by finding a person with the same icy blue eyes or cherry hair; it manifests itself through compassionate touch. Within Ponyboy's society of unlocked doors and shared beds, lost boys find comfort letting others rub their aching shoulders and guard them in their sleep. Hinton's scenes of male domesticity and physical affection upend traditional ideas about boys; they also add weight to the novel's argument that brothers reach for, and belong to, each other. By *The Outsiders'* end, Ponyboy has lost much, yet he has also gained full membership in his family and come to a deeper understanding of his brothers.

The novel's opening chapter foregrounds Ponyboy's interest in resemblance politics. "I have light-brown, almost-red hair and greenish-gray eyes," he confides, adding that "I wish they were more gray, because I hate most guys that have green eyes" (Hinton, *Outsiders* 5). Later in the text, Ponyboy bristles when being told that he resembles his brother Sodapop, "except your eyes are green" (58). His strange preoccupation is rooted in his attempt to differentiate himself from Darry, the authoritarian older brother with "cold" eyes "like two pieces of pale blue-green ice" (9). *The Outsiders'* fascination with eye color illuminates the complicated politics of family inheritance, both physiological and spiritual. Middle son Sodapop, for instance, carries "Dad's eyes," and is thus claimed in Ponyboy's eyes as his dead parents' own (10). Yet it "seems funny," thinks Ponyboy, that his oldest brother Darrel "should look just exactly like" the boys' father "and act exactly the opposite from him" (9). By meditating on eye color and physical resemblance, Ponyboy seeks to understand the meanings of kinship: how can brothers be born of the same parents but turn out differently? To whom does Ponyboy belong?

Hinton juxtaposes this adolescent struggle for identity with the novel's moral argument *against* judging a book by its cover. Readers come to see the fragile Johnny, self-confident Dally, pugnacious Steve and other friends as full characters whose humanity and complexity exceeds the stigmatized "greaser" label imposed by society. Ponyboy himself underscores the theme of misrecognition when he complains about the Socs' advantages because they "look decent." In reality, it is often "just the other way around," he continues, as "half of the hoods I know are pretty decent guys underneath all that grease, and from what I've heard, a lot of Socs are just cold-blooded mean—but people usually go by looks" (Hinton, *Outsiders* 123). He begins to learn his own lesson in complex recognition first when he perceives the humanity of Randy, a peace-loving Soc, and later when he meditates on a Soc's yearbook photo. The character Bob, who ignited a chain of events that led to Johnny's death, is a source of narrative pain. Yet as Ponyboy gazes on his picture, he notices "a grin that reminded [him] of Soda's" and "dark eyes— maybe brown, like Soda's, maybe dark-blue, like the Shepard boys." Maybe, Ponyboy considers, Bob had even "had black eyes. Like Johnny" (140). Ponyboy makes two important moves here, finding Bob's eye color ultimately *ambiguous* (and thus rejecting the notion that boys can be easily placed into kinship groups) and discovering commonality across class lines, even going so far as to link Bob's irises to Johnny's.

Hinton develops a nuanced representation of male eyes in this and other passages; it is worth noting that female characters in the novel—traditionally, objects of desire for heterosexual male narratives—are scanned with less enthusiasm. Ponyboy harshly judges Johnny's neglectful mother, finding a "cheap and hard" soul in her black eyes (Hinton, *Outsiders* 108). His own late mother fares better and is associated with the shining innocence of the color "gold" as well as the brown of a lovingly baked chocolate cake. Yet she is absent from the ongoing discussion of brotherly resemblance. Female peers, meanwhile, are visually read with indifference.

When Ponyboy pulls a switchblade for science dissection, a girl calls him a "hood," and he comment opaquely that "She was a cute girl. She looked real good in yellow" (17). Similar flattened discourse surfaces when Ponyboy and Cherry Valance agree that a shared angle of vision is possible from their different class positions. "She had green eyes," he reflects. "I went on, walking home slowly" (114). These rather disjoined observations nod to Ponyboy's perfunctory heterosexuality. The novel, though, does not bother linking girls' appearances to larger questions of identity and belonging; relationships among males remain its core interest.

Male bonding is strengthened by touch as well as visual recognition. *The Outsiders* is, of course, known for its depiction of fighting, yet there are more scenes of tactile comfort between boys than there are antagonistic ones. Members of Ponyboy's group slap, spin, and elbow each other in good-natured ritualistic play. Within the Curtis family, the brothers use maternal touch, often in the vulnerable space of near-sleep. Through a bedroom door, for instance, Ponyboy witnesses Darry, a manual laborer, receiving a backrub from Sodapop. Protection during sleep is also Sodapop's fraternal duty; while he is on the lam, Ponyboy dreams of being "home in bed, safe and warm under the covers with Soda's arm across me" (Hinton, *Outsiders* 47). After Ponyboy's rescue, Darry strokes his hair while Ponyboy collapses against him and listens "to his heart pounding through his T-shirt" in an image that recalls a reunited mother and child (88). He is further infantilized at home, where Darry "picked [Ponyboy] up and carried" him into his own room again, while Soda undresses his younger brother and guards him in sleep (92).

Clearly, even in the most vulnerable state of slumber, Ponyboy welcomes his brothers' caring touches. When bereft of their presence, he replicates their community with Johnny, his spiritual brother. Ponyboy describes for readers how he "stretched out and used Johnny's legs for a pillow" during their hideout (Hinton, *Outsiders* 57). Hinton repeatedly describes cuddling between the boys; Johnny "stretched out beside" Ponyboy, "resting his head on his arm," while later Ponyboy puts his "arm across his shoulders to warm" Johnny (60, 66). As the pair's hours in hiding pass gloomily, they drift in and out of consciousness. Ponyboy recalls waking up "late that night" to find himself "asleep on [Johnny's] shoulder," while hours later the pair "slept huddled together for warmth" (67, 68). By consoling the un-parented, un-cared for Johnny, Ponyboy *applies* the domestic care he received from his own brothers.

In *The Outsiders*, boys cry, wrap their arms around each other, crash on each other's couches, and eat Darry's nutritious "baked chicken and potatoes and corn" before going out to a fight (Hinton, *Outsiders* 115). Hinton's families are shaped by parental absence and neglect, but in response boys—brothers—pour their feelings of care and connection into relationships with one another. Siblings, writes Jeffrey Kluger, are "good at the subtler business of gently picking one another's locks, feeling how the emotional tumblers fall, and opening a sibling up in a way no professional, or even parent, ever could" (171). Darry, Sodapop, and Ponyboy are ultimately unafraid to be vulnerable with one another, and each makes the others better. "We ought to be able to stick together against everything," Sodapop declares at the end of the novel, summarizing the ways in which they have become one another's worlds. "If we don't have each other, we don't have anything" (152).

Hating the Person You Love Most in the Whole World: *That Was Then, This Is Now*

In her leaner, darker second novel, Hinton examines negative fraternal relationships and their impact on boys' moral development. Hinton's new protagonist Bryon grows apart from his beloved foster brother and best friend Mark as the boys make different moral choices with respect to girls, drugs, and crime. Through the character of Mark, Hinton constructs a problematic vision of fraternal love that is anti-intellectual, anti-authority and anti-feminine. While Bryon does not fully reject this model or move to a new way of thinking, by the novel's close he has recognized its insufficiency, and turned Mark into the police.

Just as the opening pages of *The Outsiders* place Ponyboy both within and without his fraternal gang, *That Was Then, This is Now* emphasizes the importance of male youth loyalty. The first three words, "Mark and me," foreground the novel's core dyad. Mark, "the person [Bryon loves] best in the world," is his foster brother's emotional center (Hinton, *That* 55). "I feel like you're my brother. A real one," Mark confides in Bryon in one of many comments on their closeness (63). "We've always been friends. I can't remember when we weren't," he adds (115). As in *The Outsiders*, the intensity of the fraternal relationship is heightened by family loss and violence. Mark's parents died by domestic homicide, and though Bryon's mother is kind, she is a distant figure in his life because of illness and a grueling work schedule. The loss of kinship structures further isolates Mark and Bryon; Hinton's second novel is self-consciously "post-gang," and characters rhapsodize for a lost way of life where boys fought "like brothers, not just you and me, but all of us together" to total "up to somethin'" (68).

The twinned boys of *That Was Then, This is Now* would seem to offer a rich research opportunity for social scientists; raised together and deeply interdependent, they nonetheless make different moral decisions. Social science research on intimate sibling relationships has found a "collusion dynamic" that promotes delinquent behavior. Having "an intimate relationship *with a sibling who engages in risky behavior*," researchers conclude, heightens the risks of reckless behavior and illegal activities (Solmeyer, McHale, and Crowder 601). Such coercive behavior, they note, is found "particularly among brother pairs" and may be attributable to "a stereotypically masculine culture" more accommodating of boys "recalling stories of previous deeds or laughing about friends' transgressions" (601). While both boys certainly express the collusion dynamic by affirming each other's roguish stories and nuisance behavior, Bryon's consciousness of the wider world beyond Mark—specifically the new frontiers opened through education and romance—allows him to escape the worst effects of his brother's influence.

The brothers construct boyhood in stark opposition to femininity, as evident on the first page, when Bryon introduces a central character as "the older brother of this chick I used to like" whose friendship survived "when this chick and me broke up" (Hinton, *That* 9). His observation, coupled with the dismissive use of the word "chick," indicates the extent to which Bryon prioritizes male friendships. Throughout the text, Bryon unconvincingly swaggers around as a playboy and doles out advice never to "be too eager with chicks" lest you give them "ideas" (32). Mark is little better; he lashes out at Bryon's girlfriend Cathy in jealousy, and physically assaults another classmate. Miles Groth has observed that for adolescent "boys on the way to manhood" nearly "everything considered to be feminine must be expelled" according to Western cultural norms (9). Yet Bryon learns the limits of objectifying women when he engages in a meaningful and mutually supportive relationship with Cathy. Mark, by contrast, appears to be unable to create bonds with anyone besides his brother.

"I really do like listening to stuff that's happened to other people," the intellectual Bryon reflects early in the novel. "I guess that's why I like to read" (Hinton, *That* 34). S. E. Hinton's enduring interest in boys who read and apply the empathy and perspective gained from education is particularly meaningful considering Boy Crisis discourse, which displays an "upsurge of concern for the literary achievement of boys" and "a kind of moral panic" over boys' perceived educational failings (Weaver-Hightower 273). Bryon becomes immersed in literature and subsequently interested in the "stories" of the wider world; by contrast, Mark, "too lazy or too uninterested to read himself," has little imagination (Hinton, *That* 66).

Bryon's responsiveness to other perspectives makes him pensive; he tells Mark of his regret for the latter's assault on their female classmate and engages abstract ethical questions about the lack of justice in the world. Mark repeatedly asks him to "shut up" and stop "*thinking* about" things (Hinton, *That* 115, 117). "You can't keep trying to figure out why things happen, man," he snaps; "quit trying to reason them out" (117). Yet the novel's conclusion finds Bryon *employing*, rather than disregarding, his intellect. He connects, and causally links, the effects of Mark's drug dealing to an addicted friends' intense suffering and finds the courage to turn Mark over to the police.

By metaphorically "twinning" Bryon and Mark in the novel and providing them with opposing fates, Hinton plays with the biblical first brothers, Cain and Abel. She also invokes visuality in a darker, more skeptical way. Whereas in her earlier novel Ponyboy searches male faces and eyes for physical confirmation of belonging, Hinton now utilizes color to indicate *mutability*. Mark, who is attractive and charismatic, is depicted by the boys' friend Charlie as "Golden Boy" (Hinton, *That* 82). He wears "a gold sweat shirt and wheat-colored jeans" to a public event, and is depicted with eyes sporting a "faint ring of gold around them" (48, 59). These eyes, which turn "a bright yellow" as his pranks continue, have the effect of making Mark look like "an innocent lion" (75). However, Mark's halo begins to decay as he commits crimes, including drug dealing and physical assault. The text's leonine imagery becomes more menacing, replacing *The Outsiders'* connotation of "gold" as goodness and innocence. At last glimpse, Mark morphs into a beast, with skin stretched "over his bones" and "the golden, hard, flat eyes of a jungle animal" (157-8). Full of "sinister knowledge," Mark paces his cell "like an impatient, dangerous, caged lion" (158). Behind cinder-block walls, the animalistic Mark is literally and symbolically separated from the brother of his heart.

Hinton's play with color can be read back through the lens of *The Outsiders'* famous death scene, in which the frail dying Johnny urges Ponyboy to embrace innocence and goodness by "staying gold." Mark failed to "stay gold," or innocent; perhaps it is the concept of staying gold itself—remaining in the uncomplicated realm of childhood—that is as illusory as his initial halo. *That Was Then, This is Now* ends on a melancholy note, as Bryon yearns for the days he was "a kid again, when [he] had all the answers" (Hinton, *That* 159). Yet the novel's denouement also reveals the extent to which he has chosen a different moral path, or un-twinned, from his foster brother. The person who "had all the answers" was never Bryon, but always the "untouched, unworried, unaffected" and confidently amoral Mark (16). Social scientists would tell us that by disrupting his fraternal bond with a "delinquent" brother, Bryon will achieve more positive outcomes in his social and financial lives. While this may be true, Hinton's tarnished ending captures what data cannot—the numbing pain and bewilderment brought about by the slicing of brotherly bonds.

I'm Going to Look Just Like Him: *Rumble Fish*

Four years after Mark and Bryon confront each other through barred windows, Hinton published her third novel *Rumble Fish*, expanding a story she originally wrote for her University of Tulsa alumni magazine. The novel chronicles the shifting world of Rusty-James, a neglected boy who lives in the shadow of his enigmatic older brother, the colorblind "Motorcycle Boy." Ultimately, Rusty-James is powerless to stop the Motorcycle Boy's death at the hands of police. Jay Daly's characterization of the novel as "murky" and "haunted" captures its shadowy world (67). Color, in fact, serves as a structuring absence for Rusty-James, who is abandoned by his mother, overlooked by his father, and let down by the Motorcycle Boy. Returning to Hinton's interest in the visual politics of family resemblance, *Rumble Fish* again addresses the limits of fraternal hero worship and emphasizes the need for familial community by showing the consequences of its *absence*.

Rumble Fish's narrative is catalyzed by misrecognition. When old friend Steve asks Rusty-James, "[Y]ou know who you look just like?" traumatic memories resurface, and he is forced into remembering the story of his brother's loss (Hinton, *Rumble Fish* 5). Readers encounter Rusty-James as an anti-intellectual who clings to the strict rules and physical release found in street fighting. His older brother, the Motorcycle Boy, who has perfect grades and a highly developed vocabulary, is better at everything, including combat. Declaring his older brother "the coolest person in the whole world," Rusty-James asserts, "I was going to be just like him" (35). Throughout the novel, he hunts for similarities, finding assurance in having "the same color of hair, an odd shade of dark red, like black-cherry pop" and the same "color of a Hershey bar" eyes (33). Yet the world sends Rusty-James a different message. His friend Steve flatly denies any physical similarity between the boys. A pool shark deems the Motorcycle Boy "a prince" and "royalty in exile," dismissing his younger brother with "you ain't never gonna look like that" (83). A friend even tells Rusty-James "you might make it a while on the Motorcycle Boy's rep, but you ain't got his brains" (107). The lesson that shared biology may not lead to shared destiny is a bitter one for the younger brother. "I always got [the Motorcycle Boy's] clothes when he outgrew them, but they never looked the same on me," he complains (90).

While Rusty-James clearly worships his older brother, readers of *Rumble Fish* can perceive the fraternal relationship in a more worrisome light. While the Motorcycle Boy is a mysterious, charismatic figure, he is also a highly flawed, inattentive pseudo-parent. Hinton's novels frequently offer powerful social commentary about how poverty constrains the potential of Oklahoma's working-class boys. In both *The Outsiders* and *Tex*, characters frequently ruminate on the sacrifices made by talented older brothers who have put their own dreams aside to provide parental care for their families. *Rumble Fish*'s Motorcycle Boy, in contrast, throws away his evident academic talents and provides insufficient nurturing. He leaves school, frequently deserts Rusty-James for weeks on end, and maintains an aimless, itinerant existence. Rejecting the concept of possessions, he finds little joy in any pursuit, deriding romance, fighting, and joining organizations.

Rumble Fish's exploration of fraternal divergence is somewhat similar to the argument of *That Was Then, This is Now*, yet in Hinton's third novel it is further complicated by the haunting absence of the boys' mother and the implication that they may have inherited her dangerous instability. Hinton removes the boys' father, an alcoholic living off government assistance, from the family picture early in the story. "Me and the Motorcycle Boy didn't look anything like him," Rusty-James insists. "He was a middle-sized, middle-aged guy, kind of blond and balding on top, light-blue eyes. He was the kind of person nobody ever noticed" (Hinton, *Rumble Fish* 51). While Rusty-James admits to few memories of his mother, claiming "it was like she was dead. I'd always thought of her as being dead," her face lives on in her sons (77). On rare occasions when the boys' father pays them any attention, he will comment that "you are exactly like your mother" (53).

During an emotionally intense conversation, the two boys walk downtown amidst a backdrop of intense color, music, and noise. The Motorcycle Boy reveals an ugly family secret. Long ago, their mother ran off with only the Motorcycle Boy; subsequently, toddler Rusty-James was *also* deserted by the boy's father. The abandoned child spent three days in the family home alone. Completely indifferent to the trauma these revelations induce in Rusty-James, the Motorcycle Boy discloses that he has recently seen their "dead" mother in California. "I'd forgotten we both had the same sense of humor," he says, and his repeated use of the word "funny" to describe their family situation emphasizes his emotional disconnection (Hinton, *Rumble Fish* 78). Now understanding the depth of his mother's instability, Rusty-James recalls his father's assertion of maternal inheritance and thinks "maybe he didn't mean" the boys "just *looked* like her," a revelation that makes him sweaty and fearful (77).

Rusty-James' mother and brother are portrayed as stark, cruel *absences*, a characterization reinforced by the latter's colorblindness. Hinton's previous novels relied on connotative color schemes, whether Darry's authoritarian ice blue eyes, the comforting chocolate cake of Ponyboy's mother, or Mark's complex leonine gold. *Rumble Fish*, by contrast, is leached of hue by the Motorcycle Boy's presence. Possessed of "strange mirror eyes" and a "toneless, light and cold" voice, the opaque, unnamed Motorcycle Boy sees the world only in shades of black, white, and gray (30, 88). Jay Daly intriguingly asserts that the Motorcycle Boy's inability to perceive color is "not a congenital condition at all" but rather self-attained, "a product of his life" (75).

Color reappears jarringly in the novel's finale to emphasize the two boys' different moral visions. Rusty-James provides a drawn-out description of the titular fish, which he and the Motorcycle Boy have been visiting in a pet store. "I never saw fish like them before. One was purple, one was blue with long red fins and red tail, one was solid red and one was bright yellow" (Hinton, *Rumble Fish* 110). Their bold colors signal their wildness and directly contrast with the most common of domestic pets, the goldfish. Selfishly, the Motorcycle Boy takes the fish with him on a suicidal mission that ends with police gunfire; they lie "flipping and dying around" the Motorcycle Boy, both aliens in strange environments, red blood mixed with their garish hues (118). In the aftermath of the shooting, Rusty-James experiences his brother's "glass bubble" and "graveyard" quiet existence as he goes temporarily colorblind (119). Daly has read the novel's dark conclusion as validating "the monotone world of the Motorcycle Boy" and exposing Rusty-James' world of "light and color . . . as an illusion, a child's vision" (73). While Rusty-James does indeed end the novel in pain and disillusionment, he also comes back from the brink, swimming through consciousness to find that "the colors were back" (119). In the novel's bleak end, the state's juvenile correctional system parents Rusty-James, which may—strange as it is to say—offer a more stable environment for him than the dangerously unattached mother/brother dyad he longs to resemble.

Brothers, Going and Staying: *Tex*

"There are people who go, people who stay," intones a fortune teller in Hinton's 1979 novel *Tex*. Turning to the titular character, she decrees: "you will stay" (39). Hinton's fourth novel returns to her common theme of an all-male, secret-harboring family's emotional and financial struggles against a violent Oklahoma backdrop. The genial, chatty Tex gets into many scrapes thanks to his joking nature. At home, his primary support system is his tough but loving brother Mason, who raised Tex but now longs to escape their tiny hometown by way of a college scholarship. Tonally, *Tex* hearkens back to *The Outsiders*, redemptively celebrating the power of familial love to promote adolescent maturation. As he grows, Tex learns that boys' lives can, and sometimes should, go in different directions. Diverging paths, however, are not the same as fraternal breaks for the sake of self-preservation, as was the case for the younger brothers of *That Was Then, This Is Now* and *Rumble Fish*. Hinton even reintroduces a past character—*That Was Then*'s Mark—to emphasize the power of fraternal mentoring over biology. Mark resurfaces in the midst of a criminal mission; during his encounter with Tex, it is implied that the two are biological half-brothers. Mark's intrusion into the novel offers Tex a different model of masculinity, but Tex rejects it, choosing instead his McCormick brother, Mason. A testament to the enduring power of brotherly love, *Tex* provides a lyrical example of what social scientists call "presence in relationship," a barometer of adolescent fulfillment that prioritizes companionship if not verbal sharing of feelings.

Critic Jay Daly comments on the "rare generosity" of Tex as a narrator, lauding his "ability to break out of the prison of himself and to feel a sympathy for others" (107). The audience is privy to Tex's honest, and sometimes humorous, revelations. He has not thought to look for another book by his favorite author because he "figured writing one book ought to last somebody a lifetime" (Hinton, *Tex* 71). Girls, mysteriously, are "getting so cute" when "last year they hadn't been so great" (93). In between these typical adolescent threshold moments, one relationship remains constant: the parental relationship between Tex and the three-years-older Mason.

Tex initially pits the brothers against each other, for Mason has sold several horses, including Tex's beloved pet. While the younger brother complains that Mason is "bossing" him, readers understand the compassion underlying the difficult decision (Hinton, *Tex* 8). "We couldn't feed them through the winter," Mason admits. "I wasn't going to watch them starve to death" (14). Money is scarce, thanks to their shiftless father, and Mason, who "took care of all the bills and business stuff," must supply food, gas, and groceries in his absence (10). Mason supplies Tex with social and moral guidance as well as basic needs. He answers questions about sex honestly, rails against the dangers of drugs, and passionately defends Tex against their snobbish neighbors. In scenes of comfort that recall *The Outsiders'* Curtis brothers, Mason further shows maternal care; he cleans Tex's cuts with iodine and pats him "on the head like a puppy" (29). Tex's limited understanding of his family dynamic, however, makes him impatient with Mason's mothering and too forgiving of a shiftless father who openly admits to disfavoring Tex because of their dissimilar DNA. Good-hearted Tex finds out he is not his father's son in either personality or genetics, but when a biological relative disrupts the narrative and models a different form of adult masculinity, Tex is forced to choose his role models.

The antihero of *That Was Then, This Is Now*, Mark Jennings, reappears as an initially charming hitchhiker who sticks a gun in Mason's ribs and orders the two brothers to drive with "a funny kind of little grin on his face" (Hinton, *Tex* 114). As two golden-eyed boys born of a rodeo cowboy, Tex and Mark are, it is heavily implied, heretofore unknown half-brothers. Tex is struck by déjà vu when encountering Mark, and later remarks he "knew who it was that guy had reminded me of. It was me" (124). Yet their values are antithetical. A malevolent prison escapee, Mark now boasts of being a murderer, and having seen "how some get to liking" homicide (116). In a rhetorically complex moment, Tex negotiates his future against this stranger with his own face. As Mark tells the terrified brothers about confronting a victim he intended to kill (the victim, it is implied, is Bryon), Tex recalls his English teacher's lesson about "monologue" and "dialogue." There is no productive way to engage the antisocial Mark in dialogue, so Tex uses his physical gifts instead, spinning the car into a ditch. As Mark grabs Mason to prevent falling out of the car, the two boys' "eyes [meet] for a second" before Tex pulls his brother to safety (119). Tex's actions in the scene affirm his existing brotherhood with *Mason*; the depth of their bond endures the genetic disruptions of paternity crisis. Mark is rejected as a potential brother, and he is killed by a police officer, shot with a "bitter expression in his strange-colored eyes" (121).

The reemergence of a past brother serves as a cautionary tale in Tex's moral development. In the novel's finale, Mason invokes Mark when explaining why he withheld the truth about his paternity; he didn't want Tex to turn bitter and bad like "that hitchhiker" who "hated everything and everybody" (Hinton, *Tex* 210). "Pop used to drive me crazy, he treated us so different," Mason reflects. "I was sure you'd start wondering why, the same as I did. I don't see how you could help hating everybody, if you found out. Especially me" (210). Yet Tex never *did* find out the paternity secret or feel treated differently, despite his father's clumsiness, because of

Mason's intense fraternal nurturing. This unspoken revelation is as meaningful as the brothers' understated verbal reconciliation.

Though neither Tex nor Mason frequently finds the words to discuss how much the other means to him, their harmonious relationship is a literary model of "presence in relationship," a way for boys and girls to "experience connection and closeness." Judy Y. Chu and Niobe Way have theorized that, while adolescent developmental psychology has focused upon "voice," or the "ability to speak openly about one's thoughts and feelings," this may be a "less optimal" frame for "understanding adolescent boys' experiences of self in relationships" (52). When describing supportive relationships, they note, "adolescent boys often placed greater importance on whether they felt they could talk and share their innermost thoughts and feelings, if they wanted to, than on whether they actually talked" (55). The McCormick brothers provide that sort of companionable silence for one another; as the novel closes, they are about to go fishing together. Ultimately, they will separate when Mason goes to college, but the tension between "going" and "staying" in this novel is not the same as Hinton's earlier "then" and "now." Genuine fraternal love endures, Hinton concludes, whatever the distance or the DNA.

Stories Don't Have Endings, Just Pauses: Taming the Star Runner

Coming nearly a decade after the release of *Tex*, *Taming the Star Runner* seems like a significant departure from Hinton's world of lost brothers. The novel chronicles the gradual maturation of Travis, a teen delinquent banished to his uncle's rural, horse-crazy town as punishment. It remains Hinton's only young adult novel to use third person narration; it also inhabits a harsher 1980s sensibility, referring to yuppies and AIDS blood tests and containing forbidden words like "bitch" and "ass." Finally, Travis' only child status deviates from Hinton's typical interest in brotherly pairs.

Taming the Star Runner does, in fact, continue Hinton's interest in tracing young men's process of maturation through others; it simply transfers the role of fraternal nurturer to other characters.

Travis' young uncle, Ken, physically resembles Travis and serves as a mentor who models caring, responsible fatherhood. A masculinized *girl*, Casey, also teaches Travis patience and self-discipline in a sibling-like capacity. Hinton once joked that she aged out of writing YA after her fifth novel, saying "it's very difficult for me to get in the mind-set again. I'm pretty much out of that now. I don't get suicidal over a bad haircut anymore" (qtd. in Michaud). As the last novel in her cycle, *Taming the Star Runner* is an intriguing evolution in her work on family bonds and suggests she still has more to say.

Like many of Hinton's protagonists, Travis devours the literary world. A lonely, alienated boy, he describes his eyes—"gray-green and as cold as the Irish sea"—in terms of a book he read about F. Scott Fitzgerald (Hinton, *Taming* 5). Unlike most of his compatriots, however, Travis is a soon-to-be *published* author, having secretly completed, and sold, a young adult manuscript before the events of the novel begin. Hinton's description of the acquisition and editorial process parallels her own. Jay Daly traces many self-reflexive moments in the novel, including "the nervous phone conversations and meetings between the unsophisticated author and the urbane but sympathetic editor" and the editor's critique of Travis' "'imaginative' spelling" (118).

Travis speaks of having "two languages"—"one in my head and one in my mouth"—and while he is deeply expressive on the page, he lacks a social dialect (Hinton, *Taming* 114). Other people appear to him as intrusion on private space; he condescends to his mother, and lashes out at his abusive stepfather with "smoldering embers of hate licking at his insides" (7). In suicidal despair, he is shipped off to his uncle's rural home. Amongst new peers, his good looks and sarcastic personality are unappreciated. Travis "had always assumed that being a loner was something you chose," but "now he knew the other people could choose it for you" (39). Highly accomplished yet highly alienated, Travis writes stories, but he also *lives* his own story. Like most of Hinton's male protagonists, he chooses his adventure based upon the influence of his family.

Travis' Uncle Ken, to whom he is exiled, provides physical resemblance and paternal guidance. Travis describes Ken as "younger than I thought he was," adding that "people seem to think we look alike and I'm not real insulted, expect he has some gray hair" (Hinton, *Taming* 23). The duo's hands bear an "amazing resemblance," and Ken's wife tells Travis "God, you look more like Ken than Christopher [Ken's toddler son] does" (58, 44). While Travis initially chafes under Ken's restrictions on alcohol and insistence on talking to him, he soon grows to appreciate his paternal responsiveness. "Ken seemed to think everything Christopher did was cute, and took it for granted that everything revolved around him," Travis thinks, adding that he "hated to admit it, but maybe he was a bit jealous" (53). Even discipline soon begins to feel comforting to the alienated Travis; after a fight in which "Ken yelled at him," he realizes he "didn't feel so lonesome anymore" (81).

Travis' friend Casey helps his story take root as well, and her character suggests some shift in Hinton's traditional gender politics. While most of Hinton's boy protagonists regard women with a mixture of confusion, fear and desire, Travis' chauvinism seems more harshly expressed. He blames his mother for failing to protect herself from a violent husband, arguing "she could leave" and "if she wanted to put up with that garbage, she could" (Hinton, *Taming* 7). "Donna the Hon," as he sarcastically calls his mother, is preoccupied with "soft frettings" about silly things, and Travis is equally dismissive of the heavily feminized horse-jumping subculture (3). Female riders and trainers are generally portrayed as dithering or overly sexualized, and a mother obsessed with matching her daughters' hair and horse is held up for ridicule. Travis seems most incensed that girls' love for horses diverts their heterosexual energy; he complains "it was almost sick," that girls "petted the horses, fussed over them, combed and brushed them like they were going to a prom" and "baby-talked them and even kissed them!" (12).

The head trainer, Casey (her gender-ambiguous name is actually KC, short for Katherine Caroline), confounds Travis' preconceptions about gender norms. Initially, Travis struggles to place his attraction to her vitality in traditionally gendered terms. "Her eyes were interesting, green as traffic lights," he observes, before qualifying that "actually, if she'd had on some makeup and a different hairstyle, she might not have been so plain" (Hinton, *Taming* 26). While her legs are "way too muscled up" in his opinion, he finds her "green eyes were a much warmer color than his own. They saved her face from plainness" (42). Travis' *admiration* for the character is clear and mimics the older-brother worship in Hinton's other novels. From working as her barn groom, Travis learns patience, responsibility and discipline (89). His heroics in decapitating a snake do not impress her, but she praises his domestic abilities, specifically helping to "clean up that mess you made" and not being "afraid to ask when you don't know things" around the barn (150). He begins to correct his short temper when he witnesses her patience dealing with overbearing parents: "It's my paycheck," she says to him simply. "I need to earn a living. It comes with the territory" (91). Most of all, he understands that her quest to discipline the wild horse Star Runner is not an attempt to domesticate him but rather to optimize his own power, since this is also Travis' story.

Thanks to the steady mentoring he receives from Ken and Casey, Travis writes himself a different path from delinquency. He rejects his old friends' paths of drugs and crime and returns to Ken's family. In another indication that Casey takes on the brothers' traditional role, she and Travis do not end up together romantically; rather, they maintain a close, trusting bond. Having recognized that "stories didn't have endings, only pausing places," Travis sits down at the typewriter to write a new chapter in his own narrative (Hinton, *Taming* 179). *Taming the Star Runner*'s ending alludes to Hinton's own career while also circling back to *The Outsiders'* Ponyboy Curtis, who put pen to paper to narrate the real story of lost boys stigmatized as greasers.

Over the course of three decades, S. E. Hinton's novels have conversed with one another about the formative nature of fraternal relationships in boys' lives. Hinton's books show us that brothers who are at the core of family life, like Darrel Curtis or Mason McCormick, can create emotionally responsive, altruistic worlds that challenge traditional masculine ideology. Meanwhile, those who trespass on community norms, like the Motorcycle Boy or Mark Jennings, offer negative models that force boys to examine and refine their own moral decision-making processes. Hinton's young adult novels provide an invaluable resource for parents, teachers, and researchers interested in boys' needs and their emotional connections. In an age when the public increasingly interrogates "toxic" masculinity, her works also offer a promising pro-social narrative in which boys facing tough odds form meaningful relationships. S. E. Hinton's work is an established landmark in the field of young adult literature, and it is becoming a major marker in the evolving map of boyhood studies.

Works Cited

Chu, Judy Y., and Niobe Way. "Presence in Relationship: A New Construct for Understanding Adolescent Friendships and Psychological Health." *Thymos: Journal of Boyhood Studies*, vol. 3, no. 1, 2009, pp. 50-73.

Daly, Jay. *Presenting S. E. Hinton*. 1987. Twayne, 1989.

Groth, Miles. "'Has Anyone Seen the Boy?': The Fate of the Boy in Becoming a Man." *Thymos: Journal of Boyhood Studies*, vol. 1, no. 1, 2007, pp. 6-42.

Hinton, S. E. *The Outsiders*. 1967. Dell, 1989.

_____. *Rumble Fish*. 1975. Dell, 1983.

_____. *Taming the Star Runner*. 1988. Dell, 1989.

_____. *Tex*. 1979. Dell, 1989.

_____. *That was Then, This is Now*. 1971. Penguin, 2008.

Kluger, Jeffrey. *The Sibling Effect: Brothers, Sisters, and the Bonds that Define Us*. Riverhead, 2011.

Michaud, Jon. "That Was Then, This is Now: S. E. Hinton in the Twitter Age." *The New Yorker*, 8 Nov. 2013, www.newyorker.com/books/page-turner/that-was-then-this-is-now-s-e-hinton-in-the-twitter-age/.

Skurnick, Lizzie. "The Brotherhood of S. E. Hinton." *The Chicago Tribune*, 31 May 2008, articles.chicagotribune.com/2008-05-31/entertainment/0805300355_1_ponyboy-curtis-hinton-outsiders/.

Solmeyer, Anna R., Susan M. McHale, and Ann C. Crouter. "Longitudinal Associations between Sibling Relationship Qualities and Risky Behavior Adolescence." *Developmental Psychology*, vol. 50, no. 2, 2004, pp. 600-610, dx.doi.org/10.1037/a0033207/.

Weaver-Hightower, Marcus B. "Inventing the 'All-American Boy': A Case Study of the Capture of Boys' Issues by Conservative Groups." *Men and Masculinities*, vol. 10, no. 3, 2008, pp. 267-295.

Wooden, Shannon R., and Ken Gillam. *Pixar's Boy Stories: Masculinity in a Postmodern Age*. Rowman & Littlefield, 2014.

S. E. Hinton's *The Outsiders* and Theories of Moral Development

M. Katherine Grimes

The question of what is right and what is wrong seems easy: Honesty is right; stealing is wrong; obeying one's parents is right; hitting is wrong. But with that list we can almost always find exceptions: Miep Gies should lie about hiding Anne Frank and her family from the Nazis; someone who is starving can certainly be forgiven for stealing a loaf of bread; if a parent sends a child out to sell drugs, disobeying that parent is admirable; and if someone is attacking an innocent person, a police officer is expected to hit the attacker to stop the assault.

Psychological theorist Lawrence Kohlberg (1927–1987) found that moral decision-making is even more difficult than having a list of rules and finding exceptions. In his research in the middle of the last century—at about the same time as S. E. Hinton was writing her novel *The Outsiders*—he showed that what we see as right and wrong changes as we mature. While physical maturation is obvious by observing children as they grow from infancy through young childhood to teenaged years, other types of maturation require more study, and a number of psychologists have conducted such research. As almost anyone who has taken a psychology class knows, Austrian psychoanalyst Sigmund Freud (1856–1939) proposed theories of personality and of psychosexual maturation, or the stages we go through in reaching our sexual identities. Freud's theories were based primarily on observation and speculation. Later theorists used both observation and research to support their ideas. Most notably, Swiss psychologist Jean Piaget (1896–1980) studied cognitive development, which is the way we learn; and German American theorist Erik Erikson (1902–1994) studied psychosocial maturation, which is the way we grow in interaction with other people.

Kohlberg focused on the way we mature morally, the way we determine what is right and wrong and the evolution of those methods of determination throughout our childhoods and even into adulthood. He studied numerous adolescents in the mid-twentieth century and found clear patterns of moral development, patterns that were nearly universal. Based on questions related to moral reasoning, he and his team of researchers found that almost everyone goes through at least four stages of development, with some people advancing through two additional stages. The first two stages are self-centered; the second pair moves to larger groups that support the self; the final two move outward to larger groups and to more abstract principles.

In S. E. Hinton's *The Outsiders*, most characters are firmly entrenched in the third stage, as we would expect them to be, based on their ages and environment. Having gone through stages in which the idea of what is right and wrong is based on fear of punishment or fulfilling one's own desires, most of these boys are in the stage in which they make moral decisions based on what they see as best for their own group, either family or gang.

American society teaches confusing and conflicting lessons about right and wrong. We expect everyone, especially children, to know what is moral, but we rarely provide clear guidelines for defining the concept.

One example of this lack of clarity is found in the M'Naghten rule, established in England in the mid-nineteenth century to determine insanity: a person was sane unless he or she "at the time of committing the act . . . was laboring under such a defect of reason, from disease of the mind, as not to know the nature and quality of the act he was doing or, if he did know it, that he did not know what he was doing was wrong" (qtd. in "Insanity Defense"). The problem is that the M'Naghten rule[1] does not tell us how one determines whether "what he was doing was wrong."

In religious teachings, definitions of right and wrong are even more confusing. The Judeo-Christian tradition would have almost certainly served as the religious center of 1960s Oklahoma (the Pew Research Center finds that 71 percent of adults in Oklahoma currently identify themselves as Christian ["Religious Landscape"]). We know that Ponyboy attended church even after his parents' deaths (Hinton 66), so he would have been familiar with the confusing admonitions concerning right and wrong in the Christian Bible, in which at first God wanted people only to obey, forbidding them to know good and evil (Genesis 2-3), but then gave them specific commandments (Exodus 20), and in the Christian tradition sent Jesus to teach people how to live (New Testament, especially the gospels: Matthew, Mark, Luke, and John).

So our society provides vague and even contradictory ways for determining what is right and what is wrong. Lawrence Kohlberg's scheme does not tell us whether our behavior is morally correct. What it does is show us how people at different stages in their lives make moral decisions. Based on this research, he postulated the following scheme, as he and colleague Richard H. Hersh outline in a 1977 article in the journal *Theory into Practice* and as Kohlberg and associate Carol Gilligan discuss in a 1971 essay in the journal *Daedelus*: We begin determining our moral ideas in the Preconventional Level, when the individual sees right and wrong in terms of the consequences to him- or herself. In the first stage of this level, the "punishment and obedience orientation" (Kohlberg and Hersh 54), children see moral correctness as what allows them to avoid punishment. Therefore, once children are punished for an action, they will see that behavior as bad. In the second stage, "instrumental-relativist orientation" (Kohlberg and Hersh 54), what gets us what we need or want is good. Therefore, sharing one's toys is seen as morally good to children in that stage because it gets others to share toys with them.

As we get older, we move into the Conventional Level, in which we make moral decisions based on others, but others whom we still see as related to us. The third stage of Kohlberg's scheme is the first Conventional stage—what Kohlberg and Hersh call the "interpersonal concordance or 'good boy-nice girl' orientation" (55). In this stage, behavior that children see as good earns them praise or is acceptable to their family or other small group. Kohlberg and Gilligan point out the importance of "conformity to stereotypical images of what is majority . . . behavior" in stage three (1067). Kohlberg and Hersh call the fourth stage the "'law and order' orientation" (55); in this stage, children see as morally right following the rules and laws of their society and obeying an authority beyond just the superiors in their own small groups. They believe that they have a duty to this larger group, their state or nation, perhaps, even though they do not personally know the people who make the rules or the people who benefit from their compliance, because of the importance of "the maintenance of the social order" (Kohlberg and Hersh 55).

Kohlberg and Hersh call the third level "Postconventional, Autonomous, or Principled" (55). Kohlberg and Gilligan found that adolescents often begin to think on this level, which the theorists say is "characterized by a major thrust toward autonomous moral principles which have validity and application apart from authority . . ." (Kohlberg and Gilligan 1066). In the two stages in this level, people make moral decisions less on the basis of what they are told is right and wrong and more on what they themselves determine to be so. In stage five, "social-contract, legalistic orientation," the idea is that moral right is based on what is good for society, not because some lawmakers said so but because the person whose moral belief system is being developed believes that it is good for the majority (Kohlberg and Hersh 55). If the law is not good, then people in stage five would want the law changed, even if they would not specifically benefit. Therefore, when white people in the 1960s worked in favor of legal rights for African Americans, they could be seen as using stage five moral reasoning. Stage six is perhaps the most difficult to understand. Kohlberg and Hersh call it the "universal-ethical-principle orientation" and define it in this way:

> Right is defined by the decision of conscience in accord with self-chosen ethical principles appealing to logical comprehensiveness, universality, and consistency. These principles are abstract and ethical (the Golden Rule, the categorical imperative); they are not concrete moral rules like the Ten Commandments. At heart, these are universal principles of justice, of the reciprocity and equality of human rights, and of respect for the dignity of human beings as individual persons. (55)[2]

The moral development of the characters in S. E. Hinton's 1967 novel *The Outsiders* is central to an understanding of that work. As readers know, the book is about a group of boys and young men in Tulsa, Oklahoma, and the encounters of these fellows, who call themselves "greasers," with young men and women from the group called "Socs" (from the word "socials"). The greasers and Socs (S. E. Hinton's spelling and capitalization) are enemies, fighting one another in rumbles reminiscent of *West Side Story* and attacking individual members of the other group. They are fiercely loyal to their own groups, and each group is antagonistic to the other. As greaser Keith "Two-Bit" Mathews explains, their first rule is "Stick together" (Hinton 29).

In most of *The Outsiders*, as one would expect, the main characters appear to be in stage three, the one in which they see good as what gets them praise from their own group. In the case of the orphaned Curtis brothers—Darrel, twenty; Sodapop, sixteen; and Ponyboy, fourteen (the narrator), their first group is their family. Since their parents' fatal automobile accident, the brothers take care of one another. Darrel, or Darry, works in construction to support his younger brothers and keep them from being separated and put into a county home by the authorities. Sodapop quits school to help by working in a service station. Ponyboy tries to gain their approval by doing well in school and holding his own in fights with the Socs. The Curtis brothers cook and bake for one another, rub one another's backs, and obviously love one another, despite Darry's strictness with Ponyboy, which is obviously related to fear for the youngest brother's well-being.

The group also extends to the gang, the other young men in the neighborhood. The Curtis home is open to other greasers who need a place to crash, either to get away from the police (Dallas, or Dally, Winston) or to escape a horrible home life (Johnny Cade). If one member of the gang is in trouble, the others step up to help or support him.

Only one character in *The Outsiders* really articulates a moral philosophy at the Preconventional Level: Dally Winston. In the scene in which Johnny Cade and Ponyboy Curtis go into a burning church building to rescue children who most certainly would have died had the young heroes not saved them, Dally yells to the boys, "For

Pete's sake, get outa there! That roof's gonna cave in any minute. Forget those blasted kids!" (Hinton 93). In short, Dally is urging his friends to behave in stage two, to do what will help themselves, not others. But although he articulates a stage two philosophy, his own motivation and behavior, like those of almost every other character in the novel, are nearly always stage three, which is in the Conventional Level. Even as he tells Ponyboy and Johnny to act in their own self-interest, he moves to help them because they are his group, just as he has helped Ponyboy and Johnny to hide after Johnny kills Bob Sheldon, a Soc. Johnny also tells Ponyboy about another time that Dally took care of his friends:

> "[O]ne night I saw Dally gettin' picked up by the fuzz, and he kept real cool and calm the whole time. They was gettin' him for breakin' out the windows in the school building, and it was Two-Bit who did that. And Dally knew it. But he just took the sentence without battin' an eye or even denyin' it. That's gallant." (Hinton 76)

That might be "gallant," but Dally's behavior is also the epitome of stage three—focusing on one's small group, not oneself (stage one or two) or society in general (stage four). For example, he says he wouldn't want Johnny to go to prison and get "hard," like he did (Hinton 89-90).

One could argue that the young men in S. E. Hinton's novel are in stage two, with each fighting for and supporting the others so that they will step up for him. That is not an illogical argument, as we see when Johnny explains his killing of the Soc Bob to Ponyboy. Johnny says, "I had to [kill him]. They were drowning you, Pony. They might have killed you. And they had a blade . . . they were gonna beat me up . . . ." (Hinton 57; ellipses Hinton's). Johnny kills Bob to protect Ponyboy, true, as a person in stage three would do, but Johnny is also looking out for himself, as a person in the Preconventional Level would do. Quite a lot of small-group behavior is self-preservation, just as birds flock together as protection from predators.

However, much evidence in the novel suggests that most of the characters are in stage three. They care what others in their group think of them, as we see when Ponyboy won't admit to not wanting to shoot animals for fear that Dally will think he is "soft" (Hinton 86). Darry and Sodapop work to keep their family together and to keep Ponyboy in school. Johnny kills Bob to prevent the Socs from drowning Ponyboy. When Johnny and Ponyboy need to escape, Dally gives them money, a gun, and advice and later comes to visit them, then tries to keep them from getting hurt in the church fire. When Johnny decides to turn himself in, he vows to protect Dally from charges of aiding and abetting fugitives. And when Johnny is in the hospital, his friends visit him. Upon Johnny's death, Dally is so distraught that he commits "suicide by cop." The bonds among the young men are real, and they see moral good as doing what is best for the family or the group of friends.

It is worth noting that Kohlberg's colleague Carol Gilligan (1936–) asserts based on her own studies that men and women mature morally in different ways, particularly with regard to relationships. She writes,

[R]elationships, and particularly issues of dependency, are experienced differently by women and men. For boys and men, separation and individuation are critically tied to gender identity since separation from the mother is essential for the development of masculinity. For girls and women, issues of femininity or feminine identity do not depend on the achievement of separation from the mother or on the progress of individuation. Since masculinity is defined through separation while femininity is defined through attachment, male gender identity is threatened by intimacy while female gender identity is threatened by separation. Thus males tend to have difficulty with relationships, while females tend to have problems with individuation. (8)

Gilligan goes on to say that because girls and women emphasize relationships, women are weighed in the balance and found wanting on moral scales constructed by men who have primarily observed males (18). She asserts that women should be weighed not on men's scales but on their own. Thus, moral maturation might look different for people of different genders. Girls, she says, learn empathy, while boys learn competition; girls learn human relationships while boys learn rules (10-11). Perhaps the fact that for centuries women cared for their families, a task that requires consideration and cooperation, while men went into the much more public world of paid work, which requires more competition, contributes to the difference that Gilligan has found in her research.

The Outsiders provides a complicated look at Lawrence Kohlberg's and Carol Gilligan's views of moral development. While some behaviors fairly clearly fit the Kohlberg scheme, others are much more in the Gilligan mold. The fights between the greasers and the Socs illustrate Kohlberg's stage three connections with small groups, as well as the competition and emphasis on rules that Gilligan says are common with men. Cherry Valance's attempts to understand others and to negotiate demonstrate Gilligan's assertions that women focus on relationships.

Further adding to the complication is the fact that the Curtis boys are orphaned. While adolescent boys, says Gilligan, are trying to separate from their mothers and become self-reliant, Ponyboy has had that separation thrust upon him far too early, so he clings to Sodapop, whom he sees as sympathetic towards him, and tries to separate from Darry, whom he sees as harsh. In the first relationship, Ponyboy is like a child; in the second, he is like the adolescent that he is. Perhaps Sodapop is illustrating the maternal role more, and Darry, the paternal. Johnny's reaction to his mother at the hospital might seem to illustrate this adolescent separation, but Johnny rejects his mother because she has not behaved in a maternal way toward him. S. E. Hinton's writing of the scene, on the other hand, might illustrate that desire for separation.

While biographical criticism, looking at the life of the author in relation to the work, and focus on authorial intent, what the author means to be saying, can be limiting in literary criticism, the fact that the author of this book about teenaged boys was a teenaged girl when she was writing her novel is inescapable. Therefore, individuation is depicted as dangerous—both Johnny and Ponyboy get jumped when they're alone—and relationships are shown as good. Think of the way Johnny and Ponyboy cling to one another while they are hiding and the affection Sodapop shows to his younger brother. Johnny and

Ponyboy read to one another; they look at sunsets together; Ponyboy recites poetry while Johnny listens, and Ponyboy says that he would not do that around other members of his group (Hinton 77-78).

Thus, while *The Outsiders* is a maturation novel about boys, S. E. Hinton celebrates their stage three relationships even as she realizes that they must move beyond them. Ponyboy does not stay in stage three. As is true in almost any maturation novel, the main character must move forward; he or she must have an experience or go through a series of events that change the character, usually as the result of a major revelation about the self or the world, a revelation called an epiphany or epiphanic moment.

One such series of events for Ponyboy begins with his near-drowning by Bob and his realization that his friend Johnny has killed Ponyboy's attacker. His first reaction is to run, to avoid punishment, a typical reaction for almost anyone, especially a teenager. Running is not a moral or immoral decision; it comes from the basest of instincts: self-preservation. Ponyboy says to Johnny, "What are we gonna do? They put you in the electric chair for killing people! . . . I'm scared Johnny. What are we gonna do?" (Hinton 57). So the boys run. But later, Johnny decides to turn himself in. He does this for three reasons: he is tired of hiding; he thinks he might be "let off easy" because he "ain't got no record with the fuzz and it was self-defense"; and because "[i]t ain't fair for Ponyboy to have to stay up in that church with Darry and Soda worryin' about him all the time" (Hinton 87). Johnny's decision indicates stage two reasoning—getting away from the hide-out; stage three—doing what is best for Ponyboy, Sodapop, and Darry; and a glimmer of stage four—obeying the local authorities and trusting the justice system to do what is right to maintain social order, including not punishing him unduly and following the rules about self-defense.

Although Lawrence Kohlberg and Carol Gilligan assert that we all must go through each stage, never skipping one and continuing to move forward through them (1068-69), we do not really see Ponyboy Curtis in stage four. He does not disagree when Johnny wants to turn himself in, but he also does not argue that surrendering is the right decision, the right thing to do. However,

S. E. Hinton, also a teenager when she wrote the book, shows us a glimpse of her own stage four thinking in the courtroom scene: the judge listens to all sides, acquits Ponyboy and sends him back to his brothers, and basically behaves like a nice man (167-68). The judge represents authority and social maintenance, and in painting him as an admirable and just person, Hinton shows us that we, too, can trust our society. This scene allows the young reader to feel free to move into stage four, to follow rules and trust authority, as the hearing is presented through the eyes of the character with whom readers most identify, the narrator, Ponyboy.

Carol Gilligan might assert that Ponyboy spends little time in stage four because that stage is about connection with the wider society, not with other individuals. Again, because S. E. Hinton is a woman, the value of individual relationships will outweigh the value of separation and individuation. Whereas most heroes perform their brave deeds alone, when Johnny and Ponyboy enter the church building to save the children, they do so together. Acting alone, as Dally does when he goes out with his gun after Johnny dies, is seen as foolish or dangerous.

The most important moral maturation in the novel is Ponyboy's movement into stage five, an impressive leap for a fourteen-year-old boy. Instead of seeing himself as an individual separate from others (Kohlberg's Preconventional level) or a member of an impersonal larger society (stage four, which is in the Conventional level), when Ponyboy moves forward morally, he sees himself connecting with other people, but this time with those outside his family or group of close friends. We see him make the transition to Kohlberg's fifth stage, part of the Postconventional level, in three events.

Ponyboy begins moving outside stage three early in the novel when he and Johnny talk with the Soc girl Sherri "Cherry" Valance and her friend Marcia at the drive-in movie. If Ponyboy and Johnny had been completely and irredeemably stuck in stage three, they would have joined Dally in the verbal sexual assault on the two Soc girls or would have remained silent, for Dally is a member of their own group, and Cherry and Marcia belong to the enemy camp, the Socs. Ponyboy makes clear that their friends Keith "Two-Bit"

Mathews and Steve Randle and even his own brother Sodapop would have "gone right along with [Dally], just to see if they could embarrass the girls" (Hinton 20-21). But Johnny says to Dally, who is older and tougher than Johnny and Ponyboy, "Leave her alone, Dally" (Hinton 24). Witnessing Johnny's courage and gallantry in standing up to their friend, Ponyboy begins to see that loyalty to one's group is not the only determinant of virtue. He admires Johnny's courage in standing up to their friend to protect the girls Dally was harassing. Ponyboy writes, "I was still staring at him. It had taken more than nerve for him to say what he'd said to Dally—Johnny worshiped the ground Dallas walked on, and I had never heard Johnny talk back to anyone, much less his hero" (Hinton 25).

Cherry herself then models the beginnings of stage five reasoning, talking with Ponyboy and Johnny, even though they are members of a group that her group generally despises. When she and Ponyboy are alone, she talks about Johnny: "[H]e's been hurt bad sometime, hasn't he? . . . Hurt and scared" (Hinton 31). Her observation of the pain in a person outside her clique—indeed, outside her social class—shows that Cherry is not stuck in the Conventional Level of Lawrence Kohlberg's moral scheme. After the movie, when she and Marcia are walking with their two young heroes and the boys' friend Two-Bit, Cherry tries both to understand Ponyboy and his culture and to explain hers to him. She is trying to make connections beyond her own group when Socs Bob and Randy show up, threatening the greasers; Cherry goes with them to prevent trouble for her new friends.

Later as the Socs and greasers plan a rumble, Cherry serves as the intermediary, negotiating for both sides to try to ensure a fair fight with as few injuries as possible. She wants the world to be just, and she sees herself as someone who can help make it so. In many ways, she is in stage five, not trying to enforce rules made by those in authority, as she would have done had she been in stage four, but helping to make rules that ensure justice for everyone instead of just creating an advantage for members of her own group.

For a time, Ponyboy cannot understand Cherry's motivation. Still in stage three, he tells her, "You're a traitor to your own kind and not loyal to us" (Hinton 129). In other words, Ponyboy expects his moral values to be hers. He believes that loyalty to one's group is the determinant of good. He goes on, "Don't you ever feel sorry for us. Don't you ever try to give us handouts and then feel high and mighty about it." But Cherry replies from her position in stage five: "I wasn't trying to give you charity, Ponyboy. I only wanted to help. . . . You're a nice kid, Ponyboy . . . . Wouldn't you try to help me if you could?" (Hinton 129). Her leadership helps Ponyboy move forward morally as well. He thinks, "I would. I'd help her and Randy both, if I could" (Hinton 129). Here we see Ponyboy start his moral journey from stage three to stage five, to caring about other people and not just having loyalty to his own small group.

Johnny's and Ponyboy's saving of the children from the burning church building is also an action that most would see as based on stage five reasoning. Lawrence Kohlberg would probably agree. Ponyboy and Johnny save the children not to avoid punishment or to receive a reward. They do not have time to consider whether they will be praised for their heroism or whether saving the children contributes to a better society. They save the children because the children will die if the boys do not rescue them and because Ponyboy and Johnny think, probably correctly, that they themselves left a cigarette burning and started the fire. If their motivation is guilt, then perhaps their actions represent Preconventional reasoning: saving the children will keep them from being punished, or it will give them absolution. But it is much more likely, given the fact that the boys have almost no time to consider their actions, that they risk—and, in Johnny's case, give—their lives to save the children because they inherently believe, without even thinking about that belief, that all human life has value and deserves to be preserved. Whether they could articulate that belief is unclear, but they obviously hold it.

It is in Ponyboy's talk with the Soc Randy Adderson before the rumble that we see Ponyboy's movement into stage five most clearly. During this conversation the rules of both their small groups and their larger society are called into question and ultimately rejected.

At first Randy makes assertions that would put him clearly in the Preconventional Level, saying that he would have let the children burn rather than risk his life the way Ponyboy and Johnny did, but Ponyboy responds with the possibility that Randy would have rescued the children too (Hinton 114). Then Randy makes another speech that separates him from stage three, but this time in the other direction: he argues that Bob Sheldon would have gotten in less trouble if his parents had made, communicated, and enforced rules. Rules are a stage four concept. After discussing Bob's parenting or lack thereof, Randy says that he can talk to Ponyboy in a way that is different from what he says to his friends, other Socs. Again Randy is moving outside his small stage three group mentality, but he is also moving toward another person, one he recognizes as a "kid," not a "greaser" (Hinton 117), moving toward the idea of equality that marks stage five. Ponyboy then says to his friends that Randy "ain't a Soc . . . .[H]e's just a guy" (118). Ponyboy recognizes the humanity in Randy because Randy is torn between "being marked chicken" if he refuses to take part in the rumble, a very stage three attitude, and hating himself if he fights, for "it doesn't do any good, the fighting and the killing" (117), a realization that marks more moral maturity, perhaps stage five thinking.

Carol Gilligan recognizes this rejection of fighting as part of an "ethic of care," which she sees as the way women view the world, whereas men follow an "ethic of justice" (174). She writes, "While an ethic of justice proceeds from the premise of equality—that everyone should be treated the same—an ethic of care rests on the premise of nonviolence—that no one should be hurt" (174). Gilligan asserts that both beliefs are signs of maturity, and viewed together they can help us all become more morally advanced (174).

In the end of Hinton's novel, Ponyboy is thinking about "hundreds and hundreds of boys living on the wrong sides of cities," and he writes, "Suddenly it wasn't only a personal thing to me" (179). At this point, Ponyboy's feelings and thoughts go beyond his family, beyond his group to "boys going down under street lights because they were mean and tough and hated the world, and it was too late to tell them that there was still good in it . . . ." He thinks that "[t]here should be some help[,] . . . [s]omeone to tell their side of the story." He hopes that "maybe people would understand then and wouldn't be so quick to judge a boy by the amount of hair oil he wore" (Hinton 179).

So Ponyboy Curtis sets out to write the story of the boys who are judged by the length of their hair rather than by the content of their character, choosing this time a different kind of heroism, not one that risks his life but one that tries to make the world a fairer place. He combines the stage five moral development of Lawrence Kohlberg, which aims to make the world more just for all, with the relational morality advocated by Carol Gilligan.

In the mid-1960s, S. E. Hinton made the same decision. For five decades teenaged boys and girls have seen themselves in Ponyboy and Johnny and Randy and Cherry. And those young readers are better for it.

Notes

1. While the M'Naghten rule is still used in some states to determine insanity, it was modified in many by the Model Penal Code of 1972, a more progressive understanding of insanity, and by the Insanity Defense Reform Act of 1984, which is more restrictive ("Insanity Defense"). However *The Outsiders*, published in 1967, predates both of these changes.

2. This concept was previously articulated by Kohlberg in the article "From Is to Ought" in the book *Cognitive Development and Epistemology*, edited by Theodore Mischel, Academic Press, 1971, pp. 164-65.

Works Cited

Gilligan, Carol. *In a Different Voice: Psychological Theory and Women's Development.* Harvard UP, 2003. *ACLS Humanities e-book*, 0-hdl. handle.net.library.acaweb.org/2027/heb.32978.0001.001/.

Hinton, S. E. *The Outsiders*. 1967. Platinum ed., Speak / Penguin, 2012.

"Insanity Defense." *Legal Information Institute*. Cornell Law School, Jul. 2016, www.law.cornell.edu/wex/insanity_defense/.

Kohlberg, Lawrence, and Carol Gilligan. "The Adolescent as a Philosopher: The Discovery of the Self in a Postconventional World." *Daedelus*, vol. 100, no. 4, Fall 1971, pp. 1051-86. *JSTOR*.

Kohlberg, Lawrence, and Richard H. Hersh. "Moral Development: A Review of the Theory." *Theory into Practice*, vol. 16, no. 2, 1977, pp. 53-59. *JSTOR.*

"Religious Landscape." *Pew Research Center*, www.pewforum.org/religious-landscape-study/state/oklahoma/. Accessed 28 Jan. 2018.

Robert Frost's Seasons of the Self in *The Outsiders*

Mary Baron

Nothing Gold Can Stay

Nature's first green is gold,
Her hardest hue to hold.
Her early leaf's a flower;
But only so an hour.
Then leaf subsides to leaf.
So Eden sank to grief,
So dawn goes down to day.
Nothing gold can stay.

(Robert Frost)

In one of the best-remembered scenes from S. E. Hinton's novel *The Outsiders*, the narrator, Ponyboy, visits his dying friend Johnny in the hospital. The last thing Johnny tells him is to "stay gold," referring to the Robert Frost poem that both boys admire (Hinton 148). Yet the poem itself says that Johnny's admonition is impossible, its last line insisting that "Nothing gold can stay."

In Frost's New England, birch trees first respond to the spring sun by sprouting tiny, tightly wrapped golden yellow buds. As these open, they look like small flowers. But within hours the trees make chlorophyll, turning the buds green and opening them into brackets of green leaves, so "leaf subsides to leaf."

In line six of his poem, Frost writes, "So Eden sank to grief"; the fields of New England are replaced in this line by the Garden of Eden, where there is neither growth nor decay. Nothing subsides; nothing becomes less or more than perfection. However, gold cannot stay in Eden, either, as Adam and Eve are banished from the garden and the promise is lost, leaving grief where there once was paradise.

Most critics see the expression "stay gold" as hopeful, even a blessing; yet it is an impossibility. The poem throws us out of Eden and into nature, within whose progressions "nothing gold can stay." As readers, we also are "outsiders"; like Adam and Eve, we have to live within time. We are subject to nature and her cycles. Glorious dawn becomes mundane day. We must live through the inevitable sadness of time and change. Unlike nature, human life does not consist of cycles. Instead, we move through stages. Once "dawn goes down to day," we do not get another dawn. Adolescence must give way to adulthood. Like Adam after the expulsion, and like his brothers before him, Ponyboy will have to earn his bread by the sweat of his brow. There is no return to Eden.

Johnny, however, sees beyond reality, finding good in a terrible world, a world in which boys from different social classes fight and torment one another. He prays that Ponyboy may remain pure, unchanging in the midst of change. That cannot be, but Ponyboy does learn to write out the prophecy, or forth-telling, of his own life. He can change his story, and that will change his life.

In the same way, adolescents are all, always, outsiders, neither child nor adult but inexorably moving away from childhood and toward adulthood. Both the protagonists and readers must move on to adulthood—and to death. To use J. R. R. Tolkien's term, the protagonists who write their own stories in young adult fiction are "sub-creators," inventing their own stories within time. Readers follow them as they leave childhood behind and "leaf subsides to leaf."

The last sentence of *The Outsiders* is the same as the first sentence. We end, as we began, reading Ponyboy's words. In our heads, we are still within the fiction, although we close the book. One thing has changed, however: Ponyboy now understands his past and his options; he can change the plot next time around. He can write himself a different life.

This loop of time correlates with the struggle in young adult fiction between those who have power, adults and pseudo-adults like the Socs, and those who do not, like Ponyboy. The powerless cannot at first imagine themselves as adults in charge of anything. But if they learn that they can change their story, they can imagine themselves into a different plot.

In order to forecast themselves into the future, adolescents must see themselves clearly and take responsibility for their actions. If they do so, they can inhabit an ethical world in which they can at least try to "stay gold." They can choose to stay as close to the Garden of Eden as possible, leading moral and ethical lives. There is always a choice, as Frost describes in his poem "The Road Not Taken." They must decide whether to "go along to get along" or to stand up for what they believe is right, to conform or to choose their own paths.

Once they choose, they can begin their own life stories. Ponyboy rejects escapist fiction as he leaves the movie theater. He rejects the world of make-believe, leaving behind the illusions of the movies and choosing, instead, the real world. What he writes in his journal is true, and this truth is the beginning of prophecy in the sense of forth-telling. He examines his life, using writing to clarify rather than to camouflage it; he predicts where he will go and begins the journey. He will move into adulthood on "the road less travelled."

In novel after novel written for and about young teenagers, the hardship of their lives is alleviated to some extent by the writing and rewriting of their experiences. Like Ponyboy, other characters, often the books' narrators, examine their lives, their experiences, and themselves through writing. As they explain themselves to the readers, they develop an understanding of their worlds and their places in them.

We see this process in Alex Flinn's *Breathing Underwater*, the story of an abused boy who becomes an abuser. The story is told from the boy's own point of view. Nick Andreas is sentenced by a judge to anger management classes and ordered to keep a journal detailing his abuse of his girlfriend, Caitlin. As he writes and shares this story in class, he comes to clarity; he rewrites and re-envisions the story of his life. But he will go on without Caitlin. That story is over.

Virginia Hamilton's *Sweet Whispers, Brother Rush*, winner of multiple awards, is the story of child abuse within an African American family in the Midwest. The teenage protagonist, Teresa, called Tree, is visited by the ghost of her Uncle Rush. The visions that he shows her reveal their mother's abuse of her older brother, Dabney, and the illness, porphyria, from which he suffers.

In one scene in Hamilton's novel, Tree reads aloud to Dab the chapter "The Time I Got Lost" from Warren Miller's 1959 novel *The Cool World* (Hamilton 57). Set during the times of slavery in the rural South, the chapter tells a story the children yearn for, the tale of a family that searches for and rescues a lost child. This, however, is not their story, for their mother has essentially abandoned them.

The novel ends with Dab's death, while Tree is legally emancipated from her mother. What she has learned from her ancestor, whose ghostly intervention is accepted in African American culture, makes this possible. Tree wonders,

> *Why had he come to her, with his dark secrets from a long-ago past? What was the purpose of their strange, haunting journeys back into her own childhood? Was it to help Dab, her retarded older brother, wracked with mysterious pain who sometimes took more care and love than Tree had to give? Was it for her mother, Vy . . .?* (Hamilton 84)

It was all for lies, fictions, her mother told her. But Tree realizes that now, because she has heard her story so far, she can move on to plan her future and find her own truth, then write the rest of her story herself.

Sandra Cisneros' *The House on Mango Street* sets story against story against story. It is told by the protagonist, Esperanza Cordero, who talks about her family and the people of her barrio in tiny vignettes, almost a chain of flash fiction with a poetic flavor. Like the author herself, Esperanza is Chicana, and the book both tells and refuses to believe in the cultural fictions that would keep her as a female "in her place" inside the house. She says of her great-grandmother, "I have inherited her name, but I don't want to inherit her place by the window" (Cisneros 11).

Family history and old stories will not do for her. Esperanza, whose name means "hope," must leave, write, and inhabit her new story and then return with her writing as a tool to help others. Her initial leaving is not escape, but the intentional journey of an artist who needs to learn her craft as she refashions her life. She states at the end of the book that she will return; "I have gone away to come back" (Cisneros 109-10).

In all four novels, moving away from childhood involves loss and asks the question that ends Frost's poem "The Oven Bird." What can we make of "a diminished thing"? If dawn has become day, what shall we do with our daylight? Perhaps the daylight, even though it is less lovely than the dawn, can help us see more clearly.

The Oven Bird

> There is a singer everyone has heard,
> Loud, a mid-summer and a mid-wood bird,
> Who makes the solid tree trunks sound again.
> He says that leaves are old and that for flowers
> Mid-summer is to spring as one to ten.
> He says the early petal-fall is past
> When pear and cherry bloom went down in showers
> On sunny days, a moment overcast;
> And comes that other fall we name the fall.
> He says the highway dust is over all.
> The bird would cease and be as other birds
> But that he knows in singing not to sing.
> The question that he frames in all but words
> Is what to make of a diminished thing. (Robert Frost)

"The Oven Bird" reads like a calendar of human emotion in the face of time. We will all die, and we don't like that. Further, it says that time alters what artists, who, like the bird, ask questions, can tell themselves. It is foolish to believe one can "stay gold" when "leaves are old" and we will face "that other fall we name the fall," our mortality.

In her book *In the Middle: New Understanding about Writing, Reading and Learning*, Nancy Atwell says that sometimes students see themselves as golden, not fated to join the world of adults just as inevitably as "dawn goes down to day" (43). While Johnny on his deathbed begs Ponyboy to "stay gold," Hinton warns her young readers not to squander their youth but to use it as a stage on which to build their futures, a page on which to write their own forth-tellings.

Works Cited

Atwell, Nancy. *In the Middle: New Understanding about Writing, Reading and Learning*, 2nd ed., Heinemann, 1998.

Cisneros, Sandra. *The House on Mango Street*. Vintage, 1972.

Flinn, Alex. *Breathing Underwater.* Perfection Learning, 2011.

Hamilton, Virginia. *Sweet Whispers, Brother Rush*. Reissue ed., Amistad, 2001.

Hinton, S. E. *The Outsiders.* Viking, 1967.

Miller, Warren. *The Cool World*. Fawcett Premier Book, 1959.

Modleski, Michael. "'Stay Gold,' Students: Helping Young Readers Connect to *The Outsiders." Middle School Journal*, vol. 40, no. 1, September 2008, pp. 12-18.

"Soda attracted girls like honey draws flies": *The Outsiders*, the Boy Band Formula, and Adolescent Sexuality

Michelle Ann Abate

In what has become an oft-repeated comment, S. E. Hinton's 1967 young adult novel, *The Outsiders*, inaugurated an entirely new style of writing for young people. As Michael Cart has written, prior to the release of Hinton's text, narratives for teens "were set in a *Saturday Evening Post* world of white faces and white picket fences surrounding small-town, middle-class lives where the worst thing that could happen would be a misunderstanding that threatened to leave someone dateless for the junior prom" (20). *The Outsiders* provided a counterpoint and even a corrective to this trend. With its presentation of teenage gangs, street violence, and poverty, the narrative contained profoundly different literary themes, characters, and subject matter. In a *New York Times Book Review* editorial about books for teens, Hinton offered the following explanation for her creative choices: "The world is changing, yet the authors of books for teen-agers are still 15 years behind the times" ("Teen-Agers"). This assessment was accurate. The 1960s were a time of tremendous social upheaval in the United States. The decade witnessed an array of profound and irrevocable transformations, including the agitation for civil rights by the black, women's, and gay and lesbian communities; the protests against the Vietnam War; and the shocking assassinations of prominent political and social activist figures Medgar Evers and John F. Kennedy in 1963, Malcolm X in 1965, and Martin Luther King Jr. and Robert F. Kennedy in 1968.

Young people were neither unaware of nor disengaged from these events. According to the Library of Congress, "At its height in the 1960s, the Civil Rights Movement drew children, teenagers, and young adults into a maelstrom of meetings, marches, violence, and in some cases, imprisonment" (par. 1). Likewise, the compulsory registration of young men ages 18–25 for military conscription spurred many college and high school students to join in antiwar protests; after all, they were the ones being drafted to fight in Vietnam. Yet the changing social, cultural, and political climate for American youth was not reflected in the literature written for them. As Hinton asked in her *New York Times* article, "where is the reality?" ("Teen-Agers").

The Outsiders was written to provide this missing element. Featuring a group of working-class protagonists living in an environment riddled with gang violence, the narrative was a radical departure from its literary predecessors. Jay Daly aptly summarized the difference: "Nobody worries about the prom in *The Outsiders*; they're more concerned with just staying alive till June" (i). The text's treatment of gritty subject matter, its focus on sociological themes, and its use of blunt language caused critics to credit Hinton with founding both young adult literature and the literary style of "New Realism" with which it is powerfully associated (Campbell 177; Daly 15). As Cart has asserted in a book by the same name, *The Outsiders* marked the moment when narratives for young people shifted "from romance to realism."

While contemporaneous events such as the Vietnam War and the civil rights movement undoubtedly influenced Hinton, this essay makes a case that front-page headlines were not the only medium that may have shaped *The Outsiders*. If the 1960s were a time of massive political, social, and economic change, the decade witnessed equally profound developments in the realm of popular culture, especially music for teens. In 1964, The Beatles exploded onto the American musical landscape, generating hysteria wherever they went. Two years later, The Monkees made an equally big impact on national entertainment, dominating both television ratings and radio airwaves. Taken collectively, these phenomena changed the nature of Top 40 songwriting in the United States while they simultaneously gave rise to what would become known as the "boy band." Writing about the hallmark traits or signature qualities of these groups, Sharon R. Mazzarella comments that the boy band formula is to combine somewhere between three and six (typically four or five) young, singing and dancing males; to have each represent a distinct personality type; to carefully choreograph their (individual and band) images as closely as their dance steps; and to mass-market them to an audience consisting mostly of preteen and teenage girls. (131)

Whether exemplified via past examples such as The Beatles and The Monkees or more recent ones such as the Backstreet Boys and One Direction, boy bands are known as much for being teen heartthrobs as for singing infectious pop songs—perhaps even more so.

The Outsiders was conceptualized, composed, and released against the backdrop of the rise of the boy bands. In what has become an oft-mentioned biographical detail, Hinton was only sixteen years old when the novel was released. Thus, she belonged to the demographic that was both the primary audience and the most enthusiastic fan base for these groups. It is difficult to imagine that anyone during the mid-1960s—adult or child, male or female, upper class or working class—could have been unaware of the mania generated by The Beatles or The Monkees, but least of all a teenager.

Perhaps not surprisingly given these details, *The Outsiders* can be seen as incorporating a variety of elements from the emerging formula for boy bands. The book features a group of young male protagonists whose diverse array of personalities echoes the range of individuals commonly featured in all-male pop singing troupes. In addition, the young men engage in a variety of pranks, mischief, and high jinks that mirror the impish antics of The Beatles and The Monkees. Moreover, the narrative spends a great deal of time describing the physical appearance of each character: his hair, eyes, face, and especially physique. The narrator-protagonist's middle brother, for example, is so handsome that his effect on women is described in a manner that recalls Beatlemania: "Soda attracted girls like honey draws flies" (9).

Examining *The Outsiders* in light of developments in popular music during the 1960s in general, and the emergence of boy bands in particular, places the book in fuller dialogue with the historical era in which it was written and released. Uncovering the ways in which Hinton's novel incorporates aspects of the boy band formula adds a new and previously overlooked dimension to both the book's initial attraction and its enduring appeal. While young readers, both in the 1960s and in the present day, are commonly seen as being drawn to *The Outsiders'* gritty portrayal of working-class life, they might also be attracted by its hunky portrayal of the handsome male protagonists. Hinton's novel certainly caters to adolescents' desires for more candid information about the world, but it doesn't hurt that it also caters to their budding sexuality.

For nearly fifty years, *The Outsiders* has been seen as ushering in a new era of literary realism for young adult readers. The pages that follow demonstrate that, contrary to previous assumptions, doing so did not mean wholly abandoning romance. In what has become an oft-quoted remark by the author about her motivation for writing her debut novel, she notes that "There was no realistic fiction being written about teenagers when I was in high school—everything was 'Mary-Jane Goes to The Prom'" ("Speaking" 185). While Hinton may have eschewed the fictional formula featuring teen girls attending high school dances, she may have been consciously or unconsciously tapping into another theme emerging during this era that likewise involved teen girls: all-male pop music groups.

"Underestimate sexual hysteria at your own peril": Boy Bands in American Popular Music and Youth Culture

In the apt words of David Smay, "Boy Bands rule the world and they always have" (par. 1). For over half a century, musical groups of this nature have been a fixture of American popular culture. Whether via past examples such as The Jackson 5, the Bay City Rollers, and Menudo, or more recent ones including New Kids on the Block, *NSYNC, and One Direction, all-male pop singing troupes have been the source of chart-topping songs as well as teenage crushes for generations. Indeed, for those who might be tempted to dismiss boy bands as inconsequential juvenile fads or insipid lyrical fluff, Smay warns: "you underestimate sexual hysteria at your own peril" (par. 1).

Boy bands have their origins in the burgeoning youth culture that emerged in the years following the Second World War. As Mazzarella has written, the phenomenon can be traced in many ways "to the doo-wop groups of the 1950s" (131). Performances by groups such as The Coasters, The Drifters, and The Ink Spots contained elements that would become hallmarks of the genre: they were composed of a handful of handsome young men, clad in matching outfits, singing catchy pop tunes usually about courtship and romance, and engaging in carefully choreographed dance routines. Yet the true birth of the boy-band phenomenon occurred in the decade that followed, with the advent of Beatlemania. While many rightly regard The Beatles as the progenitors of modern rock and roll music, they were also the originators of this new type of all-male pop singing group. Indeed, as Smay has flatly stated, "the Boy Band as we know it first emerges with the Beatles" (par. 5).

The Fab Four were able to achieve their tremendous popularity through a synergistic combination of style and substance, content and commercialism, catchy music, and even more clever marketing techniques. First and perhaps foremost, The Beatles attracted throngs of adoring young fan girls because of the type of music that they created. Not only did they release infectious, danceable pop tunes, but the majority of these songs were about courtship and romance. In Smay's apt words, in examples such as "Love Me Do," "She Loves You," and "I Want to Hold Your Hand," "their Pronoun Phase of early hits rarely rises above bubblegum standards lyrically" (par. 5). Enhancing the romantic appeal of these tunes, The Beatles themselves were handsome young men. However, they were not look-alike clones; each had a distinctive appearance and a unique style. Accordingly, one of the crucial differences separating boy bands such as The Beatles in their initial incarnation from the doo-wop groups of the 1950s was the way in which the members were marketed, advertised, and promoted. Unlike their progenitors, the Fab Four became fabulous in part because they capitalized on the different nature of each band member and used these details as a means to attract fans. As Andrew Sobel has written, "The individual Beatles became brands within the brand" (par. 18).

This feature is powerfully evidenced via the tremendous print coverage that the group received. In the mid-1960s, there was no shortage of newspaper articles and especially magazine stories about John, Paul, George, and Ringo. Profiles showcased their distinct personalities, individual likes and dislikes, and unique views of the world. *Tiger Beat* magazine, for example, released its first issue in September 1965. Created by former high school teacher Charles Laufer, the publication was dedicated to "Covering what mattered to girls from 8 to 14" years old (Martin 387). In Douglas Martin's summary, these subjects largely concerned handsome male heartthrobs from the realms of music, television, and film (387–88). The Beatles helped to create this phenomenon, and they also used it to their advantage. As Martin recounts, "In 1965 [Laufer] published a one-shot magazine crammed with Beatles photos. It sold 750,000 copies in two days. Later in 1965 he started *Tiger Beat*" (387). The Fab Four employed these platforms in transforming themselves from a homogenous band into a collection of diverse personalities targeting equally diverse niches of potential female fans. According to Smay, "it was their image as four complementary cuties that gave us the working model for Boy Bands ever after" (par. 5).

This new formula for success was quickly put to use. Throughout the remainder of the 1960s and continuing into the '70s, a variety of boy bands emerged on the American music scene. These groups (and their respective heydays) included The Monkees (1966–70), The Jackson 5 (1969–70), The Osmonds (1971–76), the Bay City Rollers (1973–76), and Menudo (1981–89).[1] The specific nature of these boy bands would vary. Not all of the groups, for example, contained only four members; exceptions included The Jackson 5 and the British trio "Bros." In addition, some boy bands formed of their own volition, like the Bay City Rollers, while others were assembled by producers, as in the case of The Monkees. Furthermore, the specific type or style of pop music that they played varied: The Jackson 5's sound was heavily influenced by R&B, while Menudo released music that had a Latin flair.

These differences aside, one aspect of boy bands both during the 1960s and in the present day has remained the same: they are known as much for their romantic appeal as for their hit songs. As Maura Johnston has written, "for young people trying to figure out the thorny world of sexuality, the boy band can serve as a sort of palette, a way to safely work out the boundaries of love and lust" (par. 6). In everything from the lyrics to their songs to their own dreamy good looks, boy bands provide a benign arena in which to experiment with romance. Heterosexual adolescent girls—not to mention homosexual adolescent boys—can indulge in romantic infatuation without assuming any of the physical or emotional risks. Boy bands, therefore, serve an important psychosexual purpose. In the words of Kristin Tillotson, "Whether they form organically or are manufactured in a pop-cultural petri dish," they serve as the transition between abstract and actual romance as well as between intimate relationships that are merely imagined and those that are experienced (par. 5).

As even this brief overview demonstrates, whether or not one is a fan of boy bands one must recognize that they have exerted undeniable power over popular music and especially youth culture in the United States. For more than fifty years, all-male pop singing groups have dominated both the record charts and the hearts of the nation's teenagers. As one Web site dedicated to the phenomenon asserts, "It's hard to imagine the music industry without boy bands" ("Top 10" par. 1). It is equally difficult to imagine adolescence without them. Beginning with Beatlemania in the 1960s and extending through the hysteria over One Direction in the 2010s, "boy bands have become a cornerstone" of youth culture in the United States (Mazzarella 132). They constitute a common feature of growing up and especially of coming of age—socially, psychologically, and sexually.

From Bubblegum to Sodapop: *The Outsiders* and the Boy Band Formula

In the Frequently Asked Questions section on her Web site, Hinton reveals that she began writing *The Outsiders* in 1965. By this point, Beatlemania had thoroughly permeated the American popular music scene and, especially, youth culture. After making their debut on

---

The Ed Sullivan Show on 9 February 1964, the Fab Four had become fixtures not simply on the radio, but in film and on television as well. Indeed, The Beatles were seemingly everywhere in 1965: they starred in their second feature-length film, *Help!*; they had a record-setting six songs—"Eight Days a Week," "Ticket to Ride," "Help!," "Yesterday," "Day Tripper," and "We Can Work It Out"—reach number one on the US pop charts; they released their sixth studio album, *Rubber Soul*; and they even appeared as a weekly animated cartoon show (McKinney 51–85).

The following year, in which Hinton continued to compose and edit *The Outsiders*, saw another landmark in Beatles history. In August 1966, the group released a new album, *Revolver*, which included the hit songs "Eleanor Rigby" and "Good Day Sunshine." Moreover, by year's end, The Beatles would add two more number one singles to their already impressive catalog of hits: "Paperback Writer" and "Yellow Submarine." By this point, any radio station in the United States that played popular music—including those in Tulsa, Oklahoma, where Hinton was living—routinely featured songs by The Beatles (McKinney 86–177). If the budding author listened to the radio at any point while working on her manuscript, it is likely that a song by the group was literally playing in the background.[2]

Of course, The Beatles were not the only all-male pop music troupe to provide the possible soundtrack to Hinton's composition of *The Outsiders*. In a powerful indication of both the commercial success and the cultural influence of the Fab Four, within one year of their appearance on *The Ed Sullivan Show* they had given rise to an imitation group. Matthew Stahl reports that "The Monkees were formed in 1965 by two young television producers who pitched the idea of a weekly comedy TV show featuring a young band having wacky, surreal, intertextual adventures that would trade on and draw its inspiration from Richard Lester's 1964 Beatles film *A Hard Day's Night*" (310). The television show debuted in 1966 and ran for two years. Meanwhile, The Monkees were even more successful as a band. They "had several hit records, [and] they toured the US, Europe and Australia" (Stahl 310).

The Outsiders was not simply written and released amid massive transformations in popular music during the 1960s, but engaged with those events. In a detail that is difficult to see as merely coincidental, both the first and the most frequent references to a musical group are to The Beatles. In the opening paragraph of Chapter 3, Ponyboy reflects on the similarities and differences between his friends and Cherry Valance and her crowd: "It seemed funny to me that Socs—if these girls were any example—were just like us. They liked the Beatles and thought Elvis Presley was out, and we thought the Beatles were rank and that Elvis was tuff, but that seemed the only difference to me" (37). Then, near the end of the book, such references to popular music recur. As the Socs begin to arrive for the big rumble, Ponyboy muses, "They looked like they were all cut from the same piece of cloth: clean-shaven with semi-Beatle haircuts, wearing striped or checkered shirts with light-red or tan-colored jackets or madras ski jackets. They could have just as easily been going to the movies as to a rumble" (141). In these examples, popular music is used as an index of aesthetic taste and, more importantly, as a marker of sociocultural identity. Yet while Ponyboy likens members of the rival gang to The Beatles at several points in the novel, it is his group, the greasers, that possesses an array of traits commonly associated with all-male pop singing troupes such as The Beatles. From their distinctive personality types and playful camaraderie to their crush-worthy looks and even their penchant for mischief, the greasers are patterned in many ways after signature features of boy bands.

The Outsiders begins by naming an undeniable teen idol of the 1960s: "When I stepped out into the bright sunlight from the darkness of the movie house, I had only two things on my mind: Paul Newman and a ride home" (1). As Tom McDonough has written, "The 1960s would bring Paul Newman into superstar status, as he became one of the most popular actors of the decade" (par. 2). Portraying young rebels in such films as *The Hustler* (1961), *Hud* (1963), and *Cool Hand Luke* (1967), Newman earned him Academy Award nominations for Best Actor, while his boyish good looks made him a Hollywood heartthrob for millions of young girls and his self-confident swagger provided a role model for their male counterparts. Newman's physical attractiveness is far from inconsequential to *The Outsiders*. On the contrary, Ponyboy both notices and envies it. "I was wishing that I looked like Paul Newman," he reflects as he leaves the theater, "he looks tough and I don't" (1). That said, Hinton's narrator-protagonist goes on to console himself with the thought that "I guess my own looks aren't so bad" (1). Over the next several sentences, Ponyboy provides a detailed description of his appearance: "I have light-brown, almost-red hair and greenish-gray eyes" (1). Not satisfied with this matter-of-fact accounting, he goes on to provide additional details: "My hair is longer than a lot of boys wear theirs, squared off in back and long at the front and sides, but I am a greaser and most of my neighborhood rarely bothers to get a haircut. Besides, I look better with long hair" (1). A few pages later, Ponyboy returns to the subject of his appearance, this time commenting on his physique: "I'm kind of small for fourteen even though I have a good build" (4).

Ponyboy also devotes a great deal of time, attention, and detail to the physical appearance of his two older brothers and the other greasers. As James C. McKinley observes, a key facet of boy bands is that the members "have distinct hairstyles and are deemed by their fans to be cute in different ways . . . part of the fun is having a favorite member to pine for" (par. 7). This feature is certainly true of the six young men who form the central characters of *The Outsiders*. Not only do Darry, Sodapop, Dally, Johnny, and Two-Bit possess markedly different physical features, they are also described in a manner that suggests that they are "cute in different ways." Readers learn, for example, that Two-Bit "was about six feet tall, stocky in build, and very proud of his long rusty-colored sideburns" (9–10). Meanwhile, Dally "had an elfish face, with high cheekbones and a pointed chin, small, sharp animal teeth, and ears like a lynx" (10). In addition, "His hair was almost white it was so blond, and he didn't like haircuts, or hair oil either, so it fell over his forehead in wisps and kicked out in the back in tufts and curled behind his ears and along the nape of his neck" (10). By contrast, Johnny looks remarkably different. As Ponyboy explains: "He was the youngest, next to me, smaller than the rest, with a slight build. He had big black eyes in a dark tanned face; his hair was jet-black and heavily greased and combed to the side, but it was so long that it fell in shaggy bangs across his forehead" (11). Ponyboy's eldest brother, Darry, is physically distinct from both Johnny and Dally. Readers learn that "Darry is six-feet-two, and broad-shouldered and muscular. He has dark-brown hair that kicks out in front and a slick cowlick in the back—just like Dad's—but Darry's eyes are his own. He's got eyes that are like two pieces of pale blue-green ice. They've got a determined set to them, like the rest of him. He looks older than twenty—tough, cool, and smart" (6–7).

At numerous points, Ponyboy's descriptions of the physical appearance of the greaser gang get so lengthy and detailed that they go far beyond the purpose of providing mere character portraits; instead, they begin to suggest the write-ups in teen idol magazines such as *Tiger Beat*. This aspect or quality of Hinton's novel is perhaps most evident in the presentation of Sodapop. In a lengthy passage, Ponyboy's middle brother is described as a bona fide hunk:

> Soda is handsomer than anyone else I know. Not like Darry—Soda's movie-star kind of handsome, the kind that people stop on the street to watch go by. He's not as tall as Darry, and he's a little slimmer, but he has a finely drawn, sensitive face that somehow manages to be reckless and thoughtful at the same time. He's got dark-gold hair that that he combs back—long and silky and straight—and in the summer the sun bleaches it to a shining wheat-gold. His eyes are dark brown—lively, dancing, recklessly laughing eyes that can be gentle and sympathetic one moment and blazing with anger the next. (7–8)

In these and other passages, Ponyboy doesn't want his readers merely to get a mental image of what the greasers look like; he wants the audience to see them as dreamboats. Michele Landsberg, in one of the few negative reviews of Hinton's novel when it was first published, described *The Outsiders* as being written in the style of "fan-magazine prose" (qtd. in Cart 50). While Cart deems this assessment "a bit harsh," he concedes that the "phrase does accurately capture the tone of Ponyboy's gushing descriptions of the other boys" (50). Given the amount of time and attention the novel pays to the physical attributes of its central characters, Cart concludes that "Hinton herself . . . obviously had an adolescent crush on most of the boys she created" (51).[3]

When Ponyboy moves away from the outward appearance of the greasers and begins describing their inner personalities, the similarities to boy bands continue. One defining hallmark of all-male pop singing groups is that they all possess "very distinct personalities" ("5 Kinds," par. 1). This characteristic originated with The Beatles. As Heather Jones and Emily Maltby have written: "While the lads quickly distanced themselves from their largely fabricated image as mop-topped Beatlemania-inspiring dreamboats, their blueprint for a successful boy band—smart one (John Lennon), cute one (Paul McCartney), quiet one (George Harrison) and funny one (Ringo Starr)—lives on" (par. 1). This general formula has been modified slightly over the years. Most discussions of the constitutive personalities for boy bands now name five or even six types. Some critics add the "bad boy" or "rebel," whose origins can be traced in many ways to the popularity of Mick Jagger from The Rolling Stones; others list the "older brother" figure, a wholesome, conservative carry-over from earlier doo-wop singers such as The Four Seasons' Frankie Valli. Whether an all-male musical group is composed of just three of these types or all six of them, they draw from these ingredients. As Jones and Maltby rightly note, "With few substitutions, [this is] the formula that keeps on winning" (par. 1).

The personality types of the six young men who constitute the greasers exactly match those of a boy band. First, there is Ponyboy, who occupies the role of "the smart one." Hinton's narrator-protagonist establishes this trait about himself on the second page of the novel, revealing that "nobody in our gang digs movies and books the way I do" (2). At numerous points throughout the novel, Ponyboy mentions various texts that he is either currently reading or has recently read. In examples ranging from lengthy Victorian tomes such as *Great Expectations* (15) and Jack London's naturalistic novels (143) to works of popular fiction such as Harold Robbins's *The Carpetbaggers* (177) and poems such as Robert Frost's

"Nothing Gold Can Stay" (77, 178), his bibliophilia forms the basis for the literary allusions that appear in the text. Moreover, Ponyboy does not occupy the role of "the smart one" in *The Outsiders* simply because he is bookish. As Hinton makes sure that readers know, he is also exceedingly intelligent. While talking with Cherry, Ponyboy reveals that he is a freshman in high school, even though he is only fourteen, because "I got put up a year in grade school" (23).

If Ponyboy serves as "the smart one," then his middle brother Sodapop occupies another essential boy band archetype, "the cute one" or, as he is also sometimes known, "the heartthrob." As one Web site explains, this boy band figure is "the one who was put there to draw the Squee of millions of adoring teenage girls (at least, the most Squee)" ("Boy Band," par. 4). Not only does Ponyboy spend a great deal of time describing Soda's physical attractiveness, but he also makes repeated references to how the girls find his brother irresistible. Indeed, Hinton's narrator-protagonist remarks in the opening chapter, "I wondered how he could stand being so handsome. Then I sighed" (18). Then, a few pages later, Cherry reiterates this observation: "Man, your brother is one doll" (23).

Ponyboy's eldest brother, Darry, embodies another important boy band figure: that of "the older brother." Although this type does not appear in every all-male pop group, when he does he is the "cool, reassuring figure that the girls can relate to" ("Boy Band," par. 4). While Darry is exceedingly smart and also exceedingly hunky, his primary role and even main identity in *The Outsiders* is as an older brother, both literally and figuratively. First and foremost, when their parents die unexpectedly in a car accident, Darry becomes the legal guardian of his two young brothers, forgoing college and getting a job working as a roofer to support them (6). Not content with being the protective, responsible, and supportive older brother for his siblings, Darry also serves this function for the other members of the greasers, for whom he is "the unofficial leader, since he kept his head best" (89). Through these and other examples, Darry embodies Jill Tooley's overview of the "older brother type" in all-male pop singing groups: "How could we forget about the slightly older band member who looked out for everyone else? The older brother type wasn't the most popular guy in the group, but he was responsible and kind-hearted" (par. 10).

Whereas only some boy bands have an older brother type, all of them have a figure who is "the quiet one" or "the shy one." This position sometimes overlaps with the smart one, but in many cases it is embodied by a separate individual. According to one commentator, the boy band member who occupies this role has "the cutest baby face and as much as you know he's traveled the world and experienced way more than you in life, you just can't help wanting to take care of him" ("5 Kinds," par. 3). Johnny Cade fits this description in *The Outsiders*. He is the figure who seems helpless and whom the other greasers want to protect and even nurture. Indeed, as Ponyboy openly admits, "He was the gang's pet, everyone's kid brother" (12). The reason why Johnny is so shy and the other greasers feel so protective of him is easy to understand. As readers learn, "His father was always beating him up, and his mother ignored him, except when she was hacked off at something, and then you could hear her yelling at him clear down at our house. I think he hated that worse than getting whipped" (12). Given this brutal home life, "If it hadn't been for the gang, Johnny would never have known what love and affection are" (12). Indeed, lest Hinton's readers might not see this shy character as sufficiently adorable, Ponyboy says of Johnny: "If you can picture a little dark puppy that has been kicked too many times and is lost in a crowd of strangers, you'll have Johnny" (11).

One of the original boy band personality types is also one of the most perennially popular: "the joker" or, as he is sometimes known, "the class clown." As Tooley explains, "Every group had a fun-loving guy who cracked jokes and played an occasional prank on other members. That's not to say he never got down to business, but rather that he liked to enjoy the lighter side of things" (par. 9). Once again, *The Outsiders* contains a character who fits this role and serves this purpose: Two-Bit Mathews, whom Ponyboy describes as "the oldest of the gang and the wisecracker of the bunch. . . . He had gray eyes and a wide grin, and he couldn't stop making funny remarks to save his life" (9–10). Although Two-Bit's actual name is Keith, he has acquired the nickname because "You couldn't shut up that guy; he always had to get his two-bits worth in" (10). In a powerful demonstration of how "Life was one big joke to Two-Bit" (10), Ponyboy reveals that his penchant for wisecracking knows no limits: "he was always smarting off to the cops. He really couldn't help it. Everything he said was so irresistibly funny that he just had to let the police in on it to brighten up their dull lives" (10). On numerous occasions, Two-Bit's humor injects some much-needed levity into the group and their situation. Near the end of the novel, for example, as the greasers prepare for the big rumble against the Socs, "Two-Bit yelped, and nearly fell off the cabinet from laughing so hard. I had to grin, too. He saw things straight and made them into something funny" (113).

The final, but far from insignificant, boy band persona is that of the "bad boy" or "the rebel." As the name implies, this figure is subversive and edgy in ways that the other members are not. "The 5 Kinds of Boy Band Members" says about this persona that "He seems dangerous . . . and sometimes even looks like he could steal a car—or your heart—like it was no big deal" (par. 2). Of course, the character of Dallas "Dally" Winston in Hinton's novel matches this description. Ponyboy foregrounds this feature of his personality from the beginning, introducing Dally to readers in the following way: "His eyes were blue, blazing with ice, cold with a hatred of the world. Dally had spent three years on the wild side of New York and had been arrested at the age of ten. He was tougher than the rest of us—tougher, colder, meaner" (10). When Cherry Valance sees him in person at the drive-in, she echoes this assessment, remarking to Ponyboy and Johnny, "I've heard about Dallas Winston, and he looked as hard as nails and twice as tough" (26). Dally's reputation as a "bad boy" is far from a false public persona. As Ponyboy reveals, "They have a file on him down at the police station. He had been arrested, he got drunk, he rode in rodeos, lied, cheated, stole, rolled drunks, jumped small kids—he did everything" (11).

Boy bands, especially during the 1960s, have also been associated with a specific socioeconomic demographic. As Tim Sommer has documented, The Beatles were routinely cast in mainstream media coverage as "four sassy, young, working-class men" (par. 4). The Monkees, both in their song lyrics and on their television show, routinely presented themselves in the same way. The first line that Mike utters in the very first episode of the series, in fact, is "Well, the cupboard's bare and it's not about to get any fuller unless we play a gig" ("Royal Flush"). That said, even when the members of a boy band did not hail from a working-class background, they were linked with upward mobility. In a narrative that directly overlaps with the American Dream of success, members of all-male pop singing groups are plucked from the masses and rise to fame and fortune because of their talent, hard work, and ambition.

Of course, class dynamics loom large in the lives of Hinton's central characters. All of the young men who belong to the greasers hail from working-class backgrounds. Furthermore, the source of tension between the greasers and the members of the opposing gang, the Socials, arises largely from the difference in their class status. As Ponyboy comments about his neighborhood, "the warfare is between the social classes" (11).

The areas of overlap extend further, however. In yet another feature that likens Hinton's characters to members of a boy band, although they are all presented as hunky heartthrobs, they are not sexually intimidating. As Kristin Tillotson has written, "Boy bands are about as sexually suggestive as a teddy bear, and thus just as non-threatening, safely dreamy objects upon which to hurl unbridled— and unconsummated—affection. No 11-year-old wants to daydream about some bearded, cursing, pelvis-thrusting rocker—and her parents want that even less" (par. 10). These observations apply to seemingly every past and present all-male pop singing group, from The Beatles with their G-rated early singles such as "I Want to Hold Your Hand" to One Direction with their equally sweet chart-topping hits such as "What Makes You Beautiful."

All of the young men in *The Outsiders* can be seen in an analogous manner. Even though they may be members of a working-class street gang who carry switchblades and get into rumbles, they are not physically frightening, personally intimidating, or sexually threatening. Indeed, Hinton's characters act more like cuddly teddy bears than ferocious grizzlies. Although Dally is eighteen years old and Darry is twenty-one, Ponyboy never refers to any of his fellow greasers as "men." Instead, throughout the novel, he calls them "boys." In addition, these tough gang members are extremely sensitive, demonstrative, and emotive: they "constantly burst into tears, stroke each other's hair, or put their arms around each other or their heads in each other's laps and go to sleep" (Cart 51). As Cart has observed,

> all of these boys are even further softened by their names—almost all of them diminutives. Pony's older brother's given name may be Darrell [*sic*], but everyone calls him "Darry"; the toughest Greaser in the gang is Dallas, but everyone calls him "Dally." Of course, we also have Johnny, and since the name "Pony" can't be further diminished, Hinton adds "boy" to a name matched in silliness only by his older brother's: "Sodapop." (Cart 51)

Ponyboy's middle brother is especially chivalrous. Although his girlfriend is forced to leave town after becoming pregnant, Darry makes it clear that Soda is not the father: "When Sandy went to Florida . . . it wasn't Soda, Ponyboy. He told me he loved her, but I guess she didn't love him like he thought she did, because it wasn't him" (174). In spite of the young woman being impregnated by another man, Soda demonstrates his upstanding moral character by offering to do "the right thing": "He wanted to marry her anyway, but she just left" (174). Finally, while Ponyboy reports that Dally spoke "awful dirty" to Cherry and Marcia at the drive-in (20), none of his language is actually relayed in the text. This tactic not only allows the readers to mentally supply their own examples of what they consider "awful dirty" talk, but it also preserves Dally's image as a "bad boy" who is not actually all that bad.

One factor that enables both past and present boy bands to be sexually appealing yet unthreatening to adolescent girls is the exceedingly effeminate masculinity that they embody. As Tillotson has written, most members of all-male pop singing groups "have (or had) faces that are at most gender-neutral, some of them downright girlish, and they sing tenor, or even falsetto" (par. 9). Many boy bands, in spite of their seemingly singular focus on appealing to teenage female sexuality, contain strong homoerotic overtones. Judith Halberstam has commented on this phenomenon, writing about how these groups have "drawn our attention to the homoerotic subtext to much teen culture. Boy bands . . . produce and manage anxieties about gay modes of gender performance" (329).[4] All-male pop singing troupes have strong emotional bonds, and they are frequently photographed engaging in physical horseplay, with their arms draped over each other, with one guy being held up by the others, or with one member having playfully hopped on the back of a bandmate. In so doing, boy bands make visible the strong "homoerotic dynamics . . . between the boy performers" (Halberstam 329).

The Outsiders features boys who possess a nonthreatening, effeminate form of masculinity, and the book is also laden with homoerotic overtones. The central male characters frequently touch, cuddle, and express their affection for each other in intimate ways: "I looked through the door. Sodapop was giving Darry a back-rub," Ponyboy relates in the opening chapter (16). On the following page, readers learn that the narrator-protagonist and his middle brother do not simply sleep in the same bed, but snuggle together at night: "'You cold, Ponyboy?' 'A little,' I lied. Soda threw one arm across my neck" (17). When Ponyboy runs away with Johnny near the middle of the book, he longs for this physical intimacy and the sense of comfort and security that it brings. "I was sleepy and freezing to death," he remarks, "and I wanted to be home in bed, safe and warm under the covers with Soda's arm across me" (52). Soda and Darry likewise engage in intimate physical contact. While at the hospital after the church fire, Hinton's narrator-protagonist relays how, after "stretching out on the long bench, [Soda] put his head in Darry's lap and went to sleep" (101). Darry is less physically expressive with his youngest brother, but he still speaks to him in tender ways. When Ponyboy asks Darry whether he thinks the judge will split them up at the hearing near the end of the novel, his older brother responds, "I don't know, baby, I just don't know" (157).

These moments of emotional intimacy and displays of physical tenderness point to another broad quality about boy bands: their relational affiliation. Zara Kazi has discussed two major phenotypes for boy bands. In the first, and arguably original, model, the members are biologically related (3). Past examples such as The Osmond Brothers and The Jackson 5 along with more recent ones such as the Jonas Brothers and Hanson demonstrate both the popularity and the longevity of this trend. Yet while boy bands may have had their origins as "Brothers Bands," an alternative and what would come to be a far more common model for the composition of all-male pop singing groups quickly emerged: one in which the members are not biologically related, but teamed up out of their own volition— as with The Beatles—or because they were assembled by a music producer, as with The Monkees (9). Even when the members of boy bands are not biologically related, they commonly remark in articles and interviews that they have such a strong connection that they feel like family. In comments that have been uttered in various forms by numerous other all-male pop groups, Nicky Byrne from the Irish boy band Westlife said about his fellow group members: "We have become so close and we are like brothers" (Rowley).

The Outsiders draws on both of these models in its depiction of the greasers. Exactly half of the members of the gang hail from the same nuclear family—Ponyboy, Sodapop, and Darry are brothers— while Dally, Two-Bit, and Johnny are unrelated to them or to each other. Regardless, echoing the sentiments of many boy band members, Ponyboy notes that the bond that they share makes them feel like family: "We're almost as close as brothers; when you grow up in a tight-knit neighborhood like ours you get to know each other real well" (3).

Whether boy bands are composed of family members or of young men who are not biologically related, they are known for their engagement in pranks, goofy shenanigans, and mischief. Indeed, while most of these bands contain a member who is considered "the clown" or "the jokester," such antics are typically not confined to this individual. On the contrary, as one Web site dedicated to the boy band phenomenon explains, the group as a whole is known for "doing silly stuff . . . like riding bumper cars or having the ultimate pillow fight" ("5 Kinds," par. 3). The first feature-length film starring The Beatles, *A Hard Day's Night* (1964), highlighted this aspect of the group. The movie is a comedy that showcases the band's penchant for silly antics. For example, The Beatles goof around in the bathroom of their hotel, with George using shaving cream to draw a face on the mirror and John playing with toy submarines in the bathtub. Later, in perhaps the most famous scene from the film, The Beatles give a series of humorous and often nonsensical answers to reporters at a promotional party. When John is asked, "Tell me, how did you find America?" he responds with a deadpan "Turn left at Greenland." Likewise, Paul offers the following droll reply to the question, "Do you often see your father?": "No, actually, we're just good friends." Finally, when an interviewer inquires of Ringo, "Are you a mod or a rocker?" he shoots back with a clever portmanteau: "No, I'm a mocker."

While The Monkees emulated nearly every aspect of The Beatles—their music, their clothing, and even their hairstyles—they gave special significance to the former's penchant for comedic capers. The chorus of their television theme song, in fact, showcased the group's penchant for wacky behavior: "Hey, Hey, we're The Monkees / And people say we monkey around." Affirming this quality, the montage scene that plays during the opening credits presents the group engaging in a variety of goofy antics, including riding unicycles with training wheels, turning somersaults while frolicking in a field together, and wearing nightgowns while pushing Davy in a brass bed down a busy street.

Once again, *The Outsiders* can be placed in dialogue with this phenomenon. The greasers engage in a variety of high jinks over the course of the novel. For example, while at the drugstore with Johnny and Dally, Ponyboy reports, "We bought Cokes and blew the straws at the waitress" (19). Later, in a scene that recalls both the clever answers that The Beatles gave to reporters in *A Hard Day's Night* and the frequency with which The Monkees donned military uniforms for their pranks, Ponyboy tells the farmer in Windrixville who wonders why he is asking the location of Jay Mountain, "We're playing army and I'm supposed to report to headquarters there" (65). Finally, and perhaps most powerfully, the boys tease, goof around, and engage in shenanigans. In the opening chapter, for example, Two-Bit sneaks up behind Johnny and Ponyboy at the drive-in, startles them by pretending to be a Soc, and then delights in his prank, "grinning like a Chessy cat" (27).

Even the more serious forms of mischief in which the greasers engage—which include committing various acts of petty theft, participating in rumbles, and carrying switchblades—still do not make them seem dangerous. As Halberstam has written, from their origins, boy bands have participated in "socially acceptable forms of rebellion" (329). She goes on to point out, for example, that group names like the "*Backstreet* Boys" highlight this feature by "conjur[ing] up images of working-class youth" (329; emphasis in original). Much of the so-called delinquent behavior in *The Outsiders* is presented as harmless or, in some instances, even helpful. Ponyboy, for example, tells Cherry that a rumble in which the participants can use only their fists not only "isn't rough," it is enjoyable (29). As he explains, a fight of this nature "blows off steam better than anything" (29).[5]

The way in which the greasers traffic in the silliness commonly associated with boy bands such as The Beatles and The Monkees does more than simply connect Hinton's book with events in popular music. These elements also make the narrative's presentation of unsupervised young men roaming the streets as part of a tough gang more palatable. Much has been written about *The Outsiders* in relation to postwar concerns about the growing rate of juvenile delinquency in general and teenage gangs in particular. As I have remarked elsewhere, "unsupervised youths [who] roamed the streets either individually or in 'gangs' and engaged in an array of illicit and sometimes illegal activities, ranging from smoking, drinking, and racing cars to fighting, robbery and vandalism" were a subject of national concern and even anxiety after the Second World War (Abate 67). *The Outsiders* certainly connects with this issue. However, the way in which the greasers participate in the high jinks associated with boy bands complicates and even contradicts

---

this portrait. These details make Ponyboy, Johnny, and even Dally less frightening to adolescent readers. By showing them blowing straw wrappers, cracking jokes, and engaging in horseplay, Hinton smoothes the rough edges of these young men, transforming them from hardened juvenile delinquents into goofy harmless guys. In this way, the link that the greasers have to this feature of boy bands also undercuts the book's claims to unflinching social verisimilitude. At the very least, Hinton is using the benignity associated with groups such as The Monkees and The Beatles to make the edgier form of realism in her book more culturally palatable, socially acceptable, and—ultimately—commercially viable.[6]

At the same time, the overlap between the social bonds present in boy bands and among Hinton's greasers raises another, and even more radical, implication: that the teenage gangs of the postwar era may have played a role in the formation of boy bands.[7] With their working-class backgrounds, intense loyalty among members, and engagement in mischievous fun, groups such as The Monkees and The Beatles can be read as a sanitized version of the all-male gangs that became a focus of extensive media attention as well as widespread public anxiety in the postwar years. In this way, far from existing as separate sociocultural phenomena, the all-male gangs of the 1950s and the boy bands that emerged during the following decade may have occupied a complex feedback loop.

When *The Outsiders* is viewed in light of the growing popularity of boy bands during this era, the perceptions of a variety of additional, and seemingly unrelated, narrative elements change. For example, the greaser girls occupy a position very similar to that of groupies. Presented as sexually loose young women who follow the six protagonists around in hopes of becoming romantically involved with them, they closely mirror the girls who attempt to get backstage in the hopes of kissing—or engaging in further erotic activities with—their favorite musician. The greaser girls are so sexually perilous, in fact, that both Ponyboy and Johnny get a cautionary lecture about them that mirrors the ones often given to newly famous musicians by their managers, promoters, or handlers about getting involved with groupie girls. As Ponyboy relates,

Once, while Dallas was in reform school, Sylvia started hanging on to Johnny and sweet-talking him and Steve got hold of her and told her if she tried any of her tricks with Johnny he'd personally beat the tar out of her. Then he gave Johnny a lecture on girls and how a sneaking little broad like Sylvia would get him into a lot of trouble. As a result, Johnny never spoke to girls much, but whether that was because he was scared of Steve or because he was shy, I couldn't tell. (35)

The narrator-protagonist goes on to reveal, "I got the same lecture from Two-Bit after we'd picked up a couple of girls downtown one day . . . and he told me some stories that about made me want to crawl under the floor or something" (35).

The Soundtrack to Young Adult Literature: Boy Bands, *The Outsiders*, and the Rise of Youth Culture

In the United States, music has played a central role in the construction of youth culture in general and adolescence in particular. Grace Palladino, Thomas Hine, and Kelly Schrum have all documented how, beginning as early as the 1920s and accelerating rapidly in the decades following the end of the Second World War, teenagers used popular songs as a means to construct their own identity, form their own culture, and even generate their own lingo. In Hine's words, "Every outburst of youth culture has a soundtrack" (230). From dancing the Charleston to jazz in the 1920s, to jitterbugging to the swing bands of the 1940s, to enjoying the new sounds of rock 'n' roll in the 1950s, music was both a catalyst and a point of collection for emerging new forms of youth expression and identity (Schrum 97–127; Hine 194–95; Palladino 190–205).

During the 1960s, of course, boy bands participated in this phenomenon. Palladino devotes an entire chapter in her book *Teenagers: An American History* to Beatlemania. As she discusses, the throngs of adolescent girls screaming over the Fab Four embodied more than simply a new cultural fad; they signaled a paradigm shift in the national conceptions about youth and the societal construction of youth culture. The Beatles demonstrated "the power of baby-boom teenagers to turn 'youth culture' into a national phenomenon" (196).

The Fab Four's arrival shaped the identity of an entire generation, influencing their musical tastes, fashion trends, and popular slang. Even more significantly, Palladino notes, they marked the moment when "teenagers could set national trends" (198).

Popular music in general and boy bands such as the early Beatles in particular have long been seen as having a profound influence on youth and youth culture. Given the role that these elements play in Hinton's landmark novel, they may have also exerted a powerful, and heretofore overlooked, influence on the construction of young adult literature. Phrased in a different way, the historical simultaneity concerning the appearance of boy bands and the advent of young adult literature is no coincidence. These events emerged in tandem because they were produced by a similar set of sociocultural circumstances. Therefore, the way in which *The Outsiders* incorporates elements from the boy band formula invites a consideration of larger cultural, commercial, and creative parallels between the genre of young adult literature and the tradition of all-male pop singing groups. After all, both are publicly popular and economically successful, but both have also struggled for critical respectability and aesthetic esteem. Furthermore, both young adult literature and boy bands pivot on issues of authenticity and originality. The questions that critics commonly ask about these phenomena are remarkably similar: Are they innovative or imitative? Authentic or artificial? Driven by creative impulses or by commercial ones? As even this brief discussion suggests, the overlap between young adult literature and boy bands demonstrates the need for further scholarly examination of not only the possible connections but also the forms of cross-pollination between these two important features of American youth culture.

The Outsiders has long been seen as having a profound impact on popular culture for young people. After the publication of the novel in 1967, the literary themes, individual writing style, and narrative subject matter for adolescents changed irrevocably. Yet critics have sometimes seen this influence as working in only one direction. Claudia Durst Johnson, in comments that have been echoed by several other critics, remarks on the surprising lack of references to current events in Hinton's novel. "Although the setting for *The Outsiders* is roughly the mid-1960s," she writes, "the novel has more of a 1950s flavor because few of the concerns of the 1960s are mentioned. The Vietnam War, the Civil Rights movement, Women's Liberation, the sexual revolution, and the blossoming drug culture form no part of this narrative" (116). An awareness of the way in which the newly created formula for boy bands permeates *The Outsiders* changes the text's engagement with its original historical context. Far from omitting any references to sociocultural events from the 1960s, Hinton's narrative contains a tacit, but traceable, connection to at least one of them. The way in which the central characters in *The Outsiders* echo the boy band formula suggests that Hinton's text did not simply exert an influence on youth culture in the future; she was influenced by the happenings in her own era as well.

On 16 August 1966, The Monkees released their debut single, "Last Train to Clarksville." The song quickly soared to the top spot on the US pop charts and was featured on their self-titled first album. Roughly a year later, in *The Outsiders*, two young men hopped the first train to Windrixville. However unexpected and even unlikely, the novel's portrayal of a tough boy gang possesses a multifaceted kinship with that of the era's teddy bear-esque boy bands.

Notes

1. These dates are all taken from a chart that appears in Heather Jones and Emily Maltby's discussion of the history of boy bands, published in the digital edition of *Time* magazine.

2. That said, the year 1966 is also commonly regarded as the final one in the group's teenybopper-friendly "Beatlemania" period. In 1967, The Beatles released *Sgt. Pepper's Lonely Hearts Club Band*, a record that revamped the band's image as teen idols with its strong links to the hippie movement, the drug counterculture, and the antiwar protests. For more on this issue, see Kenneth Womack.

3. Of course, when Francis Ford Coppola made Hinton's novel into a feature-length film in 1983, his casting choices both echoed and extended the hunky nature of the six central male protagonists. As Michael Malone said of the movie, "It's significant that many of the

young men who played in Coppola's 1982 [*sic*] film of *The Outsiders* were to become adolescent idols within the next few years: [Matt] Dillon, Rob Lowe, Tom Cruise, Emilio Estevez, Patrick Swayze" (278). This aspect of the movie was clear when it was released. An article that appeared in *People* magazine about Coppola's production, for example, reads more like coverage of Beatlemania than a discussion of a cinematic adaptation of a critically acclaimed novel by an Academy Award-winning director: "The scene: Lone Star Elementary School in Fresno, Calif. Hordes of teenage girls are howling for Leif Garrett, Patrick Swayze, Matt Dillon and other heartthrobs starring in Francis Coppola's *The Outsiders*. When the fab hunks emerge from their tour of the school library, the girls mob them, requesting autographs and stealing kisses" (McHugh 125). Even the general age of the movie's fans echoed that of boy bands: "'How old are they?' Garrett, 21, wonders aloud after a blizzard of passionate smooches. 'Their bodies say 12 and their kisses say 18'" (125). A number of reviews of Coppola's version of *The Outsiders* lamented that the target audience for the film was not young adults but adolescents. "It's a true kids' movie," David Denby sneered in his review in *New York* magazine, "thirteen-year-olds should love it" (73). David Ansen's assessment of the film for *Newsweek*, which bears the derisive title "Coppola Courts the Kiddies," is similar: "*The Outsiders* is unashamedly a movie for kids. Fourteen-year-olds will love it" (74). Coppola's film is still widely known and beloved, not merely because it is such a skillful adaptation of Hinton's novel, but also because it features such handsome actors. A number of customer reviews posted on Amazon.com in just the past two years, for example, call attention to the "CUTE all-star cast" (Andrew par. 1), gush about "all the 80's hunks [*sic*]" (CC par. 1), and gleefully note that "all the actors are really attractive!!" (jen par. 1). Finally, but far from insignificantly, when Coppola released the "Complete Novel" edition of the movie in 2005, he changed the soundtrack. Whereas the original theatrical release contained "a dramatic orchestral score by Coppola's famous musician father, Carmine Coppola," the "Complete Novel" edition "includes rock and roll music from the period—specifically a number of songs by Elvis Presley" (Kwiatkowski par. 3). Although the new soundtrack does not include any songs by The Beatles—or any other boy bands from the era, for that matter—this change reveals the important role that popular music from the era played in Hinton's story. As Dennis Kwiatkowski has written, "It had always been Coppola's intention to use the Presley songs, music the characters in the film would have actually listened to" (par. 3).

4. As both Gayle Wald and Halberstam have written, boy band fandom also ironically contains an undercurrent of lesbianism. In Halberstam's words, "there is something all too powerful about a nearly hysterical audience of teen girls screaming and crying together" (329). For more on this issue, see Wald, as well as the *Studio 360* "American Icons" episode on WNYC about *The Outsiders*, which discusses the book's erotic dynamics for lesbian readers.

5. A final feature of boy bands is that many engage in carefully choreographed dance routines. As Jessica Holland has commented, in past groups such as The Osmonds and The Jackson 5 as well as more recent ones including the Backstreet Boys and *NSYNC, synchronized moves—both in music videos and onstage during live performances—are a key feature of performing style. A variation on this feature appears in *The Outsiders*. While Hinton's characters never engage in a choreographed dance number, they do indulge in physically complex, carefully practiced, and often precisely timed acrobatics. As the group leaves the Curtis home on the way to the big rumble near the end of the book, for example, "Leaping as he went off the steps, Darry turned a somersault in mid-air, hit the ground, and bounced up before Soda could catch him" (135). This impressive display does not end there: "'Yeah!' screamed Soda as he too did a flying somersault off the steps. He flipped up to walk on his hands and then did a no-hands cartwheel across the yard *to beat Darry's performance*. The excitement was catching. . . . Steve went running across the lawn in flying leaps, stopped suddenly, and flipped backward" (135–36; my emphasis). Ponyboy explains the origin of this shared skill: "We could all do acrobatics because Darry had taken a course at the Y and then spent a whole summer teaching us everything he'd learned on the grounds that it might come in handy in a fight" (136). A variety of past and present critics have commented that it seems odd that young men who are allegedly so tough would engage in such preposterous antics (Cart 50–60). However, the way in which *The Outsiders* echoes the boy band formula provides a possible explanation for this element. The

greasers' engagement in acrobatics may be out of step with their identity as a tough neighborhood gang, but it is wholly in keeping with their kinship to all-male pop singing groups.

6. I am indebted to an anonymous outside reader of this manuscript for pushing my thinking in this direction.

7. Again, I would like to thank an anonymous reader for this insight.

Works Cited

Abate, Michelle Ann. "'Always Gettin' in Trouble': The *Li'l Tomboy* Comic Book Series, the Good Female Consumer, and the Fifties Bad Girl." *Journal of Graphic Novels and Comics* 6.1 (2015): 59–90.

"American Icons: The Outsiders." *Studio 360*. New York Public Radio. WNYC, New York. 4 May 2012. 1 Oct. 2016. <www.wnyc.org/story/205279-american-icons-outsiders/>.

Andrew, S. "It sure ain't the book, but CUTE all-star cast. . . ." Customer review. *Amazon.com*. Amazon.com, Inc., 31 Mar. 2015. 15 Nov. 2015.

Ansen, David. "Coppola Courts the Kiddies." *Newsweek* 4 April 1983: 74.

"Boy Band." All the Tropes Wiki. *Wikia: Home of the Fandom*. Wikia, Inc., 1 Oct. 2016. <allthetropes.wikia.com/wiki/Boy_Band>.

Brien, Alan. "Childsplay." *New Statesman* 19 Aug. 1983: 29.

Campbell, Patty. "*The Outsiders*, Fat Freddy, and Me." *Horn Book Magazine* (Mar./April 2003): 177–83.

Cart, Michael. *From Romance to Realism: 50 Years of Growth and Change in Young Adult Literature*. New York: HarperCollins, 1996.

CC. "80's cool movie." Customer review. *Amazon.com*. Amazon.com, Inc., 23 Oct. 2015. 15 Nov. 2015.

Daly, Jay. *Presenting S. E. Hinton*. Boston: Twayne, 1987.

Denby, David. "Romance for Boys." *New York* 4 April 1983: 73.

"The 5 Kinds of Boy Band Members—Who's Your Type?" Posted by melanieann. *Gurl.com*. 19 Nov. 2012. 30 Oct. 2015. <www.gurl.com/2012/11/19/boy-band-personality-survey/>.

Halberstam, Judith. "'What's That Smell?' Queer Temporalities and Subcultural Lives." *International Journal of Cultural Studies* 6.3 (2003): 313–33.

A Hard Day's Night. Dir. Richard Lester. Perf. John Lennon, Paul McCartney, George Harrison, Ringo Starr. Proscenium Films, 1964. DVD.

Hine, Thomas. *The Rise and Fall of the American Teenager.* New York: HarperCollins, 1999.

Hinton, S. E. *The Outsiders.* 1967. New York: Penguin, 1995.

_____. "Teen-Agers Are for Real." *New York Times Book Review* 27 Aug. 1967: BR 14.

Holland, Jessica. "The Boy Band's Eternal Allure." *The National.* 9 Dec. 2010. 1 Oct. 2016. www.thenational.ae/arts-culture/music/the-boy-bands-eternal-allure.

jen. "A great Film." Customer review. *Amazon.com.* Amazon.com, Inc., 14 Oct. 2014. 15 Nov. 2015.

Johnson, Claudia Durst. *Youth Gangs in Literature.* Westport, CT: Greenwood, 2004.

Johnston, Maura. "The Enduring Allure of Boy Bands." *New York Times* 2 Dec. 2012.

Jones, Heather, and Emily Maltby. "The Boy-Band Blueprint: From the Beatles to One Dirction, all the young dudes are 'NSync." *Time* 6 Feb. 2014.

Kazi, Zara. " Evolution of the Modern Day Boy Band." *Prezi.com.* 4 Feb. 2013. 30 Oct. 2015. <https://prezi.com/0duxb-2dfj9x/evolution-of-the-modern-day-boy-band/>.

Kwiatkowski, Dennis. "Review—The Outsiders: The Complete Novel (DVD—2005)." *Celluloid Dreams.* 2005. 1 May 2016. <www.celluloiddreams.net/id22.html/>.

Library of Congress. "Youth in the Civil Rights Movement." 3 Nov. 2015. <https://www.loc.gov/collections/civil-rights-history-project/articles-and-essays/youth-in-the-civil-rights-movement/>.

Malone, Michael. "Tough Puppies." *The Nation* 8 Mar. 1986: 276–80.

Martin, Douglas. "Charles Laufer—Founding *Tiger Beat*: The Inside Story." *The Obits 2012: The New York Times Annual.* Ed. William McDonald. New York: Workman Publishing, 2011. 387–88.

Mazzarella, Sharon R. "Boy Bands." *Encyclopedia of Children, Adolescents, and the Media.* Vol. 1. Ed. Jeffrey Jensen Arnett. London: Sage, 2007. 131–32.

McDonough, Tom. "Paul Newman—Biography." *International Movie Database*. 18 Nov. 2015. <www.imdb.com/name/nm0000056/bio?ref_=nm_ov_bio_sm/>.

McHugh, Jim. "Fresno Teenagers Get an Insider's Look at the Matt Dillon Movie They Inspired." *People* 4 April 1983: 125.

McKinley, James C., Jr. "Boy Bands Are Back, Wholesome or Sexy." *New York Times* 24 Mar. 2014.

McKinney, Devin. *Magic Circles: The Beatles in Dream and History*. Boston: Harvard UP, 2004.

The Monkees. NBC. 1966–1968. *YouTube.com*. YouTube, LLC. Television series.

The Monkees. "Last Train to Clarksville." *The Monkees*. RCA, 1966.

Palladino, Grace. *Teenagers: An American History*. New York: Basic, 1996.

Rowley, Eddie. *Westlife on Tour: Inside the World's Biggest Boy Band*. London: Ebury, 2002.

"Royal Flush." *The Monkees*. NBC. 12 Sept. 1966. *YouTube.com*. YouTube, LLC.

Schrum, Kelly. *Some Wore Bobby Sox: The Emergence of Teenage Girls' Culture, 1920–1945*. New York: Palgrave Macmillan, 2004.

Smay, David. "A Brief History of Boy Bands." *Bubblegum Music*. 25 April 2006. 30 Oct. 2015. <bubblegum-music.com/a-brief-history-of-boy-bands/>.

Sobel, Andrew. "The Beatles Principles." *Strategy + Business Magazine*. 28 Feb. 2006. 15 Feb. 2016. <www.strategy-business.com/article/06104?gko=8e481/>.

Sommer, Tim. "For Your (Re)Consideration: The Social and Cultural Roots of the Beatles." *The Observer*. 13 Aug. 2015. 1 May 2016. <observer.com/2015/08/for-your-reconsideration-the-social-and-cultural-roots-of-the-beatles/>.

"Speaking with S. E. Hinton." *The Outsiders*. By S. E. Hinton. New York: Penguin, 1995. 182–86.

Stahl, Matthew. "Authentic Boy Bands on TV? Performers and Impresarios in *The Monkees* and *Making the Band*." *Popular Music* 21.3 (2002): 307–29.

Tillotson, Kristin. "How One Direction and New Kids Give Us That Fan Girl Feeling." *Star Tribune.* 15 July 2013. 1 Oct. 2016. <www.startribune.com/how-one-direction-and-new-kids-give-us-that-fangirl-feeling/215232201/>.

Tooley, Jill. "Boy Bands and Teamwork: Balancing Diverse Personality Types in the Office." 30 Oct. 2015. <http://www.qualitylogoproducts.com/blog/boy-bands-teamwork-balancing-personality-types/>.

"Top 10 Most Successful Boy Bands of All Time." *Top10HQ.* 2016. 21 Sept. 2016. <www.top10hq.com/top-10-successful-boy-bands-time/>.

Wald, Gayle. "I Want It That Way: Teenybopper Music and the Girling of Boy Bands." *Genders* 35 (2002): n. pag.

Womack, Kenneth. *Reading The Beatles: Cultural Studies, Literary Criticism, and the Fab Four.* Albany: State U of New York P, 2010.

Copyright © 2017. Children's Literature Association. This article first appeared in *Children's Literature Association Quarterly*, Volume 42, Issue 1, Spring 2017, pages 43-64.

Greasers and Gallants: Writing Realism, Romanticism, and Identity in *The Outsiders*⸺

Paige Gray

Not long after the climactic moment in S. E. Hinton's *The Outsiders* (1967)—when the shy, sixteen-year-old "greaser" Johnny kills Bob, "the handsome Soc" (64)—Johnny and Ponyboy find themselves hiding out in a dilapidated, abandoned church in rural Oklahoma. It's a temporary space of escape for the two young greasers until they figure out what they "can do about this mess" (68). Though these two sensitive teenagers have been thrown into a dark situation that reflects the very real socioeconomic tumult faced by many American youths in the late 1960s, they still cling to and understand their reality in terms of the romantic. We see this when Johnny makes one trip for essential supplies during their hideout period, and he comes back with bread, baloney, and a copy of Margaret Mitchell's idealized saga of the American South, *Gone with the Wind*. Ponyboy eyes Johnny's purchase hungrily, proclaiming with surprised delight: "A paperback copy of *Gone with the Wind*! How'd you know I always wanted one?" (79).

Mitchell's romanticized narrative of the Civil War and Reconstruction—a text now rendered highly problematic through a contemporary critical lens given its handling of slavery and race—not only sustains the two boys during their long hours of simply waiting out time; it also concurrently reflects and constructs their ideas of the world and themselves. Indeed, you could argue that *The Outsiders* is a story *about* storytelling, as we discover at the novel's conclusion that the preceding pages have all been part of Ponyboy's writing assignment for Mr. Syme's English class. And as we find throughout his narrative, Ponyboy employs and reconfigures the familiar tropes of Southern gallantry that he absorbs from *Gone with the Wind* to craft his personal tale. Out of the raw, painful material that constitutes much of his young life, Ponyboy creates something that provides order, optimism, and meaning.

Literary scholars often refer to *The Outsiders* in terms of a generic realism, or more specifically, as part of the "new realism" movement in young adult literature of the late 1960s and 1970s. Yet *The Outsiders*, while dealing with the reality of violence and poverty, relies on an ideology of hope and creative invention. The novel builds its sense of new realism on the foundation of *idealism*— it evokes tropes of romance and adventure fiction through both its structures and plot devices and through references to texts such as *Gone with the Wind*. Ultimately, *The Outsiders* exposes the narrative quality of identity through the frame of Ponyboy's English assignment and suggests young people have the agency to determine their own stories.

In his entry for "Young Adult" in *Keywords for Children's Literature*, Lee A. Talley articulates what has become a truism about *The Outsiders* and its author. Quoting material from a 1967 Hinton interview, Talley writes that "Hinton calls for a young adult literature fashioned against romance—those novels about the 'horse-and-the-girl-who-loved-it' and well as the 'fairyland of proms and double dates'" (231). Certainly, Hinton chides against the formulaic mid-century narratives of privileged teenage puppy love. But the term "romance" encompasses more than stories about love and infatuation. In addition to its association with the nineteenth-century Romanticism movement that highlighted the power of imagination and was a cultural response to the reason-focused Enlightenment, "romance" also has roots in medieval tales of heroic adventures and often carries with it an underlying sense of idealism. In essence, romance and Romantic ideals bring with them a core belief in the human capacity to create from the imagination—to story-tell, to narrate. And while Hinton introduces multi-dimensional characters who question and confront the inequities of America's social-class structure system, she doesn't abandon imagination and idealism. In fact, Hinton anchors her realism in them.

Literary realism, as children's literature scholars Carrie Hintz and Eric L. Tribunella explain, "is notoriously difficult to pin down," though it can be broadly understood as being "grounded in the concept of mimesis, a Greek term that refers to imitation or representation of the physical world" (321). Simply put, realism is a collection of strategies to depict "the real," however we chose to define what "the real" is. In terms of young adult literature—a specific publishing category of fiction whose beginnings many scholars symbolically mark with the publication of *The Outsiders*—Hintz and Tribunella write that, in the latter half of the twentieth century, realism as a literary approach took on new significance, since literature written for young people often avoided depicting painful or traumatic events. The new realism of young adult literature introduced plotlines that featured issues such as substance abuse, sex, racism, teen pregnancy, and disability, among others. "These books often feature common conventions or tropes such as urban settings, a focus on the working class, and the use of vernacular (or slang)," say Hintz and Tribunella, further articulating:

> The new realism in children's and young adult fiction arose partly as a response to the social upheaval and change of the 1960s and 1970s, as adolescent readers in particular sought fiction that spoke to their immediate experiences—a concern for "relevance" and a rebellion against idealized and sanitized images of childhood and teenage life. (321)

From its opening pages, *The Outsiders* appeals to the "immediate experiences" of a more "real" subset of young people through the first-person voice of fourteen-year-old Ponyboy Curtis, a narrative choice that permits readers a sense of closeness and psychological interiority. Ponyboy feels familiar, like someone we would possibly meet (or have met) in junior high or high school—but certainly not someone whom we would expect to be the hero of a young person's novel, at least not in the late 1960s. The story's emotional verisimilitude may result from the fact that Hinton *was* a young person when she composed it. Hintz and Tribunella note that "Hinton wrote *The Outsiders* while in her teens, which deepened the impression that the book reflected genuine adolescent culture, as recounted by an insider: the quintessence of realism" (322).

Ponyboy immediately establishes his "outsider" status on multiple fronts. We learn that his "hair is longer than a lot of boys wear theirs" (Hinton 9), a damaging social-status signifier during the 1960s, since long hair at that time was still often associated with a lower socioeconomic position and even juvenile delinquency. Also marking Ponyboy as different from previous teenage protagonists is the fact that we meet him emerging from "the darkness of the movie house" *alone*. Indeed, this self-described "greaser" embarks on "a long walk home" with "no company" (9). This introduction provides a very specific portrait of our narrator, and yet this specificity engenders a type of universality. Through articulating both the physical and social "outsider" position that often accompanies—and, for many, defines—adolescence, the text normalizes the isolation and alienation that can come with young adulthood, enabling a diverse array of readers to connect with Ponyboy's story, greasers or not.

However, despite Ponyboy's stigmatized "greaser" label and all that might be associated with it, such as an assumed emotional hardness and general disregard for education, morality, and legal authority, he reveals himself to be introspective and artistically inclined. He goes to the movie alone not because he lacks friends, but because he enjoys it. "I like to watch movies undisturbed so I can get into them and live them with the actors," he tells us (Hinton 9–10). His time alone at the theater allows Ponyboy to create a psychic space where he can coexist with Paul Newman and other Hollywood heroes of the era. But more than just serving as a retreat from the difficulty of his greaser reality, Ponyboy's relationship with imaginative storytelling—from Paul Newman movies to *Gone with the Wind*—empowers him to erase the thin line between fiction and reality; the narratives he consumes frame his knowledge of self and society.

This reciprocity between art and life, fantasy and truth manifests itself in the relationship between Mitchell's work of fiction and the two greaser runaways' actualities. While taking cover in the secluded church, Johnny and Ponyboy "killed time by reading *Gone with the Wind* and playing poker" (Hinton 83). Ponyboy remarks that despite Johnny's not "know[ing] anything about the Civil War and even less about plantations," he "sure did like that book" (83). *Gone with the Wind*'s historical context and the veracity of events upon which Mitchell builds her story matter very little to Johnny and are of less consequence to Ponyboy, despite his grasp of United States history. (Ponyboy confesses, "I make good grades and have a high IQ and everything, but I don't use my head," suggesting that while conscious of facts, he prefers the imagination [12].) What matters more for Johnny and Ponyboy is the imaginative core of the novel. The constructed dramatic frame provides a means for the boys to better determine and categorize their current surroundings, as well as their past lives.

Indeed, after listening to Ponyboy read from *Gone with the Wind*, Johnny can put words to his hero-worship of Dallas "Dally" Winston, the member of the boys' surrogate family whom Ponyboy calls "tougher than the rest of us—colder, tougher, meaner" (Hinton 19). Now armed and informed by the world of Mitchell's novel, Johnny can better articulate what it is about Dally that he so admires. In essence, he uses fiction to structure his reality. In hearing Mitchell's characterizations of Confederate soldiers and Southern gentlemen, Johnny tells Ponyboy, "'I bet they were cool ol' guys,'" conflating Mitchell's more-or-less invented depictions with the actual lives of nineteenth-century Southerners (84). He then maps the story onto his own life and brings the characters into his world, saying, "'They remind me of Dally'" (84). He recalls an incident in which Dally was targeted by the police but "'kept real cool and calm the whole time,'" even though it was the boys' friend Two-Bit who committed the offense at hand (84). In taking "the sentence without battin' an eye or even denyin' it," Johnny finds his definition of "gallant" (84). For Johnny, the injustice faced by Dally because of a broken social system becomes less important than the mythic figure revealed in Dally, one based in the popular imagination's mélange of Arthurian knighthood, baroque sophistication of the eighteenth century with its attention to elegance and extravagance, and militaristic courage. The new-realism backdrop of Hinton's novel gets filtered through heroic tropes of romance, with the lofty ideals of gallantry overriding the immediate difficult struggles faced by Johnny and Ponyboy.

Gone with the Wind mentions characteristics or embodiments of gallantry more than forty times, linking the term to conflated notions of valor, fearlessness, and charm. For example, upon thinking of the Confederate soldiers fighting for the South, Scarlett O'Hara rhapsodizes, "Had there ever been such men as these since the first dawn of the world, so heroic, so reckless, so gallant, so tender?" (Mitchell 171). She shortly thereafter pities herself because of her young widowhood—and not because she's lost her husband, but because of the circumstances of his death: measles and pneumonia. Therefore, he "didn't even die in the fine glow of gallantry in battle," thus denying Scarlett the opportunity to "brag about him" (174). The adulation of the Confederacy's gallantry feels unpalatable to most of us now given its avowed duty to uphold slavery, but Mitchell's text disregards this moral incongruity, as do Ponyboy and Johnny.

The heroic notion of gallantry absorbed by Ponyboy and Johnny during their time reading *Gone with the Wind* sweeps into their own behaviors, as seen when they save a group of school children from the burning church—an event that occurs shortly after their deep engagement with the novel. "On the fifth day I had read up to Sherman's siege of Atlanta," Ponyboy recounts, so entrenched in the newly created reality of the old church and rural landscape that it feels as if he "had dreamed the outside world and there was nothing real but baloney sandwiches and the Civil War and the old church and the mist in the valley" (Hinton 87). But the fiery havoc wrought in Atlanta on Mitchell's pages follows the boys into their Oklahoma existences, actualizing into flames that consume the "old church" while Johnny and Ponyboy are in town having lunch with Dally. Upon their return and discovery of the children trapped inside the burning church, the boys, the two greasers who were previously the most likely to be "spooked" or "hurt" (16), transform into their quixotic visions of Southern gallantry, alongside the already gallant Dally, who ironically admonishes his friends not to be heroic but to protect themselves. Bounding into the burning church, Ponyboy remembers telling himself, "I should be scared" with "an odd detached feeling" while the "cinders and embers began falling" all around him and Johnny (100). Moreover, Johnny, described in the story's opening chapter as looking like a "little dark puppy that has been kicked too many times and is lost in a crowd of strangers" (19), metamorphoses into his gallant fantasy. Yet, though this bold version of Johnny who braves "falling embers" doesn't "behav[e] at all like his old self," Ponyboy says that "it looked like he was having the time of his life" (100-101). Through recycling and adapting the narrative, narrative conception of heroic gallantry into his dim reality, Johnny creates a new identity for himself.

Gone with the Wind's power over Johnny—its ability to help him reconfigure his perception of life and identity—becomes part of Johnny's legacy for Ponyboy, who eventually assumes the weighty responsibility of literary narrator. When Johnny gains consciousness in the hospital, his primary concern is returning to the imaginative space of the novel. While lying in his infirmary bed "pale as the pillow" and looking "awful," he softly asks Ponyboy, "The book . . . can you get another one?" (Hinton 128). Through "the book," Johnny has found a means to transcend the bleakness of poverty, violence, and parental neglect that has surrounded him for most his young life. But more than that, "the book" allows him to rewrite who he is; his assumption of the brave gallant effectively erases the meek former Johnny as he changes himself into a courageous soldier and martyr. And when Johnny dies, the physical copy of *Gone with the Wind* serves as his one material belonging to bequeath to Ponyboy. In other words, his only earthly vestige, his lasting visible mark is Mitchell's novel. "Johnny left you his copy of *Gone with the Wind*," Darry tells Ponyboy. "Told the nurses he wanted you to have it," Darry adds, attempting to console his grieving younger brother. Here, Ponyboy becomes conflicted and confused, as the novel and its visions of gallantry are now bound to Johnny. "I looked at the paperback lying on the table," Ponyboy says. "I didn't want to finish it. I'd never get past the part where the Southern gentlemen go riding into sure death because they are gallant" (166). Stubbornly, angrily, Ponyboy indicates that he does not want the reminder that Johnny is gone. Yet Ponyboy eventually comes to realize the same thing that Johnny did upon death—that our identities and memories are creations of narrative, and through writing, we can live forever.

However, before coming to this recognition of narrative power, Ponyboy tries to bring back his friend through his own corporeal being. Instead of accepting the supposed finality of Johnny through his death, Ponyboy endeavors to resurrect his lost friend through *himself.* (Indeed, Johnny Cade bears the same initials as the emblem of resurrection, Jesus Christ.) He first attempts this through adopting Johnny's identity and past. He tells Randy that it was he, Ponyboy, who killed Bob that night on the playground, firmly declaring, "I had a switchblade and I was scared they were going to beat me up" (Hinton 173). Rather than trying to convince Randy that he—Ponyboy—killed Bob, here Ponyboy tries to *become* Johnny; by re-imagining or re-scripting himself in Johnny's likeness, Ponyboy thinks that Johnny can be brought back to life. "Johnny is not dead," Ponyboy repeats in a "shaking" voice (173). Johnny is not dead to Ponyboy at this moment because Ponyboy incorporates Johnny's identity into himself and thus assumes his past actions. When he says that "Johnny didn't have anything to do with Bob's getting killed," Ponyboy essentially absolves Johnny of any guilt surrounding Bob's death. Through his process of psychological resurrection, Ponyboy suggests Johnny's gallant death pardoned his supposed crime of killing Bob. Ponyboy's reasoning, of course, remains tangled and chaotic as he tries to *be* Johnny and assume responsibility for Bob's death while also wanting to absolve Johnny through this pseudo-resurrection—Ponyboy's figurative means of bringing Johnny back from the dead.

Ponyboy's means of coping, his capacity to reconcile Johnny's death comes with recognizing Johnny's ability to create new life from narrative by way of the imaginative, romantic tropes of *Gone with the Wind.* Johnny refashioned himself from underprivileged, delinquent greaser into a child-saving hero by enacting and embodying the gallantry he found in Mitchell's narrative. Johnny made a part of fantasy his reality, however briefly. Ponyboy's epiphany comes after he finds the note Johnny slipped into the copy of *Gone with the Wind,* his last will and testament of sorts. "'*Ponyboy, I asked the nurse to give you this book so you could finish it,*'" the note begins (Hinton 186). Not only does the note refer to Mitchell's literary creation; it also brings in Robert Frost's poem "Nothing Gold Can Stay," which the boys discussed during their time at the church. In his final imprint on the world, Johnny suggests the imaginative, idealistic quality of existence. This young boy who lived a life filled with pain and trauma essentially contradicts the "new realism" of his own history by telling Ponyboy to stay gold—new, optimistic, and in a state of perpetual wonder—because "'[t]*here's still lots of good in the world*'" (187). The entirety of Johnny's note underscores the notion that we create the world we want through our art—our poems, films, novels. Our identities are a form of narrative informed by the idealism and realism around us. In other words, it's all a story. Johnny challenges Ponyboy to remain as he is now forever, and Ponyboy finds that preserving himself and bringing Johnny back to life can come through writing.

Ponyboy takes Johnny's letter as a call to arms. He determines that "someone should tell their side of the story," a story that will help make "boys with black eyes" remember the beauty and possibility that the world holds. Ponyboy's genuine earnestness in believing that "[t]here should be some help" for greasers like him, that "someone should tell them" about the sunsets and the stars and the good "before it was too late" spurs him to action (Hinton 187). Remembering the writing assignment that he's been putting off, Ponyboy locates an avenue for providing that "help." He discerns that in writing his story, by giving voice to a youth perspective that is not represented in popular culture and media, those other "boys with black eyes" may start to feel less alone and be able to establish stronger community and familial connections and, therefore, may be less prone to ending up like Dally or Johnny. The text suggests that because society refuses to recognize or depict greasers and other "outsiders" in literature and culture, they feel disposable, invisible. But through the process and permanence of writing, Ponyboy can inscribe social outsiders into existence, into relevance. At the same time, because of its quality of permanence, Ponyboy can also preserve Johnny—at least, the version of Johnny he wishes to preserve—by means of putting words to memories. The act of narration that he takes up for Mr. Smye's writing assignment, then, legitimates Ponyboy's "story," his identity—an identity he controls *through* writing.

The conclusion of *The Outsiders* reveals itself to be Ponyboy's carefully constructed self-narrative that authenticates his marginalized identity and agency. While it does work to complicate the landscape of youth literature that Hinton deemed unrealistic, a landscape that she saw as the aforementioned "fairyland of proms and double dates," it still underscores the overriding imaginative quality of existence and the human capacity for creation—paramount notions whether a text roots itself in romance or realism. The last sentence of the novel, which begins, "When I stepped into the bright sunlight from the darkness of the movie house," loops readers back to the book's opening scene, not only exposing the literary architecture of Ponyboy's story, but also signaling the importance of art (meaning ideas of creativity and their products) in creating identity. Ponyboy may be a greaser, but he understands himself, his family, and his dreams through Paul Newman's screen adventures in *Cool Hand Luke*. The framing device of *The Outsiders* through the exiting of the movie theater suggests a kind of self-enlightenment in the transition from darkness to the brightness of day. After engaging with the romantic, adventurous escapes of Paul Newman for a few hours, Ponyboy has the actor's world and performance "on his mind." He now sees his greaser reality superimposed against the romance of Paul Newman's film, thus changing the way he comprehends "reality" and himself (Hinton 9). *The Outsiders* demonstrates how self-identity is a narrative, creative project influenced by the stories around us, both romantic and real.

Works Cited

Hinton, S. E. *The Outsiders*. 40th Anniversary ed., Penguin-Viking, 2007.

Hintz, Carrie, and Eric L. Tribunella. *Reading Children's Literature: A Critical Introduction*. Bedford/St. Martin's, 2013.

Mitchell, Margaret. *Gone With the Wind*. 1936. Macmillan, 1962.

Talley, Lee A. "Young Adult." *Keywords for Children's Literature*. NYU Press, 2011, pp. 228–232.

Gold and Magic—Ponyboy Curtis and Harry Potter: Binaries, Hierarchies, and Privilege____

Mária I. Cipriani

> . . . [A]s psychoanalysts from Freud and Jung onward have observed, myths and fairy tales often both state and enforce culture's sentences with greater accuracy than more sophisticated literary texts.
>
> (Sandra M. Gilbert and Susan Gubar, *The Madwoman in the Attic*)

> Johnny and I looked at each other. He grinned suddenly, raising his eyebrows so that they disappeared under his bangs. Would we ever have something to tell the boys! his eyes said plainly. We had picked up two girls, and classy ones at that. Not any greasy broads for us, but real Socs. Soda would flip when I told him.
>
> (S. E. Hinton, *The Outsiders*)

Popular young adult (YA) novels reveal cultural attitudes and expectations with respect to appropriate behavior for girls and boys. With only slight variations, S. E. Hinton's 1967 novel *The Outsiders* and J. K. Rowling's 1997 *Harry Potter and the Prisoner of Azkaban* convey similar messages about suitable behavior for girls and boys. Though written more than three decades apart, both texts depict girls generally as accessories to boys; in fact, Hinton's 1967 depiction of girls' roles appears to have changed very little from Louisa May Alcott's and Mark Twain's a century earlier: girls can acceptably be clever and demure, but not sexy, and certainly not sexually active. Boys can acceptably enact and experience violence, but not sex. Gay and lesbian identity, so far from being an option that it does not exist within the pages of YA texts until 1969, carries dire consequences for YA characters when those characters do appear, and they rarely appear in books that sell millions of copies.

This essay assumes children's and YA literature serves the function of subtly showing, not telling, young readers what is acceptable or "normal," reinforcing the dominant culture's rules and expectations. This normative assumption has its roots in the well-documented history of children's literature with its dual purpose of instructing and delighting readers (Nodelman & Reimer, Hunt, Demers, Bottigheimer). These subtle messages carry far-reaching consequences in literature and everyday life. From Alcott's girls and Twain's boys onward, the history of children's and YA literature, a literature for the most part written for children and young adults by adults, traces a literary genre that has, from its beginnings, been used to model acceptable behavior for its readers. These behaviors indicate an absolute false correlation, or conflation, of sex and gender along a male/female binary[1] and make gendered assumptions about girls' and boys' appearance, education, and function in society.

The clearly-delineated gender binary informs a code of behavior presented as normal for girls and boys: the absence of any characters not clearly identified as either girl or boy implies the gender binary. Literature intended for boys and girls instructs them about acceptable behaviors through examples of clearly gender-defined, gender-identifiable characters whose sex and gender are routinely conflated without question. That instruction continued in YA literature from its inception until 2002, when Carol Plum-Ucci introduced an ambiguously gendered character, Lani, in *What Happened to Lani Garver*. Two years later, Julie Anne Peters's *Luna* featured the first explicitly transgender character in a YA novel. The YA novels of 1967 and 1997 conform to the accepted binary.

Because mainstream publishing remains a commercial undertaking, successful marketing of books depends upon satisfying the expectations of potential purchasers. Dominant expectations normally parallel the unspoken, assumed values of the dominant culture; thus the sociocultural values projected in YA literature parallel the values of the dominant culture, if only to make a book attractive to the largest number of potential buyers. The marketing decisions of YA publishers thus have the effect of inserting into the pages of YA literature normative messages for YA readers, demonstrating acceptable and unacceptable behavior in the depictions they reward, punish, or annihilate by their total absence from the pages of YA texts. The frequency with which YA texts show boys to be the active perpetrators of violence, girls to be passive and the recipients of violence, and both boys and girls to be presumed heterosexual indicate that these are "normative" values, that is, the values which are considered "normal" and thus acceptably depicted in most YA literature. The infrequency of depictions of sex and sexuality in YA texts is also normative, as is the rarity, and therefore marginality, of gay and lesbian characters in mainstream YA literature. While some forms of acceptable behavior have evolved—for example, twenty-first century YA texts depict girls as athletic, courageous, and adventuresome—much of the behavior deemed acceptable in YA literature follows traditional gender expectations. Although fan fiction of the 2010s embellishes and reinterprets individual relationships between characters (Krischer), similarities between *The Outsiders* and *Harry Potter and the Prisoner of Azkaban* demonstrate the normative messages that continue to form the foundational assumptions of YA fiction.

Called "The Voice of Youth" after its publication (Daly 3), *The Outsiders* is a coming-of-age novel narrated by "greaser" Ponyboy Curtis that depicts the culture of the 1960s and reflects, consciously or not, the gender roles and gender rules followed by the majority of young adults in the 1960s. For Hinton's teens, the question of identity begins with issues of survival, not sexuality. In *The Outsiders*, the group to which teens belong helps them survive and defines their identity. A boy's socioeconomic status determines his group, either greaser or Soc, and girls attach themselves to boys based on the same socioeconomic determination. For these teens, survival on the most basic level means dealing with home, school, and street life to stay alive into adulthood.

For *The Outsiders* teens, threats come from different quarters, depending on their socioeconomic position. Socs fall prey to gang wars and suicide; greasers perish in gang wars and police encounters. All the characters attempt to stay alive, but in the course of the novel, two greasers and one Soc die. On a socioeconomic level, well-to-do Socs attempt to survive their parents' expectations of acceptance to Harvard; working-class greasers endeavor to survive daily struggles for food and shelter (Daly 16).

Hinton's characters are predominantly male because females in the 1950s and 1960s did not have the same opportunities as males. "The world of girls was too limited for what Hinton wanted to do," asserts Antoine Wilson (20). Hinton states, "When I was young, girls never got to *do* anything" (Daly 1, emphasis in original). Thus, according to the author, and as reiterated by the critics, Hinton's "gritty realism" (Wilson 20, Daly i, Peck) reflected young adults' experience of their culture, rather than attempting to change the status quo.

Critics acknowledge that *The Outsiders*, which has sold more than 15 million copies, changed YA literature (Daly, Peck, Wilson). A novel about young adults, for young adults, and written by a young adult "set a new standard for the YA genre" (Wilson 23), offering a text more realistic, dark, and relevant to YA readers' actual experiences than other novels for teens at the time (Wilson 9). Readers were shocked, which was Hinton's intent. Hinton's raw portrayal of the difficult realities of life was radical for the time, especially in a novel by and about teens (Daly 17). The realism of the text made, and continues to make, the novel controversial. Hinton biographer Jay Daly notes that Hinton fueled the controversy by arguing in *The New York Times* that teenagers needed fiction that reflected their reality (Daly 17). While *The Outsiders* appeared on the American Library Association's (ALA) list of the Best Young Adult Books of 1975, *The Outsiders* routinely appears on the ALA's list of most frequently challenged books (ALA), for depictions of gang violence, child abuse (termed "family dysfunction"), and underage smoking and drinking, as well as for the use of slang and "strong language" (ALA). Despite the controversy, many middle schools and high schools include the novel as part of the standard curriculum.

The Outsiders focuses on a group of socially and economically disadvantaged teenagers who are "outsiders" because their lives fall outside acceptable socioeconomic norms. Just-turned-fourteen-year-old narrator, Ponyboy Curtis, a "greaser" whose parents died in an automobile accident eight months before the opening of the story, lives with his two older brothers, Sodapop and Darry. Darry, the eldest, has custody of his younger brothers and works to make ends meet. The main conflict centers on the gang war between the greasers and the Socs. Social and economic status differentiates the rival gangs, as do their prospects of graduating from high school and attending college. Unlike Socs, greasers must work for a living, are not expected to graduate from high school, and routinely experience violence, both in their homes and in the public spaces that they share with their economically privileged peers. Ponyboy's steady progression toward high school graduation makes him an exception, rendering him an "outsider" even among greasers.

The gang rivalry results in violence when a group of Socs attack Ponyboy and his friend Johnny one night after Ponyboy speaks with a Soc girl. Johnny kills a Soc who is attempting to drown Ponyboy, and Ponyboy and Johnny flee. The ensuing violence, including Johnny's death after trying to save some children from a fire, the confrontation between the gangs, and the shooting death of another greaser by the police, depicts a series of traumatic events for Ponyboy and leads to the book's conclusion that both greasers and Socs share a longing for love and a feeling of belonging, a desire to avoid shame, and a need for a meaningful identity.

In *The Outsiders*, normative messages about appropriate behavior for boys and girls are clear and unwavering. Hinton's motivation in writing the story was to "let off steam" after "nice" kids attacked one of her greaser friends without provocation (Hinton, "Bonus Materials"). It is notable that while *The Outsiders* challenges some boundaries of behavior, specifically, the idea that young adults do not smoke, drink alcohol, or engage in violence, the novel leaves gender roles unchallenged. Boys acceptably engage in fighting (2-6, 54-58, 171); experience violence from child abuse (33-34, 122-23); are involved in gang warring in the form of a "rumble" (4-6, 142-45) as well as murder (54-58); and older boys flirt, while younger ones are embarrassed simply by being around girls (25-28). However, sex, always heterosexual, falls outside the "gritty realism" of this text. Boys resort to violence publicly to cover tender feelings, although they cry privately and with their closest friends. Girls in *The Outsiders* function as possessions that boys fight over, objects for boys to own or trophies for boys to win. Other normative messages regarding girls' behavior in *The Outsiders* include being cute (25, 84, 127), smart (20, 35), manipulative (14-15, 34-35, 38-41), flirtatious (25-28), and submissive (44-45, 128).

Hinton did not intend to teach moral lessons or change the sex/gender status quo with *The Outsiders*; hence, the sex/gender depictions demonstrate that heterosexuality is the norm by the absence of any other option. Hinton's stated agenda in 1967 was to portray the harsh realities of middle- and lower-class youth who did not have the social and economic acceptability of the characters portrayed in novels written for and about teens before 1967. Hinton observed in 1967 that girls had little agency. They could help boys to effect action, but did not themselves instigate action. This type of secondary role is embodied by Cherry Valance, the only notable female character in *The Outsiders*.

Cherry appears at the beginning of the novel, precipitating the fight between Ponyboy and the Socs, and again toward the end as an intermediary between the greasers and the Socs (Hinton 128), taking no action to change the status quo. While boys fight for their territory and for their pride, girls remind boys to follow and, thereby to maintain, the class status quo. Cherry's behavior does not change, and that behavior effectively enforces the acceptable codes of gender and class presented in *The Outsiders*. She verbalizes her unwillingness to break the unspoken rules that govern class or social boundaries when she tells Ponyboy, "[I]f I see you in the hall at school or someplace and don't say hi well, it's not personal or anything" (45). Similarly, Sodapop, Ponyboy's brother, is rejected by his girlfriend because he is not a Soc, and, therefore, not someone she will marry. From the sidelines, upper-class girls follow the complex, unspoken rules that govern interactions within their own social class and never accept greasers as friends or boyfriends. Girls' activities are never described in the detail that the rumbles are— the girls, and their actions, are marginal. No girl takes part in the rumble, engages in physical violence, or holds membership in either gang, and not one is a tomboy. The normative gender message in

The Outsiders is clear: 1967 boys can be violent and can drink and smoke; 1967 girls cannot.

Hinton acknowledged contemporary gender expectations. Yet Hinton's focus in writing *The Outsiders* was not to change readers' perceptions of gender roles; it was to depict contemporary teen life realistically. Contrast this to Sally Watson's 1969 YA novel *Jade*, which presents a teenage girl in traditionally male situations (Watson portrays Jade as an expert dueler who takes beatings without flinching and liberates captive slaves from slave ships): *Jade* did not enjoy the long-enduring popularity of *The Outsiders*, despite being a well-written, well-researched story. Watson notes in her introduction to the reprinted version of *Jade* that the mostly male critics of the late 1960s panned *Jade* as "unrealistic" in its foregrounding of a girl who is an expert with a sword and who willingly becomes a pirate. This challenging of socially delineated gender roles in 1969 exceeded critical audiences' tolerance, and book sales suffered.

Hinton was a self-described "tomboy" (Wilson 9), and her principal characters, especially the narrators, are male because Hinton feared that a female point of view would invalidate her stories (Wilson 20). Her publisher subsequently reinforced that choice by identifying her as S. E. Hinton rather than Susan Eloise Hinton, fearing public rejection of a female author of a gritty, violent novel (Daly 7). This would not have been an issue had Hinton been male, but the publisher feared that "reviewers would assume a girl couldn't write a book like *The Outsiders*" (Hinton, "Bonus Materials") and would question the novel's authenticity rather than giving it a fair reading and review (Daly 7), which would affect sales (Daly 17). That marketing decision, along with Hinton's acknowledgement of then-current acceptable gender expectations, contributed to the success of *The Outsiders*, while Sally Watson's gender-norm-challenging *Jade* was dismissed by critics and was out of print two years later.[2]

Hinton's "gritty realism" acknowledged readers' gender expectations and undeniably popularized the novel, since that gritty realism did not challenge gender assumptions. Thus, by focusing on male characters—not portraying female characters experiencing or engaging in the same or similar acts of violence—Hinton was able to make the point that teens experienced violence, whether through random acts, like the accident that killed Ponyboy's parents and the fire that kills Johnny, or through deliberate acts, like the attempted murder of Ponyboy by the Socs, the rumble, or the police shooting of a fellow greaser. Hinton and her publisher correctly assumed that readers would accept the shock of violent imagery but not the challenge to gender roles.

The themes relevant to young adults' experience, including shame, belonging, and identity, coupled with portrayals of violence and death, made *The Outsiders* a best seller and created a template for a new trend in YA literature (Wilson 9, 53) that flourished in the later decades of the twentieth century. *The Outsiders* challenged the legitimacy of the tradition that prohibited the portrayal of youthful experiences of violence and death in YA texts. However, *The Outsiders*' reinforcement of gender stereotypes, its unwavering assumptions about heterosexual sex, sexual preference, and a gender binary, and its systematic conflation of sex and gender normalize these stereotypes for YA readers.

Since 1967, female agency has expanded somewhat, and women with careers and a degree of independence are more acceptable now than they were fifty years ago. Definitions of acceptable girl behavior have expanded, although acceptable boy behavior has not expanded at the same rate. Depictions of heterosexuality as the norm and clearly-delineated male and female gender roles have remained remarkably constant, especially as these depictions reinforce an artificial sex and gender binary. Changes in publishing during the past fifty years, including consolidation of many publishing companies into a few major publishers of physical books, coupled with the availability of e-books and self-publishing technology, online webpages, e-zines, fan fiction, and blogs, have enabled wide-ranging independent dissemination of queer options for young adults. However, in mainstream publishing houses—and their corresponding, richer cousins, film production companies— the texts receiving the largest proportion of readership continue to reinforce heteronormativity, a conflation of sex and gender, and the gender binary. Individualism for YA readers is supported within broadly accepted cultural norms, as long as that individuality does not fundamentally challenge the traditional binary sex/gender system that, while not articulated explicitly, is ubiquitous.

Thirty years after *The Outsiders*, the best-selling Harry Potter series continued to reinforce the same gender roles, rules, and assumptions. While Hermione, the main female character in the Harry Potter series, is more central to the action than any girl in *The Outsiders*, Hermione's actions and appearance continue to be described in distinctly feminine terms, and there are neither witches nor wizards in the Harry Potter text who are ambiguously gendered or gay. The third book of the series, *Harry Potter and the Prisoner of Azkaban* (1999), is no exception. Each volume in the series portrays normative sex and gender roles found in YA literature after 1985, any one of which might be compared with *The Outsiders*. However, the third volume presents the protagonist, Harry Potter, at approximately the same age as Ponyboy Curtis, and, like Ponyboy, Harry is prepubescent and in need of parental guidance. Thirteen-year-old Harry does not have conscious sexual feelings for girls; he does, however, need to individuate and explore his independence. Harry exhibits more self-awareness and more awareness of his status in his wizard community in the third book than he does in the first two books of the series, displaying, in this book, an age-appropriate self-awareness similar to Ponyboy's.

The Prisoner of Azkaban features Harry in his third year at Hogwarts School of Witchcraft and Wizardry. Orphaned as a one-year-old when his witch mother and wizard father were murdered by the series villain, Voldemort, Harry has the distinction of being the sole survivor of a Voldemort attack. To protect him after the attack, leaders in the magical world send Harry to live with his muggle (non-magical) aunt and her muggle husband.

The 1967 Ponyboy Curtis and the 1999 Harry Potter are similar in notable ways. Both protagonists are young teen males created by female authors, both were orphaned suddenly (Ponyboy by a car accident—the muggle cover story for the absence of Harry's parents—and Harry by the murder of his parents) and the most important relationships are with their peers. Both protagonists exhibit a combination of traditionally masculine and feminine traits. Both are described as being sensitive and good listeners, traditionally feminine traits; however, as is stereotypical of male characters, both are willing to fight. Additionally, typical of boy protagonists, both characters court trouble—both act rashly without weighing the consequences of their actions: After a late-night argument with his guardian brother, Ponyboy flees his house, placing himself in danger as a group of Socs attack him. Harry runs from the house of his guardian uncle late at night, illegally uses magic outside of school, and unknowingly places himself in danger.

Harry breaks many school rules in addition to the prohibition on underage wizards and witches using extracurricular magic. However, although Harry is the protagonist, his two friends, Hermione and Ron, assist him at critical points in his adventure. Unlike the female characters in *The Outsiders*, Hermione is not merely a two-dimensional accessory for the boys. In fact, the text depicts Hermione as intelligent, sensible, clever, and essential to many of Harry's successes. Simultaneously, however, Hermione, like Cherry, stands for the status quo, reminding the boys of the rules, though also demonstrating her willingness to break those rules when necessary. Additionally, in her resourcefulness, Hermione breaks rules that Harry and Ron do not know can be broken, such as the rules of the space-time continuum, allowing her to repeat a segment of time in order to perform an alternate activity.

Hermione is one of many female characters who "do" things in this series, and in this respect, *Harry Potter* differs greatly from *The Outsiders*. In *The Prisoner of Azkaban*, both boys and girls play on the school's four Quidditch[3] teams; girls and boys are presented with the same challenges and rewards in all subjects, including the hazardous Care of Magical Creatures and the Defense Against The Dark Arts classes; and boys and girls are represented equally in the four houses of the school, although they are segregated within the house dorms according to two sexes, thus reinforcing without question the gender binary and the sex-gender conflation.

The social and historical context at the time of the publication of *The Prisoner of Azkaban* places the text in the center of the cyber revolution in the United States and much of Europe. Thirteen-year-olds in 1997 were born in 1984. For those in the United States and much of Europe in 1997, a world without television, telephones, or computers was unknown. They faced Y2K and the onset of the new millennium, and they did not know a world without HIV/AIDS. In addition, the women's movement and the gay rights movement changed discussions of gender and sexuality in the three decades between the publication of *The Outsiders* and *The Prisoner of Azkaban*, with discussions of teen sex and sexuality moving from frank to explicit (Brennan and Durack). Possibilities for girls and activities in which girls engaged broadened materially in the same thirty years. The Harry Potter series, however, reflects only this last change.

Girls function as the agents of literary action more often in 1997 than they did in 1967, yet the gender binary remains reinforced for 61 million readers of the Harry Potter series, including silent instruction about normative sex/gender roles. Theorist Meredith Cherland notes, where there is a binary, there is a hierarchy (274), and where there is hierarchy, there is privilege. In *The Outsiders*, the hierarchy is based on class and economic status. In the world created by Rowling, boys are wizards and girls are witches, and while they have similar and usually equal powers, girls do not become wizards; boys are never witches. This characterization along gender delineations reinforces the gender binary in a way that calling all magical people "wizards" (or "witches" or something along the lines of the neologism "muggle") would not. In addition, Rowling subtlety implies a hierarchy that privileges wizards over witches: when referring to a combined group of witches and wizards (including the term "wizarding world"), the group is referred to as "wizards" (13, 14, 29, 83, 85, 118, 176). When Hogwarts's headmaster Albus Dumbledore talks about adults not believing the word of Harry and Hermione specifically, he says, "the word of two thirteen year old wizards" (286) will not convince anyone.[4] The text reinforces the fact that the wizard has a slightly higher status, and the extremely good and extremely bad magical people in this series are all wizards. Language also reinforces the slightly higher status of "wizard": in common usage, outside the Harry Potter text, "wizard" holds positive associations with wisdom, expertise, and maleness; traditionally "witch" has negative connotations (Bottigheimer 50) and associations with evil magical powers and, despite its original meaning, "wise woman," witch women are ugly, disliked, and old.[5]

The Prisoner of Azkaban depicts the equality of males and females in terms of intellectual and physical abilities in sports, magical powers, scholarship, and in both "good" and "bad" behaviors. However, the book also expresses a more subtle, insidious set of inequalities, which appear in the language and cultural myths Rowling uses to create the Harry Potter fantasy, such as in the linguistic distinction between witches and wizards noted above. Readers' perceptions of males as wizards and females as witches reinforce the separate and unequal status of the two gender-based categories, which also function in the implied difference between words such as "poet" and "poetess." This linguistic distinction provides the reason that male and female thespians are increasingly referred to as (default male) "actor" rather than "actor" and "actress." The Harry Potter book provides one example of this inequity in the statement, "Hermione was the cleverest witch in Harry's year" (9), as opposed to Hermione's being the cleverest student overall. The statement raises the question, who is the cleverest wizard? It further implies that the wizard in question might also be understood to be the cleverest student (a gender-neutral term that encompasses the entire class), a recognition that the preceding quotation does not necessarily confer on Hermione.

The hierarchy, and resulting privilege, created and enforced by binaries extends beyond the gender binary, since, like The Outsiders, The Prisoner of Azkaban also includes binaries of class, (magical people versus muggles), race and racial status among magical people (pureblood witches and wizards versus "mudbloods," magical people—like Hermione—one or both of whose parents are not magical), economics (Harry is wealthy while Ron's family is poor), and ability (among the magical people, a non-magical person whose parents are both magical is disdainfully labeled a "squib"). These binaries reflect those encountered by readers in their own lives and include the inherent hierarchy associated with each binary. With respect to the gender binary, the hierarchy is so commonplace as to be unnoticed.

The enforcement of gender norms occurs in various ways in *The Prisoner of Azkaban*. For example, despite female characters' agency within the story, the male characters' actions move the plot forward. The hero, villain, school's headmaster, and Minister for Magic are all male. Males also instigate all evil, as well as beneficial, events. None of the characters is ambiguously gendered, and none presents any serious challenge to existing gender roles or gender rules.

Rowling depicts wives as secondary and reactive to their husbands, exemplifying domesticity (Rowling 53, 54). When Arthur Weasley, his boys, and Harry are getting into trouble, Molly keeps the boys (including her husband) in line. Molly and Arthur are always portrayed together (unless she is waiting for him to come home from his job at the Ministry for Magic). Molly expresses her obviously potent magical power when performing the ultimate stereotypical "girl" spell (Bottigheimer 40): teaching the young witches how to create a love potion (Rowling 56). The entire notion of a love potion reverts back to the adjectives used for girls in *The Outsiders*, since the creation of a love potion implies girls acting cute, smart, flirtatious, and manipulative.

Rowling describes Professor McGonagall, who heads Gryffindor House, Harry's living community at Hogwarts, as a spinster (69, 196). Although McGonagall is not the only unmarried professor at Hogwarts, she is the only one to whom that adjective is applied. Rowling additionally depicts McGonagall as being motherly at times, more a function of her gender than of her predominantly authoritative, unsentimental character. The text also presents Professor Trelawney, the female teacher of the "inexact art" of Divination (25), as vague, hysterical, and comical, an object of ridicule not to be taken seriously (80-3). In fact, as critics Ximena Gallardo-C. and C. Jason Smith note, readers "of all ages and genders can identify with the Harry Potter stories, not *in spite of* the gender inequality but *because* they see in the stories a reflection of their own experiences of gender disparity" (192, emphasis in original).

The Prisoner of Azkaban variously represents the most active and resourceful female presence in the series, Hermione, as maternal (Rowling 60) and "the mature one" (63). At the same time, Hermione exemplifies acceptable gender characteristics, as she squeals (73, 110), giggles (56), screams (250, 253, 262), shrieks (291), is shrill (217), and is characterized on several occasions as a know-it-all (83, 85, 98, 101, 172, 175). None of these characterizations apply to any of the series' male characters, who routinely yell (90, 104, 110, 197, 210, 221, 227, 250), bellow (104, 306), shout (104, 114, 123, 270, 315), roar (73, 87, 89, 93, 104, 221, 285), and snarl (115, 209, 256, 258, 260), verbs not associated with any female character.

Interestingly, the gang of greasers in *The Outsiders* resembles the old "gang" at Hogwarts that consisted of Harry's deceased father and three chums[6] who return to Hogwarts in *The Prisoner of Azkaban*. The male groups in both *The Outsiders* and *The Prisoner of Azkaban* are headstrong, daring, and loyal, with Harry's father's three chums (along with Harry, who is consistently aided and coached by Hermione for the denouement) moving the story forward. Thus, while Hermione is more central and has more agency, and her actions in *The Prisoner of Azkaban* carry more import throughout the text than do the actions of Cherry Valance in *The Outsiders*, the text nonetheless relegates Hermione to much the same secondary role as Cherry—the helper rather than the principal.

The fact of a female-authored male hero presented as much of an issue for J. K. Rowling in 1997 as it did for S. E. Hinton in 1967. Although UK authors customarily use initials rather than full names, one reporter states that Rowling was "persuaded to endure the indignity of hiding behind her initials to spare young male readers the embarrassment of enjoying a book by a woman" (Holden). Three decades after the publication of *The Outsiders*, publishers continued to fear overtly identifying female authors of stories about males would adversely affect sales. The same consideration has not seemed to pose a problem for male writers of the children's and YA fiction that feature female protagonists. From Lewis Carroll's *Alice in Wonderland* (1865) to *13 Reasons Why* by Jeffrey Archer (2007), publishers have not required male authors to use gender-hiding initials when writing female characters or for female audiences.

Hinton's characters are boys because in 1967 girls did not "do" anything; Rowling, when asked why she made her protagonist a boy, answered, "I had been writing the first book for six months before I stopped and thought, 'Why's he a boy?' And the answer is, He's a boy because that's the way he came. If I had stopped at that point and changed him to Harriet, it would have felt very contrived. My feminist conscience is saved by Hermione, who's the brightest character" ("J. K. Rowling's Books"). As a reflection of values acceptable to the dominant culture, the Harry Potter series demonstrates prevailing cultural gender roles and gender expectations. Rowling, who portrays Hermione as a more interesting, active, and three-dimensional character than Cherry Valance in *The Outsiders*, ultimately conveys to YA readers the same message in 1999 as Hinton did in 1967: boys are active; girls are their helpmates.

In addition to the recapitulation of the gender binary and depiction and reinforcement of traditional gender roles, *The Prisoner of Azkaban*, like *The Outsiders*, implies sexuality only in terms of male-female relations through the portrayal of heterosexual, married couples. In the case of adolescents, the text restricts male-female relationships to momentary flirting, dutiful companionship (Rowling 191, 312), and awkward behavior (Rowling 51, 215), while non-heterosexual relationships are nonexistent. Normative messages for YA readers about relationships in *The Prisoner of Azkaban* did not change significantly from the messages for YA readers of *The Outsiders*. Both texts depict typical YA readers' desires to belong to a group, to have at least a few good and loyal friends, and to be a dependable friend in return. In addition, an explicit theme that frequently motivates characters in both novels involves avoiding shame and fear (Hinton 149, Rowling 68) at any cost.

The unarticulated message of both texts demonstrates the difficulty but worthiness of asserting one's individuality and upholding one's principles (within gendered limits). Both texts show that society will accept a certain degree of nonconformity for a poet like Ponyboy or a celebrity like Harry, but, by their absence, both texts demonstrate that deviations from heteronormativity and traditional gender roles remain unacceptable, no matter how otherwise remarkable the character.

In addition to the strict guidelines of conformity to which both *The Outsiders* and *The Prisoner of Azkaban* adhere, similarities of the male characters' agency and female characters' secondary roles also remain constant between the two texts. Rowling does not feature any character who is openly gay or lesbian, just as Hinton does not depict any gay greasers (or Socs). Neither text includes a tomboy.

The Prisoner of Azkaban demonstrates that thirty years after the publication of *The Outsiders*, YA texts depict females with greater agency. A significant number of female characters appear in the Harry Potter text who actually "do" many things. From the actions of Harry's aunt and his uncle's sister at the beginning of *The Prisoner of Azkaban* to female students actively participating at Hogwarts, and Hermione's clever machinations throughout, female characters are agents of action. While no female character has an active, significant role in *The Outsiders*, in *The Prisoner of Azkaban* one very active and purposeful female character, Hermione, has the singular intelligence, skills, and ability that help to move the plot forward. Additionally, while the teens in both texts share the need to belong to and feel part of a peer group, expectations for both male and female characters in *The Prisoner of Azkaban* are less polarized than in *The Outsiders*. Both male and female characters display self-sufficiency, reliability, and loyalty in the Harry Potter text, whereas in *The Outsiders*, only male characters evidence those traits.

Today, as in 1997 and in 1967, YA readers continue to locate themselves within a dominant heteronormative culture; and normative messages about acceptable and unacceptable behavior in mainstream YA fiction, particularly with respect to gender rules and gender roles, remain relatively unchanged: most youthful characters experience the need to be loved, to belong to a group, to avoid shame, and to have a meaningful identity. In addition, YA literature continues to embed traditional messages about acceptable sex, gender, and sexuality within the majority of YA texts, thereby reinforcing the sex/gender binary. These texts also continue to conflate, without question or comment, sex and gender as male and female, just as they persist in perpetuating the false correlation of male and female with masculinity and femininity, respectively.

A comparison of *The Outsiders* and *The Prisoner of Azkaban* confirms a continuing enforcement of traditional gender roles and, with those roles, a continuing enforcement of the gender binary. Although texts themselves reflect the expansion of girls' sphere in the 1990s, girls remain in secondary roles. As the texts continue to delight and to instruct readers, the messages and metamessages of YA texts uniformly steer YA readers to make choices that conform to gender binary, reinforcing the male-female hierarchy, and the privilege associated with that hierarchy.

Notes

1. The gender binary refers to the traditional Western conceptualization of gender as either male or female, a classification of human beings as belonging to one of only two sexes and categorizing and labeling their actions as either masculine or feminine. Feminist scholar Gayle Rubin noted in 1975 that the traditional gender binary assumes heterosexuality because this point of view dictates that the acceptable sexual preference for a female is a person of the opposite sex, a male; with the converse assumed true for males. In 1990, philosopher Judith Butler reiterated the concept that the gender binary implies heterosexuality, which in turn reinforces the gender binary (xxx), a notion subtly supported by the YA mainstream publishing industry's consistent portrayals of the gender binary and its correspondingly gender-determined actions and preferences.

2. This raises the question of whether Sally Watson's book would have received a more critically favorable review if she had been listed as S. J. Watson; presumably a male author would have been perceived as having more authority to write a pirate story, even one about the historical female pirate Annie Bonnie.

3. A rough, semi-contact sport of the wizarding world that resembles a combination of polo and soccer, played airborne on broomsticks.

4.   Perhaps Rowling invoked the traditional grammatical rule that mixed or unknown genders revert to the masculine. This traditional rule exemplifies another one of the ways in which language, here, English (but also many Indo-European and Semitic languages, among others worldwide), reinforces the gender binary and the hierarchy associated with it. In 2017, teachers of French in France made a recommendation to the French Academy suggesting gender inclusive linguistic alternatives, noting that the rationale for the grammatical rule in which the gender of a group is determined by one man (a group's gender is masculine if one man is in a group with an infinite number of women) was according to a line in a 1767 grammar book, because "the masculine gender is deemed more noble than the feminine gender because of the superiority of man over woman," (qtd. in Carmel McCoubrey, "Toppling the Grammar Patriarchy," The New York Times, 16 Nov. 2017.). The teachers were met with a resounding *"Non."*

5.   Historically a woman called a "witch" implied the notion of someone playing with the male fear of female sexuality (Pearson 37-8). Some argue that fear of female sexuality led to the witch hunts in Europe and Salem, Massachusetts, in the United States. That witch hunt, according to feminist writers Mary Daly, Andrea Dworkin, and Merlin Stone, never really ended but rather mutated into myriad forms. These feminists assert that the witch as a symbol of female sexuality and power is thus as firmly entrenched as ever, but women are now creating the image to reflect their own interests and concerns (Pearson 37). This may not be the case for Rowling's books, but it provides an explanation for why the Harry Potter series does not feature male witches.

6.   Synchronistically, Harry's father and his friends would have been approximately fourteen years old in 1967.

Works Cited

American Library Association (ALA)."100 most frequently challenged books: 1990–1999." *Banned & Challenged Books*, 2 Oct. 2012, www.ala.org/advocacy/bbooks/100-most-frequently-challenged-books-1990–1999/.

Bottigheimer, Ruth B. *Grimms' Bad Girls & Bold Boys*. Yale UP, 1987.

Brennan R. O., and D. T. Durack. "Gay Compromise Syndrome." *Lancet.* Vol. 12. No. 2 (1981): pp. 1338-39.

Cherland, Meredith. "COMMENTARY: Harry's Girls: Harry Potter and the Discourse of Gender." *Journal of Adolescent & Adult Literacy*, vol. 52, no. 4, Dec. 2008/Jan. 2009, pp. 273-82.

Daly, Jay. *Presenting S.E. Hinton.* Twayne, 1987.

Demers, Patricia. *From Instruction to Delight: An Anthology of Children's Literature to 1850.* Oxford, 2001.

Galliardo-C., Ximena, and C. Jason Smith. "Cinderfella: J. K. Rowling's Wily Web of Gender." *Reading Harry Potter: Critical Essays*, ed. Giselle Liza Anatol, Praeger, 2003.

Gilbert, Sandra M., and Susan Gubar. *The Madwoman in the Attic.* Yale Univ. 1979.

Hinton, S. E. *The Outsiders.* 1967. Platinum ed., Penguin, 2007.

Holden, Anthony. "PEOPLE: Why Harry Potter doesn't cast a spell over me: J.K. Rowling's new blockbuster will be a monster hit worldwide. But just how good is the Harry Potter series?: 'I brave the wrath of millions by saying so'." (London) *Observer*, 25 Jun. 2000, p. 1. *InfoTrac Newsstand.*

Hunt, Peters. *An Introduction to Children's Literature.* Oxford UP, 1994.

_____. *Children's Literature.* Blackwell, 2001.

_____, ed. *Understanding Children's Literature.* Routledge, 1999.

Krischer, Hayley. "Why *The Outsiders* Lives On: A Teenage Novel Turns 50." *New York Times.* 1 Mar. 2017, www.nytimes.com/2017/03/12/books/the-outsiders-s-e-hinton-book.html/. Accessed 24 Feb. 2018.

Nodelman, Perry. *The Hidden Adult: Defining Children's Literature.* Johns Hopkins, 2008.

_____, and Mavis Reimer. *The Pleasures of Children's Literature.* 3rd ed., Pearson, 2002.

"J. K. Rowling's Books That Made a Difference." *O, The Oprah Magazine*, Jan. 2001, www.oprah.com/omagazine/JK-Rowlings-Books-That-Made-a-Difference/print/1/. Accessed 24 Feb. 2018.

Pearson, Jo. "Inappropriate Sexuality? Sex Magic, S/M and Wicca (or 'Whipping Harry Potter's Arse!')." *Theology & Sexuality*, vol. 11, no. 2, 1 Jan. 2005, pp. 31-42.

Peck, Dale. *"The Outsiders*: 40 Years Later" *New York Times*, 23 Sept. 2007, www.nytimes.com/2007/09/23/books/review/Peck-t.html/. Accessed 24 Feb. 2018.

Peter, Julie Anne. *Luna.* Little, 2004.

Plum-Ucci, Carol. *What Happened to Lani Garver.* Harcourt, 2004.

Rowling, J. K. *Harry Potter and the Prisoner of Azkaban.* Scholastic, 1999.

Rubin, Gayle. "The Traffic in Women." *Toward an Anthropology of Women.* Rayna R. Reiter, ed. Monthly Review Press, 1975, pp. 157-210.

Watson, Sally. *Jade.* 1969. Image Cascade, 2002.

Wilson, Antoine. *The Library of Author Biographies, S.E. Hinton.* Rosen, 2003.

"You've Seen Too Much to Be Innocent": *The Outsiders*, the Myth of American Youth, and Young Adult Literature_____

Paige Gray

Youth has long been associated with innocence, an idea both reflected in and perpetuated by literature. But this idea is just that—an *idea*, an idealization of what the youth experience is for actual young people, one often (but not always) crafted by adults whose youth is now at a distance. Ponyboy Curtis, the fourteen-year-old "greaser" protagonist and narrator of S. E. Hinton's *The Outsiders* (1967), slyly mocks the conceit of young innocence during his first encounter with Cherry Valance, a popular girl from his high school who belongs to the "Socs," or the Socials, a group that Ponyboy describes as "the jet set, the West-side rich kids" (10). Cherry compares Ponyboy and shy Johnny Cade to their inscrutable, hard-edged friend Dallas "Dally" Winston, telling them, "[Y]ou two don't look mean." Ponyboy replies "tiredly" with a response of "Sure," flippantly adding, "we're young and innocent." Ponyboy's fatigued demeanor and ironic response indicate his weariness with the cliché and its supposed truth. But Cherry intuits this, telling Ponyboy, "No . . . not innocent. You've seen too much to be innocent" (34).

For scholars of children's literature, *The Outsiders* serves as a symbolic marker in the development of literature for young adults. While stories featuring themes and characters relevant to young adults are as old as storytelling itself, after *The Outsiders*, the publishing industry and the public at large began to recognize "young adult" as a distinct category in publishing, thus giving fuller representation to American adolescence outside the protected, privileged idea of a middle- or upper-class white childhood. "The phrase 'young adult,'" writes literary scholar Lee Talley, "reflects the history of changing perceptions of childhood, adolescence, and adulthood and how these ideas have shaped parenting, education, libraries, publishing, and marketing" (228). Indeed, *The Outsiders* disrupted the fantasy of youthful innocence. From the seventeenth century through the 1950s and 60s (and still today), much of children's literature, film, and television—ideas and art created by adults—projected and helped shape a notion that youth is a time for innocence, a time unencumbered by the harsh truths of adulthood. In order to understand how Hinton's novel helped complicate and nuance the depiction of youth, it's important to understand the historical context of how American children's literature and literary works for young people have both reflected and fashioned our understanding of American youth and innocence. With the publication of *The Outsiders*, Hinton eroded previously held cultural beliefs by giving voice to the plurality of youth experience, particularly through the depiction of violence, poverty, and socioeconomic conflict—which for many young people is part of their everyday reality. As Cherry suggests in her comment to Ponyboy, equating youth with innocence proves an ill-informed cultural assumption.

But why are childhood and youth so closely connected to innocence? The association has become so entrenched in Western society that many people take it for fact, as opposed to cultural ideology. Ideology governs the ways individuals and cultures accept and filter knowledge in order to build workable realities. In *Reading Children's Literature*, Carrie Hintz and Eric L. Tribunella further explain that "[i]deologies and discourses (ways of thinking and communicating) circulating at a given time and in a given place influence or construct how individuals see the world, making it possible to think in certain ways as well as impossible or difficult to imagine alternatives" (5).

Moreover, a space or gap generally forms between ideology and actuality, and multiple discourses—formalized thoughts and language surrounding a theory or discipline—can exist at the same time. In terms of understanding the ideology of childhood, this means that a society's beliefs about childhood may greatly differ from the reality of childhood. "Complicating the study of the history of childhood," Hintz and Tribunella contend, "is the fact that at any given moment multiple and even contradictory ideas about children and childhood coexist; what we think about children and childhood and the ways real children actually live do not always correspond" (14). *The Outsiders* attempts to show the ways in which the old ideas of youthful innocence do not correspond with the ways Ponyboy, his brothers, and their close-knit group of friends actually live, and in doing so shows the complexity and diversity of young people's worlds.

Looking back through the history of childhood, we find drastically different beliefs regarding the young, and the notion of young innocence is not a constant or even foundational tenet. With the initial 1960 publication (and eventually with the 1962 English translation) of his *Centuries of Childhood*, French historian Philippe Ariès created quite the controversy with his statement, "In medieval society the idea of childhood did not exist" (128), thereby nullifying our ideas of "natural" childhood or childhood innocence.[1] Though scholars have presented valid concerns about Ariès's evidential support and methodology, his work undoubtedly helped spur academic scholarship on youth and childhood in multiple disciplines. Children's literature scholar Marah Gubar writes that the relationship between innocence and the young is relatively recent, speaking in historical terms. Gubar explains that "prior to and during the nineteenth century many people subscribed to the doctrine of original sin, which held that human beings are born already tainted by depravity inherited by Adam" (122). In this ideology, the child was "naturally" sinful rather than "naturally" innocent. Historian Steven Mintz underscores the fallacy of belief in a "natural" state of childhood, asserting that "childhood is not an unchanging biological stage of life but is, rather, a social and cultural construct that has changed radically over time" (viii). Indeed, most of the ways in which Western cultures define or discern youth have been in flux over the centuries, according to Mintz:

> Every aspect of childhood—including children's household responsibilities, play, schooling, relationships with parents and peers, and paths to adulthood—has been transformed over the past four centuries. Just two hundred years ago there was far less age segregation than there is today and much less concern with organizing experience by chronological age. There was also far

less sentimentalizing of children as special beings who were more innocent and vulnerable than adults. (viii)

From this, we can see that one unchanging idea about youth is that our cultural conception of it is *always changing*. The inherent innocence ascribed to children in recent generations must not only be questioned, but also examined in terms of the harm such assumptions make. How are children marginalized or demeaned when they don't fit the innocence model?

The innocence model of childhood gained widespread cultural prominence in the early nineteenth century during the Romantic era. This time period followed the historic, global impact of the French Revolution and the American Revolution, in addition to developing as a social response to the science-driven, reason-focused Enlightenment. The Romantic era emphasized the imagination as seen in the works of the English poets William Wordsworth, Samuel Coleridge, and William Blake. The lasting influence of the Romantic vision of childhood can be seen in Wordsworth's "Ode on Intimations of Immortality from Recollections of Early Childhood" (1807). However, as Hintz and Tribunella outline, the Romantics themselves develop alternate models of childhood innocence, with some subscribing to the theories inspired by the seventeenth-century philosopher John Locke, who asserted that "the minds of children are blank slates, and children must be molded by adults and imprinted with culture" (17). Meanwhile, "Others influenced by the Romantic tradition see children as naturally happy, carefree, innocent, or pure and thus likely to be disappointed, deformed, or corrupted by experience and maturation" (Hintz and Tribunella 17). William Blake explores this conceit in his illuminated book of poetry *Songs of Innocence and of Experience* (1789), which contrasts the privileged, sheltered child more likely to have a space to be innocent and lighthearted with the child born into poverty and forced into— and therefore tainted by—premature experience.

Young people played a pivotal role during the early days of American settlement, certainly countering ideas of innocence though they remained largely without voice or power. And the abuse

---

and cruelty endured by African youth during the development of the slave trade cannot be overlooked, as well as those difficulties also suffered by young enslaved white migrants. Historian Steven Mintz relates that between 1700 and 1775, approximately 500,000 Africans and "more than half of the 307,000 white migrants" came to America "unfree," and that a majority of them were "in their teens and twenties" (33).[2] (However, Mintz points out that "Indian children in the Eastern Woodlands enjoyed a degree of freedom from corporal punishment and household labor that was unimaginable to enslaved children, young indentured servants, or youthful apprentices and household servants" [33].) Meanwhile, for those young people who were free during the country's fledgling years, their agency was limited, as was the scope of their citizenship. Despite the fact that "persons under the age of twenty-one made up more than half of the U.S. population during the period from 1776 to 1868," Courtney Weikle-Mills argues that young people were largely ignored in the developing democracy's understanding of citizenship (2). She articulates youth's disenfranchised position amid America's "emergence of a concept of citizenship based on free birth" and its ideological rootedness in the "concept of childhood as a deficient state" (2). As a result, children and young adults became "individuals who could not exercise civic rights but who figured heavily in literary depictions of citizenship and were often invited to view themselves as citizens despite their limited political franchise" (2).

In late nineteenth- and early twentieth-century American culture, class and race were key determinants in constructions of youth. Before laws were passed regulating child labor and compulsory education, many children and young people were forced to work because of their family's economic circumstances, in both urban and rural areas.[3] And certainly, for much of the nineteenth century—and arguably still today—African American children could never experience the privilege of innocence because of slavery and its subsequent systemic, cultural discrimination. The very real history of working children invalidates the conceit of youth as a natural, free, imaginative space of innocence. Or, rather, it reveals the ways in which this now-ubiquitous notion of childhood derives from a white middle- or upper-class position. But in the Gilded Age and Progressive Era, working children could not be ignored. And, arguably, the jarring intersection between idealized childhood innocence and actual working children brought about social reform in the United States. Paula Fass says that between 1880 and 1920, "the increasing emphasis on child welfare and its relationship to social stability and national prosperity" forced states to think about how to regulate youth labor and education (vii). School attendance rose from seven million in 1870 to twenty million in 1915, and by 1920, "20 percent of all teenagers attended high school, especially boys and girls from well-off families," James Marten states (7). Marten adds that adolescents who had the ability to attend high school were afforded a space that enabled the further demarcation of the emerging teenage identity. He writes, "High school gave them a chance to participate in sports, music, and other organized activities unavailable to poor youth" (7).

With the implementation of child labor laws and mandatory schooling, along with the growth, development, and institutionalization of the American high school, the emerging category of the "teenager" acquired cultural significance, providing a stronger sense of identity for adolescents who no longer saw themselves as "innocent" children, but neither understood or believed themselves to be experienced, mature adults. Part of this emerging interest came from ideas being put forward by psychology and the other science disciplines. Thomas Hine writes in *The Rise and Fall of the American Teenager* that the social construction of the teenager "rests . . . on the idea of the adolescent as a not quite competent person, beset by stress and hormones," a problematic theory propagated by psychologist G. Stanley Hall in the early twentieth century (4). However, Hall's "data and assertions . . . have not withstood scientific scrutiny," writes Hine (4).

In addition to rising scientific interest in this later stage of childhood, Steven Mintz discusses how changes in mobility, media, and communication helped shape the distinct American-teenager milieu. "As a result of cars, telephones, and the movies," Mintz says, "the young had broken away from the world of adults and established their own customs, such as dating, which were regulated by the peer group and not adults" (214). Teens began to have their own separate reality, and many teens, like S. E. Hinton, eventually came to feel that this reality wasn't reflected in the literature written for young people by adults.

One of the most popular novels for teenagers (a category we now refer to as YA, or young adult) during the first half of the twentieth century, *Sue Barton, Student Nurse* (1936), garnered readers' approval likely for its attempts at realism, though contemporary readers may disagree with its version of "real" by today's standards. According to a 1947 librarian survey, *Sue Barton, Student Nurse* was teenagers' favorite book (Cart 9). Michael Cart, an expert on YA literature, posits that the appeal of *Sue Barton, Student Nurse* and its sequels "may have derived in large part from its verisimilitude," since the author, Helen Boylston, was a nurse and infuses the novels with details from her professional experience (9). Undeniably, the intrigue of the working world proved compelling for teen readers, and "Sue Barton was the prototype of the career story, an enormously popular subgenre among the earliest young adult books" (10).

However, by the 1960s, the relatively safe world depicted in the Sue Barton novels and similar books began to clash with actual young people's social realities. Unpacking the cultural climate in which Hinton wrote and published *The Outsiders*, children's and YA literature scholar Michelle Ann Abate explains,

> The decade [the 1960s] witnessed an array of profound and irrevocable transformations, including the agitation for civil rights by the black, women's, and gay and lesbian communities; the protests against the Vietnam War; and the shocking assassinations of prominent political and social activist figures Medgar Evers and John F. Kennedy in 1963, Malcolm X in 1965, and Martin Luther King Jr. and Robert F. Kennedy in 1968. (43)

And, of course, "Young people were neither unaware of nor disengaged from these events" (Abate 43). Though the teenager and the idea of its discrete social group became more defined over the course of the twentieth century, this did not mean these young people were not affected or involved with the political and cultural movements. Yes, young people had popular entertainment and activities that catered to them, but they were not isolated from the strife, tragedy, and turmoil of both the everyday and the historic. As Abate points out, in 1969 when the United States enforced conscription, men as young as eighteen years old were eligible to for the draft, forcing them into military service during the Vietnam War. In other words, young adults (and children, for that matter) then and now face difficult challenges in their daily lives and are touched by the socioeconomic, political, and global events around them; youthful innocence is a myth.

Hinton discerned this myth of youthful innocence in the literature for teenagers that she read while growing up in Tulsa, Oklahoma. In a 2014 *New Yorker* interview, Hinton recalls that, in 1967, "[T]here was no young-adult market," referring to the now ubiquitous—and extremely profitable—YA literary genre (qtd. in Michaud). Moreover, Hinton states that during her youth, "There was only a handful of books having teen-age protagonists: Mary Jane wants to go to the prom with the football hero and ends up with the boy next door and has a good time anyway" (qtd. in Michaud). While this more-or-less innocent storyline may have appealed to some teenagers, it didn't feel authentic or relevant to her. Prom-date concerns "didn't ring true to my life," Hinton says. "I was surrounded by teens and I couldn't see anything going on in those books that had anything to do with real life" (qtd. in Michaud). With the publication of her novel, Hinton "provided a counterpoint and even a corrective to this trend," asserts Michelle Ann Abate (43). She says that "[w]ith its presentation of teenage gangs, street violence, and poverty," *The Outsiders* contained profoundly different literary themes, characters, and subject matter" (43). As Cherry Valance says, Hinton reveals that many teenagers have "seen too much to be innocent."

After its publication, educators, librarians, and writers—and teenagers—connected to and appreciated the ways in which *The Outsiders* sidelined the hollowness of innocence ideology, thus ushering in the rise of YA literature. In an article headlined "Literature for Teens" printed in a 1969 edition of the *New York Times Book Review*, M. Jerry Weiss describes Hinton's characters as "long-haired, rough, tough, teen-agers from the wrong sides of the tracks" who have "little hopes of achieving such material pleasures of American life," though they continue to "search for a better tomorrow." Weiss calls it a "Now Generation story" (178). Certainly, there were novels before *The Outsiders* that showed the lives of teenagers outside white, middle-class America, and there were stories, art, and films depicting teen violence to some degree.[4] In particular, Michael Cart mentions Frank Bonham's Los Angeles-set *Durango Street* (1965), which focuses on teen gangs (25). However, "there was something about *The Outsiders* that captured the imagination of its readers and spawned a new kind of literature" (Cart 25).

In her work now paramount to the study of YA literature, *Disturbing the Universe: Power and Repression in Adolescent Literature* (2000), Roberta Seelinger Trites lays out the basic tenets of the genre. Notably, she contends, "The chief characteristic that distinguishes adolescent literature from children's literature is the issue of how social power is deployed during the course of the narrative" (Trites 2). In 1967, Hinton likely wasn't thinking about generic conventions or the social construction of youth and innocence. She was, however, thinking about real teen lives and what they gain or lose by not seeing themselves in the literature they read. "Teen-agers today want to read about teen-agers today," she wrote in a 1967 column for the *New York Times Book Review* (Hinton, "Teen-agers" 27). Across the centuries, teenagers and young adults have had to decide how they're going to handle the injustices and challenges that they encounter—the "social power" issue that Trites identifies, whether that social power be in the realm of age, race, gender, or class. Young people confront and grapple with these circumstances every day, despite Western culture's long-held myth of sheltered, innocent youth. Indeed, youth have never been innocent, in the sense that children and teenagers face material, social, and cultural adversity and in the sense that they acquire knowledge rapidly. As

Hinton remarks, "Teen-agers know a lot today. Not just things out of a textbook, but about living" (29). However, through more diverse representation in literature and media, ideological thought can be refashioned. Narratives can be rewritten. The stories of outsiders can come into focus.

Returning to the scene between Ponyboy and Cherry, that moment when Cherry realizes the tumultuousness of Ponyboy's young life, *The Outsiders* suggests the possibility of a story with a dim, pessimistic view on contemporary youth—a generation too jaded for dreams or hope. But in Ponyboy, Hinton creates a character whose narrative shows readers that innocence is not a requirement for maintaining joy and wonder. In Ponyboy, readers discover that they're never too old, too young, too experienced, or too innocent to "watch the sunset" and relish the promise of what tomorrow may bring (Hinton, *Outsiders* 54).

Notes

1. It's important to note that Ariès adds to his contentious statement regarding the non-existence of childhood during the medieval period that "this is not to suggest that children were neglected, forsaken, or despised" (128). Ariès writes that in terms of his argument, the "idea of childhood is not to be confused with affection for children: it corresponds to an awareness of the particular nature of childhood, that particular nature which distinguishes the child from the adult, even the young adult. In medieval society this awareness was lacking" (128).

2. Teenagers—though that term was not used at the time—actively participated in political activities leading up to the Revolution, as well as the war itself. "Teenage apprentices engaged in many mob actions that preceded the outbreak of war," Mintz writes (61).

3. Mintz asserts that "social class is the most significant determinant of children's well-being. While race, gender, and ethnicity exert a powerful influence on children's lives, socioeconomic status is intimately linked to their health care, schooling, and family stability" (ix).

4. In regard to film depiction of youth culture, Cart calls attention to the movie releases of 1955 that had adults "outraged" and teens

Critical Insights

"enthralled" with "not one but two cinematic classics of youthful disaffection," *Rebel without a Cause* and *Blackboard Jungle* (18).

Works Cited

Abate, Michele Ann. "'Soda Attracted Girls Like Honey Draws Flies': *The Outsiders*, the Boy Band Formula, and Adolescent Sexuality." *Children's Literature Quarterly*, vol. 42, no. 1, Spring 2017, pp. 43-64. [Note: Abate's essay is reprinted in this volume.]

Ariès, Philippe. *Centuries of Childhood: A Social History of Family Life.* Translated by Robert Baldick, Vintage-Random House, 1962.

Cart, Michael. *Young Adult Literature: From Romance to Realism.* ALA Editions of the American Library Association, 2011.

Fass, Paula S. "Forward." *Children and Youth during the Gilded Age and Progressive Era*, edited by James Marten, New York UP, 2014, pp. vii–ix.

Gubar, Marah. "Innocence." *Keywords for Children's Literature.* NYU Press, 2011, pp. 121–128.

Hine, Thomas. *The Rise and Fall of the American Teenager.* HarperCollins, 1999.

Hinton, S. E. *The Outsiders.* 40th Anniversary ed., Penguin-Viking, 2007.

_____. "Teen-agers Are for Real." *New York Times Book Review*, 27 Aug. 1967, pp. 27–29.

Hintz, Carrie, and Eric L. Tribunella. *Reading Children's Literature: A Critical Introduction.* Bedford/St. Martin's, 2013.

Marten, James. "Introduction." *Children and Youth during the Gilded Age and Progressive Era*, edited by James Marten, New York UP, 2014, pp. 1–16.

Mintz, Steven. *Huck's Raft: A History of American Childhood.* Harvard UP, 2004.

Michaud, Jon. "S.E. Hinton and the Y.A. Debate." *New Yorker*, 14 Oct. 2014.

Talley, Lee A. "Young Adult." *Keywords for Children's Literature.* New York UP, 2011, pp. 228–232.

Trites, Roberta Seelinger. *Disturbing the Universe: Power and Repression in Adolescent Literature.* U of Iowa P, 2000.

Weikle-Mills, Courtney. *Imaginary Citizens: Child Readers and the Limits of American Independence 1640–1868.* Johns Hopkins UP, 2013.

Weiss, M. Jerry. "Literature for Teenagers." *New York Times Book Review*, 16 Feb. 1969, p. 178.

RESOURCES

Chronology of S. E. Hinton's Life

Laurie Adams

3 April 1943	Grady Pulaski Hinton and Lillian Geneva McCormack marry.
22 July 1948	Susan Eloise Hinton is born.*
19 Dec. 1951	Hinton's only sibling, Beverly Ada Hinton, is born.
1963	Hinton begins her freshman year at Will Rogers High School.
February 1965	Hinton's father dies of cancer.
1965	Hinton begins work on the story that will eventually become *The Outsiders*. Originally titled "A Different Sunset," the story will go through four drafts on its way to publication (Rego Barry).
	Hinton's catalyst for writing the story was the real-life beating of a friend who was walking home from school, but Hinton has noted even prior to that event that she had become angry about the formation of factions of students within her high school, groups that did not intermingle but rather created unnecessary tension and exclusion. She has also cited a lack of true-to-life-as-she-knew-it fiction for people her age at that time and "wrote the book [she] wanted to read" (*Great Women Writers*).
	Hinton gives a copy of the story to the mother of a friend to read. The mother, a writer of children's books, passes the manuscript along to an agent, who begins to shop the book to publishers. It is accepted by the second publisher, Viking (*Great Women Writers*).

Spring 1966	Hinton graduates from Will Rogers High School. On the same day, she receives publication contracts for *The Outsiders*.
Fall 1966	Hinton begins classes at the University of Tulsa. Initially a journalism student, she switches tracks to education. It is here she will meet her future husband, David Inhofe, in one of her classes.
24 April 1967	*The Outsiders* is published. In its first year, it wins the first of many awards and recognitions it will receive, including the *New York Herald Tribune* Best Teenage Book and *Chicago Tribune* Book World Spring Book Festival Honor.
1968	Hinton publishes a short story version of *Rumble Fish* in the University of Tulsa Alumni Magazine supplement, the *Nimrod*.
Spring 1970	Hinton graduates from the University of Tulsa with a BA in education and undertakes a short stint as a student teacher.
Sept. 1970	Hinton marries David Inhofe.
26 April 1971	*That Was Then, This Is Now* is published.
15 Oct. 1975	Novel version of *Rumble Fish* is published.
24 April 1977	*The Outsiders* celebrates its tenth anniversary.
Oct. 1980	*Tex* is published.
1980	Hinton sells the screen rights for *The Outsiders* to Disney and *Tex* to Zoetrope.

30 July 1982	Film version of *Tex* is released, including cameo appearances by Hinton and her show horse, Toyota.
25 March 1983	Film version of *The Outsiders* is released.
21 Aug. 1983	Hinton's son, Nicholas David Inhofe, is born.
21 Oct. 1983	Film version of *Rumble Fish* is released.
28 Nov. 1985	Film version of *That Was Then, This Is Now* is released.
24 April 1985	*The Outsiders* celebrates its twentieth anniversary.
1 Oct. 1988	*Taming of the Star Runner* is published.
1988	Hinton receives the American Library Association and School Library Journal's first-ever Margaret A. Edwards Award "for significant and lasting contribution to young adult literature" ("Margaret A. Edwards").
1990	*The Outsiders* is adapted as a stage play by Christopher Sergel.
9 Aug. 1991	Hinton becomes the first writer to receive the Tulsa Library Trust Award for Young Reader's Literature.
25 March 1990	*The Outsiders* television show debuts and runs for thirteen episodes. The show is developed by Hinton, Joe Byrne, and Jeb Rosebrook and features the work of thirteen other writers ("S. E. Hinton," *IMDb.com*).
30 June 1993	Lillian Hinton dies.
1 Feb. 1995	*Big David, Little David* is published.
1 Sept. 1995	*The Puppy Sister* is published.

24 April 1997	*The Outsiders* celebrates its thirtieth anniversary.
7 Aug. 1995	Beverly Hinton dies.
1 Sept. 1995	*Hawkes Harbor* is published.
24 April 2007	*The Outsiders* celebrates its fortieth anniversary.
26 April 2007	Hinton's first short story collection, *Some of Tim's Stories*, is published.
24 April 2017	*The Outsiders* celebrates its fiftieth anniversary. It has been in continuous publication since 1967.

*Hinton's date of birth is listed in various books and articles as 1948; 1950; and, as author Jay Daly noted, sometimes 1949 and 1951 (Daly 2). Confusion remains, with various sources asserting one date or another. Daly noted 1948, as did the Oklahoma Historical Society on Hinton's author page on its site. An absolute date for Beverly Ada Hinton's date of birth was found listed on a genealogy site, along with a photo of her memorial headstone, which noted her birthdate as 1951. Beverly Hinton, as reported by Daly, was two years S. E. Hinton's junior, making 1949 the logical correct date (Daly 2), and 1949 also is in line with Hinton's entering high school in 1963, at fourteen years old, the typical age for freshmen. I elected to list the 1948 date to reflect the majority of credible sources, particularly Daly, who directly interviewed Hinton as well as family members.

Works Cited

Barnard, Matt. "*The Outsiders* Author S.E. Hinton Headlines Event at Circle Cinema." *Tulsa World TV*, n.d., www.tulsaworldtv.com/The-Outsiders-author-SE-Hinton-headlines-event-at-Circle-Cinema-32173450/. Accessed 9 Sept. 2017.

"Beverly Ada Hinton." *Geni*, 31 Aug. 2017, www.geni.com/people/Beverly-Hinton/6000000001193200085/.

Daly, Jay. *Presenting S. E. Hinton*. Updated ed, Twayne, 1989.

"Deaths: Aug. 9, 1997." *Tulsa World*, 9 Aug. 1997, www.tulsaworld.com/archives/deaths/article_8a885498-3d63-51e5-b284-05bfac7d90ec.html/.

Franklin, Joseph, and Antoine Wilson. *S.E. Hinton*. Rosen, 2016.

"Grady Pulaski Hinton." *Ancestry*. Ancestry.com. Accessed 11 Sept. 2017.

"Grady Pulaski Hinton." *Geni*. 31 Aug. 2017. https://www.geni.com/people/Grady-Hinton/6000000066037858912/.

Great Women Writers: Rita Dove, S. E. Hinton, and Maya Angelou. Hacienda Productions, 1999.

Lang, George. "S.E. Hinton recalls *The Outsiders* 45 years later—e-book due in Spring 2013." *NewsOK.com*, 10 May 2012, newsok.com/article/3770291/.

"Lillian Hinton." *Geni*, 31 Aug. 2017, www.geni.com/people/Lillian-Hinton/6000000001193200065/.

"Margaret A. Edwards Award Previous Winners." *Ala.org*, www.ala.org/yalsa/booklistsawards/bookawards/margaretaedwards/maeprevious/previousmargaret/. Accessed 13 September 2017.

Milam, Cathy. "S. E. Hinton to Get Library Award." *Tulsa World*, 17 Jul. 1991, www.tulsaworld.com/archives/s-e-hinton-to-get-library-award/article_95d76aae-d5a5-5a10-b182-43722b9ef266.html/.

Rego Barry, Rebecca. "A Few Way-Less Catchy Discarded Titles for S.E. Hinton's *The Outsiders*." *Slate.com*, 25 Apr. 2017, www.slate.com/blogs/the_vault/2017/04/25/alternate_titles_proposed_for_s_e_hinton_s_novel_the_outsiders.html/.

"S.E. Hinton." *IMDB.com*, n.d., www.imdb.com/name/nm0386023/?ref_=fn_al_nm_1. Accessed 18 Aug. 2017.

"S.E. Hinton on Location in Tulsa." *Youtube*, uploaded by micalaux, 14 Nov. 2010, www.youtube.com/watch?v=wJnfleLeOZg.

"S.E. Hinton." *Oklahoma Historical Society*, n.d., www.okhistory.org/writers/bio.php?/name=hinton&fname=s.%20E/. Accessed 6 Sept. 2017.

"S.E. Hinton on the 50th Anniversary of *The Outsiders*." *Youtube*, uploaded by Channel One News, 24 Apr. 2017, www.youtube.com/watch?v=0LXWhWG45u4/.

"S.E. Hinton.com." *S.E. Hinton.com*, n.d., www.sehinton.com/. Accessed 18 Aug. 2017.

Smith, Dinitia. "An Outsider out of the Shadows." *New York Times*, vol. 154, no. 53330, 07 Sept. 2005, p. E1. *EBSCOhost*, 0nesearch. ebscohost.com.library.acaweb.org/login.aspx?direct=true&db=f5h& AN=18139141&site=eds-live/.

Taylor, Elizabeth. "An Interview with S.E. Hinton." *Chicago Tribune*, 31 May 2008, articles.chicagotribune.com/2008-05-31/ entertainment/0805300368_1_hinton-outsiders-gender/.

Tipping, Joy. "S.E. Hinton on how *The Outsiders* Worked Its Way into the Mainstream." *Dallas News*, 18 Apr. 2014. www.dallasnews.com/ arts/books/2014/04/18/s.e.-hinton-on-how-the-outsiders-worked-its-way-into-the-mainstream/.

Works by S. E. Hinton

Books

The Outsiders, Viking, 1967

That Was Then, This Is Now, Viking, 1971

Rumble Fish, Delacorte, 1975

Tex, Dell, 1979

Taming the Star Runner, Delacorte, 1988

Big David, Little David, Doubleday, 1995

The Puppy Sister, Doubleday, 1995

Hawkes Harbor, Tor, 2004

Some of Tim's Stories, University of Oklahoma Press, 2007

Screenplays

Rumble Fish, Zoetrope Studios, 1983

The Outsiders, Television Series Zoetrope Studios, 1990

     "Pilot," 1990

     "The Stork Club," 1990

     "Only the Lonely," 1990

     "Breaking the Maiden," 1990

     "He Was a Greaser, Only Old," 1990

     "Maybe Baby," 1990

     "Storm Warning," 1990

     "Mirror Image," 1990

     "Carnival," 1990

     "Tequila Sunset," 1990

     "Winner Take All," 1990

     "The Beat Goes On," 1990

     "Union Blues," 1990

Fan Fiction

Hinton has acknowledged, but not identified, an unknown number of fan fiction posts. At the 2009 *LA Times* Festival of Books, Hinton admitted she enjoys writing fan fiction of her own work and joked to fans searching fan fiction sites for tales from *The Outsiders* universe, ". . . if you find a few good ones, they're mine" ("S.E. Hinton, *LA Times*").

Sources

"S.E. Hinton." *IMDb*, www.imdb.com/name/nm0386023/?ref_=fn_al_nm_1/. Accessed 18 Aug. 2017.

"S.E. Hinton, LA Times Festival of Books 04/26/09." *YouTube*, uploaded by christinelive, 30 Apr. 2009, www.youtube.com/watch?v=7U2tmwohMuI/.

"*The Outsiders.*" *Television Obscurities*, www.tvobscurities.com/articles/outsiders/. Accessed 25 Mar. 2017.

Bibliography

Chaston, Joel D. "S. E. Hinton: Overview." *Twentieth-Century Young Adult Writers*, edited by Laura Standley Berger, St. James Press, 1994. Twentieth-Century Writers Series. *Literature Resource Center*.

Cole, Flora. "Soft Sell." *The English Journal*, vol. 60, no. 7, 1971, pp. 931–932. *JSTOR*, www.jstor.org/stable/813218/.

Daly, Jay. *Presenting S.E. Hinton.* Updated ed., Twayne, 1989.

Franklin, Joseph, and Antoine Wilson. *S.E. Hinton*. Rosen, 2016.

Gillespie, Joanne S. "Getting Inside S.E. Hinton's *The Outsiders.*" *English Journal*, vol. 95, no.3, Jan. 2006, pp. 44-48. *EBSCOhost*.

Great Women Writers: Rita Dove, S. E. Hinton, and Maya Angelou. Hacienda Productions, 1999.

Hinton, S. E. *Big David, Little David*. Doubleday, 1995.

_____. *Hawkes Harbor*. Tor Books, 2004.

_____. *The Outsiders*. Viking, 1967.

_____. *The Puppy Sister*. Doubleday, 1995

_____. *Rumble Fish*. Delacorte, 1975.

_____. *Some of Tim's Stories*. U of Oklahoma P, 2007.

_____. *Taming the Star Runner*. Delacorte, 1988.

_____. *Tex*. Dell, 1979.

_____. *That Was Then, This Is Now*. Viking Juvenile, 1971.

Hinton, S. E. "An Interview with S.E. Hinton." Interview by Elizabeth Taylor. *Chicago Tribune*, 31 May 2008, articles.chicagotribune.com/2008-05-31/entertainment/0805300368_1_hinton-outsiders-gender/.

Hinton, S. E., and Lisa Ehrichs. "Advice from a Penwoman." *Contemporary Literary Criticism Select*. Gale Group, 1999. *EBSCOhost*.

Inderbitzin, Michelle. "Outsiders and Justice Consciousness." *Contemporary Justice Review*, vol. 6, no. 4, Dec. 2003, pp. 357-362. EBSCO*host*, doi:10.1080/1028258032000144802.

Judy, Stephen, and Susan Judy. "English Teacher's Literary Favorites: The Results of a Survey." *The English Journal*, vol. 68, no. 2, 1979, pp. 6–9. *JSTOR*, www.jstor.org/stable/815464/.

Krischer, Hayley. "Why *The Outsiders* Lives On: A Teenage Novel Turns 50." *New York Times,* 12 Mar. 2017, www.nytimes.com/2017/03/12/books/the-outsiders-s-e-hinton-book.html/.

Lang, George. "S. E. Hinton Recalls *The Outsiders* 45 Years Later—e-book due in Spring 2013." *NewsOK.com,* 10 May 2012, newsok.com/article/3770291/.

Martin, Sydeana M. "Teaching *The Outsiders* to the Real Outsiders." *The English Journal,* vol. 87, no. 3, 1998, pp. 81–83. *JSTOR,* www.jstor.org/stable/822393/.

McFarland, Kevin. "The Much-Banned YA Novel *The Outsiders* Turns Clunky Prose into Deep Emotion." *avclub.com,* 27 Aug. 2012, www.avclub.com/the-much-banned-ya-novel-the-outsiders-turns-clunky-pro-1798233112/.

Michaud, Jon. "S. E. Hinton and the Y.A. Debate." *New Yorker,* 14 Oct. 2014, www.newyorker.com/culture/cultural-comment/hinton-outsiders-young-adult-literature/.

Modleski, Michael. "Stay Gold," Students: Helping Young Readers Connect to *The Outsiders.*" *Middle School Journal,* vol. 4, no.1, Sept. 2008, pp.12-18. *EBSCOhost.*

Morgan, Linda O. "Insight through Suffering: Cruelty in Adolescent Fiction about Boys." *The English Journal,* vol. 69, no. 9, 1980, pp. 56–59. *JSTOR,* www.jstor.org/stable/816383/.

Peck, Dale. "*The Outsiders*: 40 Years Later." *New York Times,* vol.157, no. 54076, 23 Sept. 2007, p. 30. *EBSCOhost.*

Rosenthal, Kristina. *Banned Books: Young Adult Novels.* The University of Tulsa Department of Special Collections and University Archives, 13 Mar. 2014, orgs.utulsa.edu/spcol/?p=3254/.

"S.E. Hinton." *IMDB.com,* n.d., www.imdb.com/name/nm0386023/?ref_=fn_al_nm_1/. Accessed 18 Aug. 2017.

"S.E. Hinton." *Oklahoma Historical Society,* n.d., www.okhistory.org/writers/bio.php?/name=hinton&fname=s.%20E/. Accessed 6 Sept. 2017.

"S.E. Hinton Biography." *Encyclopedia of World Biography,* 2018, www.notablebiographies.com/He-Ho/Hinton-S-E.html/.

"S.E. Hinton.com." *S.E. Hinton.com,* n.d., www.sehinton.com/. Accessed 18 Aug. 2017.

"S.E. Hinton *LA Times* Festival of Books 04/26/09." *YouTube*, uploaded by christinelive, 30 Apr. 2009, www.youtube.com/watch?v=7U2tmwohMuI/.

Shi, Dan. "De-egocentricity and Socialization: A Study of Hinton's *The Outsiders.*" *Theory and Practice in Language Studies*, vol. 4, no. 4, pp. 668- 674. *AcademyPublications.com*, Apr. 2014, www.academypublication.com/issues/past/tpls/vol04/04/02.pdf/.

Simmons, John S. "A Look Inside a Landmark: *The Outsiders.*" *Censored Books: Critical Viewpoints*, edited by Nicholas J. Karolides, Lee Burress, and John M. Kean, Scarecrow, 2001, pp. 431-441.

Skurnick, Lizzie. "The Brotherhood of S.E. Hinton." *Chicago Tribune*, 31 May 2008, articles.chicagotribune.com/2008-05-31/entertainment/0805300355_1_ponyboy-curtis-hinton-outsiders/.

Smith, Dinitia. "An Outsider out of the Shadows." *New York Times*, 7 Sept. 2005, p. E1. *EBSCOhost*.

Sutherland, Zena. "The Teenager Speaks." *Contemporary Literary Criticism*, edited by Jeffrey W. Hunter and Deborah A. Schmitt, vol.111, Gale, 1999. *Literature Resource Center*, gogalegroup.com/ps/i.do?p=LitRC&sw=w&u=ferrum&v=2.1&it=r&id=GALE%7CH1100003921&asid=bea65c677ea1d967a5445a58a3581bf0/. Originally published in *The Saturday Review*, 27 Jan. 1968, p. 34.

Tribunella, Eric L. "Institutionalizing *The Outsiders*: YA Literature, Social Class, and the American Faith in Education." *Children's Literature in Education*, no. 2, 2007, pp. 87-101. *EBSCOhost*.

VanderStaay, Steven L. "Doing Theory: Words about Words about *The Outsiders.*" *The English Journal*, vol. 81, no. 7, 1992, pp. 57–61. *JSTOR*, www.jstor.org/stable/820750/.

About the Editor

M. Katherine Grimes is professor of English at Ferrum College. She earned a PhD in English from the University of North Carolina at Greensboro, an MA in English literature from the University of North Carolina at Chapel Hill, and a BA *summa cum laude* from Catawba College in English and psychology. Dr. Grimes contributed to *The Ivory Tower and Harry Potter: Perspectives on a Literary Phenomenon*, edited by Lana A. Whited, and coedited, with Dr. Whited, *Critical Insights: The Harry Potter Series*. Her work on J. K. Rowling's series has also been published in *Introduction to Mythology: Contemporary Approaches to Classical and World Myths*, edited by Eva M. Thury and Margaret K. Devinney.

Dr. Grimes is interested in maturation literature, especially works with absent mothers and those that show moral development. She is currently writing an introduction to literary studies and a couple of picture books.

Contributors

Michelle Ann Abate is Associate Professor of Literature for Children and Young Adults at The Ohio State University; she has also taught at Hollins University. Dr. Abate is the author of four books of literary criticism: *The Big Smallness: Niche Marketing, the American Culture Wars, and the New Children's Literature*; *Bloody Murder: The Homicide Tradition in Children's Literature*; *Raising Your Kids Right: Children's Literature and American Political Conservatism;* and *Tomboys: A Literary and Cultural History.* She earned a PhD and an MPhil from the City University of New York and a BA from Canisius College; all three degrees are in English.

Laurie Adams is a freelance writer who has contributed to two other *Critical Insights* volumes*: The Harry Potter Series* and *The Hunger Games Trilogy.* She has also published in the American Criminal Justice Association *LAE Journal*, the *Council on Undergraduate Research Quarterly* and, with Dr. Billy Long, the *International Journal of Business and Social Science.* Ms. Adams holds a bachelor of science degree *cum laude* in criminal justice from Ferrum College. She currently works with the nonprofit organization Diversity Serves, which seeks to develop partnerships to promote peace and prosperity in communities in South Sudan and Appalachia.

Mary Baron is professor of English at the University of North Florida. She earned a PhD from the University of Illinois at Urbana, an MA from the University of Michigan at Ann Arbor, and a BA from Brandeis University. Dr. Baron has published three books of poetry: *Letters for the New England Dead, Wheat Among Bones*, and *Mary Baron: New and Selected Poems.* She has received awards for both creative writing and teaching.

Jake Brown recently earned his master's degree in English language and literature from the University of North Carolina at Charlotte after receiving his bachelor's degree in the same fields from the University of

North Carolina at Chapel Hill. Mr. Brown is currently Project Manager at Duke Energy and plans to continue his graduate education.

Mária I. Cipriani holds a PhD in comparative literature and cultural studies, as well as certificates in gender studies and rhetoric and composition, from the University of New York at Stony Brook. Dr. Cipriani is an adjunct assistant professor who teaches American Literature at CUNY's John Jay College of Criminal Justice and American and Media Studies at SUNY's College at Old Westbury and whose primary research focus is representations of gender and trauma in young adult literature.

Robert C. Evans is I. B. Young Professor of English at Auburn University at Montgomery, where he has been named Distinguished Research Professor, Distinguished Teaching Professor, and University Alumni Professor. External awards include fellowships from the American Council of Learned Societies; the American Philosophical Society; the National Endowment for the Humanities; the UCLA Center for Medieval and Renaissance Studies; and the Folger, Huntington, and Newberry Libraries. He earned his PhD from Princeton University. Dr. Evans is the author or editor of roughly fifty books and of more than four hundred essays, including recent work on various American writers.

Paige Gray is a visiting assistant professor in the English Department at Fort Lewis College, where she teaches literature and media. She has also taught at the U.S. Military Academy at West Point and the University of Southern Mississippi. Dr. Gray specializes in children's and young adult literature and has been published in *Children's Literature*, *Children's Literature Association Quarterly*, and *Bookbird*. She is also a freelance journalist and is currently working on a book project that explores the intersection between children's literature and journalism. She holds a PhD and an MA in English from the University of Southern Mississippi, an MA in journalism from Columbia College Chicago, and a BA in English from Indiana University Bloomington.

Julia Hayes is assistant professor emerita at her alma mater, Catawba College, where she studied English and psychology and currently teaches as an adjunct instructor. She has also taught at Livingstone College. Her fields of specialization are African American literature and the war in Vietnam. Ms. Hayes earned a master's degree in English from the University of North Carolina at Charlotte and continued graduate study at the University of North Carolina at Greensboro.

Lana A. Whited is professor of English and director of the Boone Honors Program at Ferrum College. She earned degrees in English from the University of North Carolina at Greensboro (PhD), Hollins University (MA), the College of William and Mary (MA), and Emory and Henry College (BA). Dr. Whited received the Exemplary Faculty Award from the Council of Higher Education of the United Methodist Church in 2014 and was nominated in 2016 for the State Council of Higher Education of Virginia's Outstanding Faculty Awards. She is editor of *The Ivory Tower and Harry Potter: Perspectives on a Literary Phenomenon* and *Critical Insights: The Hunger Games Trilogy*. She also coedited *Critical Insights: The Harry Potter Series* with M. Katherine Grimes. Her current project is a book on American literary naturalism.

Sarah E. Whitney is director of the women's studies program and assistant teaching professor of English and women's studies at Pennsylvania State University Erie, The Behrend College. She holds an MA and a PhD in English literature from the University of Virginia and a BA in English and history from the College of William and Mary. Dr. Whitney is the author of *Splattered Ink: Postfeminist Gothic Fiction and Gendered Violence* and researches the intersections of gender, violence, and young adult literature.

Index

Bryon 119, 120, 121, 122, 123, 128

Buehler, Jennifer 25

Butler, Judith 213

Butler, Patrick 15

Byrne, Nicky 174

Byron, George Gordon 96

Cade, Johnny xiii, xv, xxii, xxv, xxvi, 5, 6, 30, 139, 169, 194, 217

Cain 54, 56, 122

Caitlin 152

Caldwell, Patrick 9

Campbell, Patty 21, 22

Caroline, Katherine 131

Carroll, Lewis 211

Carter, Ally 25

Cart, Michael 22, 156, 223, 225

Casey 130, 131, 132

Catcher in the Rye, The xvii, 21, 75

Catholicism 99

Cathy 121

Caulfield, Holden xvii

Charlie 56, 122

Cherland, Meredith 207

childhood xv, 51, 66, 97, 100, 122, 135, 151, 153, 154, 189, 217, 218, 219, 220, 221, 222, 226

child labor laws 222

child welfare 222

chivalry 172

Christopher 131

Chu, Judy Y. 129

church xiv, xv, xvi, 6, 47, 49, 56, 57, 58, 65, 90, 91, 95, 97, 98, 103, 136, 139, 141, 143, 144, 146, 173, 187, 190, 192, 195

Cisneros, Sandra 153

citizenship 221

Civil Rights Movement xi, xix, 157

Civil War xiv, 57, 89, 95, 187, 190, 192

class xi, xii, xiii, xv, xxiv, 4, 24, 31, 32, 34, 35, 48, 66, 67, 69, 72, 80, 87, 88, 91, 92, 104, 105, 114, 117, 118, 124, 135, 145, 152, 156, 157, 158, 159, 169, 171, 176, 177, 187, 188, 189, 199, 202, 207, 208, 217, 221, 222, 225, 226

Cleaver, Bill 21

Cleaver, Vera 21

Clemens, Samuel Langhorne 101

Clinton, Hillary 8, 19

Coleridge, Samuel 220

Collins, Suzanne xx

color schemes 125

Common Sense Media 125

composition 71, 163, 174

conflation of sex and gender 204

conflict xiii, 54, 91, 99, 107, 201, 218

Contender, The 21

Cool Hand Luke 164, 196

Cool World, The 153, 155

Coppola, Carmine 181

Coppola, Francis Ford xxvii, 80, 89, 180

Cordero, Esperanza 153

Corrections Corporation of America 12

Couch, Ethan 14, 18
